About the Author

Photo by Marjolein Stevens

Yvette Ho Madany 何亦玮 was born in Shanghai and educated in the US. For the past two years, she has conducted charity walks for foreigners in Shanghai to benefit migrant children and still writes for Shanghai's expatriate magazines. She and her family now live in the US. All of her royalties are donated to charity.

Shanghai
Story Walks
Walking tours through Old Shanghai

By
Yvette Ho Madany
何亦玮

EARNSHAW
B O O K S

Shanghai Story Walks

By Yvette Ho Madany 何亦玮

Designed by Frank Zheng 郑魏

ISBN-13: 978-988-18154-5-3

© 2009 China Economic Review Publishing (HK) Limited for Earnshaw Books

Shanghai Story Walks is published by
China Economic Review Publishing (HK) Limited for Earnshaw Books
1804, 18/F New Victory House,
93-103 Wing Lok Street, Sheung Wan, Hong Kong

First printing June 2009
Second printing September 2009
Third printing April 2010
Fourth printing December 2011

Preface

SHANGHAI is a city of immigrants. People from other provinces and countries have come to call the city home now and then, hence the title, "SHANGHAI STORY WALKS."

Shanghai is a vibrant, developing city, with many bikes, buses, cars, mopeds, and people. Please cross all streets carefully.

Aside from enriching our minds, the walks are for fun and for exploring an amazing city. I devised all the routes and chose what I thought would be interesting. This book is for your personal use or for use with a few friends. It is not meant as a tool for the tour guide or large groups.

Wherever you are, please use good judgment so as not to intrude upon people's privacy.

Please do not take pictures of government buildings.

And please remember that things change at a rapid speed in this city. What is here today maybe gone tomorrow.

I have used Pinyin for most names, except a few famous people whose names are spelled out in the traditional way, such as the "Soong" of the Soong sisters as opposed to the pinyin "Song."

序 言

上海是一座移民城市。外省和外国的人来到这里，从此以后会把这座城市称为他们的家，这便是《漫步上海的故事》(Shanghai Story Walks)这个书名的由来。

上海是一座生机勃勃，不断发展的城市，这里有太多的自行车、公共汽车、小汽车和行人。请小心穿越它的每一条街道。

除了能够丰富我们的精神世界，漫步是为了寻求乐趣，及对这座令人赞叹的城市的探究。我对所有的道路都作了精心设计，并选出了我认为有趣的部分。本书可供个人参考，也可为三五知己分享。它无意作为旅游指南或大型团体的工具。无论你置身何处，请保持良好的判断，以免侵犯他人的隐私。请不要对政府建筑摄影摄像。

请记住这是一座日新月异的城市。今天还在的，或许明天就已消逝。

我对大多数路名使用汉语拼音，除了少数著名人物的名字以传统方式拼写，如宋氏三姐妹的"宋"字拼写为"Soong"，有别于拼音"Song"。

Acknowledgments

I SINCERELY thank my parents Kuokkan Ho and Chongwai U for knowing either directly or indirectly many of the people mentioned on my walks and for telling me stories; Myszka Reeck for suggesting that I write a book and for her great support; Tess Johnston for her generous time and advice; Peter Madany, Shelly Aschkenase and Stephanie Welsh for proof reading my book; my expatriate friends who walked with me and gave me unwavering support; and of course my husband and children for their love and encouragement.

I thank the staff at Earnshaw Books - Graham Earnshaw, Derek Sandhaus, Andrew Chubb, and Frank Zheng.

致 谢

我衷心感谢我的父亲(何国谨)、母亲(俞仲炜)，为在我本书中所提到的、许多为他们直接或间接认识的人，以及他们对我讲述的故事；感谢瑞可·米西卡(Myszka Reeck)建议我写作本书并给予了大力支持；感谢江似虹(Tess Johnston)拨冗阅读并提出宝贵建议；感谢彼得马达尼(Peter Madany)、安爱文(Shelly Aschkenase)和Stephanie Welsh为本书所作的校对；感谢那些与我一同漫步的外国朋友，以及他们对我的坚定支持；当然还要感谢我的丈夫和孩子们，感谢他们的爱和鼓励。

CONTENTS

WALK I:
From Huashan Road to the Jing An Temple Area

华山路——静安寺

A Time to Dance,
A Time to Mourn

Jing An Hotel 静安宾馆

This walk makes a loop, starting and finishing near the same stretch of Yan'an Road (M) 延安中路 in the Jing'an area. It takes you through what was known in Old Shanghai as the Chinese Territory. From the 1840s, after the first Opium War, up to World War II, Shanghai was basically divided into sections: the British and the American sections which were combined to be the International Settlement north of Yan'an Road, the French Concession, and the Chinese areas all around these two core districts.

On this walk you will stroll through a peaceful park in the traditional Chinese style that is a part of a well-known hospital, hear love stories of actresses and dancers, and be introduced to a formerly grand mansion and a popular dance hall. You will also walk through a fashionable neighborhood of the 1930s and get a glimpse of how the local Chinese people live today.

Subway Line 2—Jing'an Temple Station—Exit 2: Go up the escalator, turn left, walk south down Huashan Road, and take the pedestrian bridge over Yan'an Road (M). The Hilton Hotel is on your right; turn right at the intersection just beyond it, staying on Huashan Road, and the Jing An Hotel is on the right.

Jing An Hotel 静安宾馆

Jing An Hotel
静安宾馆
370 Huashan Rd
华山路

This tall, white building at the end of the driveway faces a rolling lawn of 6,000 square meters. Built in 1925 in the Spanish style by Elliott Hazzard, the building was originally called Elias Court Apartments, after its Sephardic Jewish owner, a prominent financier who lived in the 9th-floor penthouse. The name was later changed to Haig Court Apartments, reflecting the Old Shanghai name of Huashan Road, Avenue Haig, named after General Douglas Haig, who commanded the British Expeditionary Forces

Elliott Hazzard

Elliott Hazzard, the building's architect, grew up on a rice plantation in South Carolina and attended the Citadel. Being with the firm of well-known architect, Stanford White, Hazzard worked on New York's Lord and Taylor building, for example. In 1920 Hazzard signed a two-year contract with the Chinese government to work as a city planning consultant, as recommended by Standard Oil. After the two years were up, he stayed in China and founded his own architectural firm. He designed several buildings in Shanghai, including another building down the street, the Brookside Apartments. He died in 1943 in a Japanese internment camp.

Huashan Hospital 华山医院

during World War I.

The building was also home to several American Foreign Service officers, including John S. Service, who was known as a "China Hand". Born to missionaries in Sichuan Province in 1909, and mastering the Chinese language at an early age, he attended the Shanghai American School before moving to California with his parents. He eventually worked for the State Department and was attached to the American Consulate in Shanghai in 1938. He lived here 1939 and 1941.

He was probably evacuated along with other consular personnel after December 7, when the U.S. declared war against the Japanese after the bombing of Pearl Harbor. Later he was sent as part of the U.S. Dixie Mission to Yan'an, to assess the Communists politically and militarily. Service reported how the Communists were energized in Yan'an and predicted they would defeat the U.S.-backed Kuomintang. However he was later heavily criticized by pro-Kuomintang U.S. politicians, and Senator Joseph McCarthy accused him in 1950 of being a communist for his optimistic appraisal of the Chinese Communists. Service was fired from his State Department job but was later reinstated by the Supreme Court.

The Jing An Hotel has been altered since 1949 with an additional floor and lower ceilings. But it was one of the few high-end hotels in Shanghai before the city's recent development, and locals still look upon the hotel favorably.

After the hotel, continue along Huashan Road to the intersection with Wulumuqi Road 乌鲁木齐路, also called Urumqi Road.

Huashan Hospital
华山医院
12 Wulumuqi Rd
乌鲁木齐路
corner of Wulumuqi and Huashan Roads, entrance on right side of Wulumuqi

Huashan Hospital, established in 1910, was the earliest general teaching hospital affiliated with the Number One Shanghai Medical University. For decades it has been one of the best hospitals in Shanghai. On the eighth floor in Building No. 1, which started operations in 2004, is the fancy new clinic for foreigners.

Bear left of the building, pass the little green space, and if you continue on this path you will come to a two-story, red brick building, numbered 10. This building originally served as the **China Red Cross Hospital 中国红十会医院**, which was the former name of Huashan Hospital. Today it is used for meetings and hosting VIPs.

Go inside the Chinese garden **华山花园** at the far west end of the hospital property, and take a stroll among the ponds, trees, and rockery. Linger by the traditional Chinese buildings with latticed doors and windows painted in red. This garden transports you to a different world in a different era, away from the hustle and bustle of a modern metropolis.

There is a story about the family connected with this garden. Once upon a time, three brothers with the family name Zhou moved from Ningbo to Shanghai to seek their fortune. Legend has it that they were so poor they could afford only

Huashan Garden 华山花园

one preserved salty egg and divided it among themselves for two meals. After the brothers learned to speak some English, one would go to the harbor to trade currencies with the sailors and merchants on the boats. Such was their humble beginning. Eventually the two elder brothers left Shanghai, but the third, Zhou Liantang 周莲塘, remained. He got to know a French priest and ran errands for him. During the late 1800s, when many foreigners moved to Shanghai, Zhou acted as a liaison between the foreigners and the local Chinese. He also started his own construction business to build and repair houses. One day the French priest decided to leave China, and he transferred all his real estate holdings to Zhou. This made Zhou an important property owner. Soon he was in business with the likes of Sir Victor Sassoon, one of the most influential names in Shanghai business.

Zhou had a very capable wife, Shui Chunlan 水春兰, to help him. She would listen behind a screen when her husband held business meetings. Afterwards she would analyze for him what went well or poorly. At the year's end, she would hand out bonuses and evaluations to employees so they knew why they got what they got. Once, when accountants who had come to check the company books were seated at a banquet table, she asked the chef why there were no delicacies ready. This made the accountants feel very important.

When Zhou died, he left two sons barely in their teens. As a result, people began to question if it was wise to continue doing business with the Zhous. When Mrs Zhou heard this, she took her two sons to visit their business partners and to assure them that as long as she was alive, the Zhou business would continue as before. This impressed the many who decided to continue their business dealings with the Zhou family.

It turned out that the two sons had excellent timing in their business dealings. Between 1911 – when there was much unrest as the Qing Dynasty was being overthrown – and the 1930s – during the anti-Japanese resistance – many rich people, ex-warlords, and ex-Qing Dynasty officials moved from places like Beijing and Tianjin to Shanghai to live in the concessions. Many businesses moved to Shanghai for its relative stability. Land prices skyrocketed several times over, and the Zhous benefited greatly. They owned many lanes of houses, and those lanes all had the character "庆", meaning celebration, in their names.

Wealth was not lost on the two brothers. The elder son, Zhou Xiangyun 周湘云, was a more conservative and traditional Chinese businessman who collected Chinese antiques. The younger son, Zhou Chunqing 周纯卿, was more Westernized and had many foreigner friends. He loved cars and yachts. Motor car registration plates in Old Shanghai were issued in numerical order, and there was great 'face' to be had from possessing a low number. When he heard a doctor was returning to Denmark and wanted to sell his car, Zhou Chunqing snapped it up for its No. 1 license plate. He imprinted his family's name on his car door handles. The last time his car was seen on Shanghai streets was during his funeral in 1945.

Zhou Chunqing was the original owner of this garden, and his family came here to spend summer days. His youngest daughter, who is in her nineties, still remembers how she and her father loved to ride horses in their garden. One of Zhou's daughters contracted tuberculosis. At that time, there was no cure – the best advice was to eat well and enjoy life – and she spent her last days here. Perhaps because of this unhappy memory, Zhou later sold the garden. Today, as part of the Huashan Hospital, it is used by patients as they recuperate.

Exit the Chinese garden, and turn left onto Huashan.

Bear in mind that this street and others nearby were very quiet residential streets before Shanghai's rapid economic development began in the 1990s. There were no cars honking or people with bikes blocking the sidewalks. No little shops or restaurants lined the street either.

Continuing west along Huashan Road, on your right side, across the street, there is a large garden with red brick walls and broken glass on top of the walls. The black gates are numbered 560 Huashan Rd. The garden inside the red brick walls now belongs to the hospital that government officials favor, Huadong, formerly Country Hospital or Hong'en 宏恩医院, off Yan'an Road. The garden was the site of the former German Garden Club, a German social center. The German Ladies' Benevolent Society, a.k.a. German Women's Club, operated here in the early 1930s. Nearby were the German Pharmacy and a German radio station, XGRS. This area was known as the German Corner.

Recently a 1949 Shanghai American School graduate, Teddy Heinrichsohn, visited Shanghai and told a shocking story about when he was living near the German Corner all those long years ago. One morning in 1945, when he was 14, Teddy took a shortcut to the German Church through the grounds of the German School on the Great Western Road (today's Hilton Hotel on Huashan Road). Suddenly, a body fell off the school's roof and landed in front of him. Teddy turned around and ran away, but he later learned that it was the radio personality, Herbert Moy, of Radio XGRS. An American-born Chinese, Moy had supported the Nazis and the Japanese occupation of China; his future looked bleak once both had been defeated.

The Children's Art Theatre of China Welfare Institute
中国福利会儿童艺术剧院
639-643 Huashan Rd
华山路
left side

Housed in a series of Y-shaped buidlings, this academy is part of the China Welfare Institue established by Soong Ching-ling 宋庆龄, the widow of Dr Sun Yat-sen 孙中山, in 1947. They were designed by Moorhead and Hals and completed in 1941 to function as Cathedral Girls' School belonging to the British Anglican Church.

The Children's Art Theatre of China Welfare Institute 中国福利会儿童艺术剧院

Shanghai Theatre Academy 上海戏剧学院

Shanghai Theatre Academy
上海戏剧学院
630 Huashan Rd
华山路
right side

This is the best theater academy in town, origi-nally housed in the two-story brick building facing Huashan Road near the entrance. Built in 1903 and remodeled in 1999, it is named after the first presi-dent of the academy, Xiong Foxi 熊佛西. Xiong was a prolific playwright who completed 27 full-length dramas and 16 one-act plays.

Zhenliu Mansion
枕流公寓
(Brookside Apartments),
699 Huashan Rd
华山路
left side

This apartment building was built in 1930, and, with fireplaces and separate entrances for masters and servants, its apartments were considered first-class. Due to its proximity to the Shanghai Theater Acad-emy across the street, many playwrights, producers, directors, and actors lived here. Painters and writers also lived here, and it was once called the "Celebri-ties Mansion". The official name, Zhenliu, came from a Chinese poem, meaning a rock beside the brook.

One of the notable tenants was actress Fu Quanxiang傅全香. She sang Yueju 越剧, a style of Chinese opera in the Northern Shaoxing dialect. A fan wrote her over 1,000 love letters over five years before he was finally granted permission to meet her in her apartment in 1955. They fell in love and had a happy marriage until Fu died in 1979.

Zhenliu Mansion 枕流公寓

There is also some tragedy connected with Zhenliu Mansion. Screen actress Zhou Xuan 周璇 lived here. She had a natural affinity for remembering songs and said when she was young that she loved to hear others sing. She would hum along and was able to sing the songs after three or four times. In 1932, when she was 13, she joined a dancing and singing troupe. In 1936 she won second prize in a radio competition in Shanghai. She was dubbed the "golden voice" during her career, in which she sang more than 200 songs. At the same time, she found fame in acting and starred in over forty movies. Her most memorable role and personal favorite was *Street Angel* in 1937. Critics said her most successful role was that of an innocent girl.

Zhou Xuan suffered numerous tragedies in her personal life. Raised by adoptive parents, she searched all her life but never found her biological parents. She was divorced once and then separated from her lover of eight years, a man who refused to recognize their son.

She went on to have a second son with another man who was later sentenced to three years in jail for cheating and raping her because she was deemed mentally incompetent to have entered into the relationship. Zhou suffered from several mental breakdowns and died in 1957 at only 39. Fortunately, the memory of this theatrical great lived on through her sons and her songs.

Ahead at the intersection of Huashan Road and Changle Road 长乐路, note the large villa and garden on the left side. Sometimes the garden walls are covered because the premises are used for shooting movies. Turn right onto Zhenning Road 镇宁路.

Zhenning Road tells the story of development in Shanghai. You will see high-rises that were put up in the last decade. You will pass shops serving coffee, selling flowers, and catering to a rising middle class. Cross under the elevated highway, Yan'an Road (W), which runs from east to west across the city. Continue on Zhenning Road, and cross Yongyuan Road 永源路/Dongzhu'anbang Road 东诸安浜路 (on the corner is a Starbucks on the right side). On the north side you will come upon some lane houses from Old Shanghai.

Yuguang Cun
渔光村
255-275-285
Zhenning Rd
镇宁路
left side

These are typical upper-middle class lane houses, though in the olden days there was no air-conditioning. To take advantage of natural light, the more important and larger rooms such as the living room and master bedroom face south, while the less important rooms such as the kitchen and

Yuguang Cun 渔光村

smaller bedrooms face north. (This design was not connected with *fengshui*.)

To this day, you will see people hanging their laundry out on long poles to dry, mostly to save money, but the local people also like to put clothes, especially heavy things such as quilts and coats, in the sun to kill germs.

Just ahead you will notice a long, pale yellow wall on your left side. This wall encloses the garden that belongs to the upcoming villa.

Villa of Yan Qingxiang
699 Yuyuan Rd
愚园路
corner of Zhenning and Yuyuan Roads

Built in 1911, this villa and extensive garden belonged to Yan Qingxiang 严庆祥, who purchased it in 1940. Yan's father was a first-generation industrialist in China who, in 1902, founded a factory called Dalong Machinery Factory 大隆机械厂 that made textile machines. Inheriting the business from his father when he was only 19 years of age, Yan eventually owned two machinery factories and five cotton mills.

Yan supported Sun Yat-sen's revolution and called Sun his teacher. Sun wrote the words "博爱" (Universal Love) on a calligraphy scroll and gave it to Yan. Yan was also a philanthropist, donating generously to charitable causes, repairing a library, fixing bridges, and feeding the hungry. After Chiang Kai-shek's 1927 massacre of thousands of communists and their sympathizers, Yan visited the wounded in the China Red Cross Hospital, the red brick building in Huashan Hospital that you saw earlier on this walk. In 1933 he represented the Chinese textiles industry by attending a world conference on labor issues in Switzerland, where he suggested changing the practice of 12-hour work days.

After 1949 Yan retired due to heart problems. He organized a Shen Xian Hui 神仙会 (Immortal Club), including famous artists such as Liu Haisu 刘海粟 and Tang Yun 唐云. They met here to visit and exchange ideas. During the Cultural Revolution, Yan was locked up for a time in a steel factory. When he got home, he discovered his wife had to live in an eight-square-meter room. In his old age, Yan wrote a book called *Kongzi Yu Xiandai Sixiang* 孔子与现代思想 *(Confucian and Contemporary Ideology)*. In 1986 Yan became a board member of the Soong Ching Ling Foundation. He died in 1988 at age 80. Some of his descendants still live here, according to a mutual family friend.

After passing Yan's villa, turn right on Yuyuan Road, going east.

Yuyuan Road 愚园路 was a most fashionable street in the 1930s because of its Western-influenced architecture. This road contains two different styles of housing: lane houses and villas with gardens. When the Communists came to Shanghai to take over the city in 1949, they came from the west, passing through Yuyuan Road.

608 Yuyuan Road, left side
Built in 1938, this lane was called Wenyuan Fang 文元坊. These are lane houses with little gardens.

611 Yuyuan Road, right side
This is a good place to take photos because of the contrast of the old lane houses and the new high-rises.

532 Yuyuan Road, left side
High ranking officials of the Kuomintang lived here. Today some of these buildings house military families.

406 Yuyuan Road, left side
This large building with a grey façade was the former Shanghai Municipal Council's Girls' School

that author Betty Barr attended as a missionary's daughter. Barr, who has lived in Shanghai on-and-off for over four decades, has written two books with her Shanghainese husband, George. These books give foreigners a glimpse of what life was like in Old Shanghai and in the New China. This building is now part of Shixi High School, next door, which was the Shanghai Municipal Council's Boys' School.

**Shixi High School
市西中学
left side**

Shixi is considered a very good high school. In 2007 it had the highest percentile of students going on to college among all high schools in Shanghai. I went there for middle school and part of high school.

Across the street is the famous Bubbling Well Lane. Please cross the street carefully.

Investing in the Future

Education is of paramount importance in Chinese cities. Children study very, very hard, and school rankings matter greatly. Parents spend much time and money on tutoring programs for their children in the hope that they will excel and eventually enter the country's best universities. This, in turn, will ensure they will have good jobs in the future.

**Yong Quan Fang
涌泉坊
(Bubbling Well Lane),
95 Yuyuan Rd
愚园路
right side**

Bubbling Well Lane came from one of two sources. One source was the bubbling well that used to be near the Jing'an Temple, ten minutes east from here. Another source was the Chinese proverb that says one will repay a droplet of kindness with a fountain of gratitude (滴水之恩涌泉相报).

These lane houses were designed by a Chinese architect and built in the early 1930s. In the beginning, each house had a single family in it. After the Cultural Revolution many families moved in. Many families had only one room each. Families had to share kitchens and bathrooms. This is called "qishi'er ge fangke 七十二个房客" in Chinese; the phrase means "Seventy-two lodgers". Recently, the local government has improved the kitchen facilities with new cabinets and paint. Also, wherever possible a private bathroom is installed for each family.

This lane of houses was built by a tobacco king, Chen Chuxiang 陈楚湘 of the Huacheng Cigarette Company. Long ago, when Chinese men smoked water pipes, Chen's workers handed out cigarettes, promoting it as a new, more convenient form of smoking. The cigarettes were hand-rolled, and that was the start of his hugely successful business.

His family originally occupied Nos. 14, 18 and 24. After 1949 Chen donated No. 24 to the government. No. 14 was sold to foreigners in recent years. Chen's descendants still live in No. 18. No. 24, at the end of the lane, houses military families and has a large garden. Despite its faded look, the large villa, covered with colored tiles, still shows traces of its former beauty.

Here is a story about a lady who lived in No. 4: Lingling (not her real name) was born to a poor family. When she was a teenager, every day before the sun rose she had to line up in front of a shoe factory to get orders to make shoes, which was how she supported her family. Eventually she became a favorite dancer at the Paramount Ballroom, down the street from Yuyuan Road, and in dance halls in Hong Kong.

Lingling fell in love with a jockey from a well-to-do Shanghainese family. His family looked down on her because she was a dancer, but he married her anyway. But soon her new husband was arrested by the government as a class enemy and sent far away to do hard labor. While he was in

Bubbling Well Lane

prison, she came to Bubbling Well Lane and rented a flat. Her husband asked her to divorce him because he said there would be no future for them and that she was still young, but she refused. Sadly her husband died without ever returning home to his faithful wife.

During the Cultural Revolution, Lingling herself was sent to do hard labor, carrying cement on a pole over her shoulders. When she was released, another family had already occupied her flat, so she was forced to sleep on the landing of the stairway.

Lingling married again. Years later she immigrated to America, where she died at age 69. Despite her tortured life, she remained an elegant lady, inside and out. A tall woman, she was statuesque in her smart clothes, and every hair was always in place. She bore whatever life brought her, and she kept a smile on her face.

Outside Bubbling Well Lane, turn right and head east on Yuyuan Road. At the intersection of Yuyuan and Wulumuqi Road, you have a choice to make: you may cross Wulumuqi and continue on Yuyuan, which will lead to the Paramount where Lingling danced in about five minutes; or you may want to make a right down Wulumuqi to see the Kadoories' grand mansion at the next street corner. This will add about 15 minutes to your walk.

Bubbling Well Lane

Bubbling Well Lane was where my grandmother brought me up. We lived in No. 9. When I was born, my grandfather had just passed away. My grandmother's name was Xia Chonghua 夏重华; my grandfather was Yu Xilou 俞锡娄. My grandparents and great-grandmother were the original occupants of No. 9. My grandmother was friends with tobacco king Chen Chuxiang's wife, Jin Cuilin 金翠琳, and I went to school with some of the Chen grandsons. Lingling of No. 4 was also a good friend of my grandparents. When she moved in, most mistresses of the other houses looked down on her because she was a former dancer, but my grandparents befriended her. Their friendship endured, through thick and thin, until her death.

Former Kadoorie Mansion, now Children's Palace
少年宫
64 Yan'an Rd (W)
延安西路

Built in 1924 and costing one million taels of silver (roughly 40 tons), this garden villa covers over 14,000 square meters. The original estate covered more space to the east with a building for the servants' quarters. With extensive use of Italian marble, such

Former Kadoorie Mansion, now Children's Palace 少年宫

as in the grand ballroom and staircases, the villa, with over twenty rooms, was nicknamed "The Marble Hall". Graham Brown, who was known to drink excessively and to have romantic inspirations under alcoholic influence, designed the mansion.

In 1880 Elly Kadoorie came from Bombay to Shanghai and worked as an employee of David Sassoon & Sons. He soon made money in the Hong Kong Power and Light Company that supplied power to half of Hong Kong. He eventually had holdings in real estate, electric power utilities, rubber plantations, and banking in Hong Kong and Shanghai. He opened the first brokerage firm in Hong Kong, and also established philanthropic institutions such as Shanghai's first pulmonary tuberculosis hospital and Yuecai High School.

Lord Kadoorie had two sons, Lawrence, born in 1899 in Hong Kong, and Horace, born in 1902 in London. Lady Kadoorie died in a fire in their home while saving her maid in 1918. His sons assisted Kadoorie in making theirs a family business.

Here at the mansion, the Kadoories held lavish parties. In 1938 the Shanghai Jewish community gathered here to call for support for European Jewish refugees. The Kadoories donated money to establish a Jewish youth institute, and Elly Kadoorie was president of the Shanghai Jewish Club. When the Japanese occupied Shanghai, they put the Kadoories in a detention camp from 1941 to 1944, where Elly Kadoorie died. When his sons were first allowed home, they turned on all the lights in the mansion to celebrate. But the celebration was short-lived – they were put under house arrest in a small building next to the grand mansion. At the end of the war in 1945, they left for Hong Kong. The mansion was then used as a club for American soldiers. After 1949,

Paramount (Bailemen) Ballroom 百乐门

the mansion became the Children's Palace under the Soong Ching Ling Foundation. The Children's Palace offers recreational classes on a regular basis to children. The palace grounds are open to the public, but please check with the guard.

Of the three influential Jewish families in pre-1949 Shanghai, only the Kadoorie family still does business in China, through the Peninsula Hotel built on the grounds of the former British Consulate in Shanghai. Now retrace your steps back to Yuyuan Road and turn right, heading east.

Paramount (Bailemen) Ballroom
百乐门
corner of Yuyuan
愚园路
and Wanhangdu
万航渡路
Rds

Completed in 1933 in the Art Deco style, this building was financed by a group of bankers and was used as a meeting place for Shanghai's elite. This lasted until 1936, when the group went bankrupt. In 1937 the Paramount was converted to a dance hall with Shanghai's famous dancing hostesses. The first floor was a restaurant, and dance halls were on the second and third floors. The floors had springs underneath, making them perfect for dancing. Although it was located in the quiet west side of town, the Paramount attracted much attention. It remained a dance hall until 1949 and afterwards became a movie theater. It has been converted back to a dance hall in recent years and is popular with the local couples, but there are no more dancing hostesses.

One of the star dancers was Chen Manli 陈曼丽, known for her curvaceous body and a cultured way of talking. She even knew how to sing Peking Opera. On the night of February 25, 1940, while she was sitting and chatting with two clients, a young man dressed in a Western suit came and shot Chen three times. Her partners were shot too. Chen and one of these men died at the China Red Cross Hospital. The reason for her murder remains a mystery. Some suspected a political connection between her and a pro-Japanese traitor during World War II, while others said he was a jilted lover.

One day, Victor Sassoon came to visit. When the waitress saw he walked with a limp, she assumed he had not come to dance and so cast him aside without much attention. Enraged, Sassoon left and decided to build his own dance hall. Ciro's Night Club was soon launched, located next to the racetrack (today's People's Park 人民广场) on Nanjing Road. Decked out with neon lights, an orchestra and dancing girls, it soon surpassed the Paramount in popularity.

Diagonally across from the Paramount is the Jing'an Temple, at the corner of Huashan Road and Nanjing Road (W).

Jing'an Temple
静安寺
Nanjing West Rd
南京西路

Having demolished the older temple, the local government built the current large, yellow temple in 1983. According to the Jing'an District Government, the very original Jing'an Temple, one of the oldest Buddhist temples in China, dates back to the Three Kingdoms Period in the third century. A bubbling well near the temple on today's Nanjing West Road was the reason why this road was named Bubbling

Jing'an Temple 静安寺

Well Road in Old Shanghai, being called the "Number Six Fountain under Heaven 天下第六泉". That well was filled in 1966.

According to several Western sources, including Frommer's, there was a Jing'an Temple Abbot prior to 1949, who had several wives and lived a rather decadent life.

Jiuguang City Plaza 久光 and Fresh Mart, *Nanjing West Rd, next to the temple*

Built over former lane houses, this is a very nice department store with an excellent grocery store called Fresh Mart in the basement. There are several bakeries, restaurants, and a pharmacy there also.

Jing'an Park 静安公园 *Nanjing West Rd, across the street from the temple*

A small, serene park built on a former cemetery for foreigners in Old Shanghai, in Jing'an Park you will find lots of trees, a rockery, a waterfall, and a pond. In the back corner on the left side of the park is a little garden in the traditional Chinese style. It is called the Jing'an Eight Scenic Spots Park (**静安八景园**), recreating the eight scenic spots in the Jing'an area from the Three Kingdoms Period (3rd century A.D.) to the 13th century. They include the Hudu Rampart built during the reign of Emperor Chen (326-342 B.C.) of the Eastern Jin Dynasty (317-420)

Jing'an Park 静安公园

to protect the local people from sea pirates, and the Green Cloud Cave that was the residence of Abbott Shouning in the Yuan Dynasty from 1208 to 1225.

Underneath the park, there is a shopping plaza near the subway station's No. 2 exit. Email Fashion Plaza 伊美时尚 has two stories full of many little shops that sell mostly women's clothes and accessories. Here you may finish your walk with a bargain: the prices are low, and you can haggle, too.

Further Reading:
Jing An Hotel:
Heritage plaque
Frenchtown: Shanghai Western Architecture in Shanghai's Old French Concession by Tess Johnston and Deke Erh, Old China Hand Press, 2000, pp. 77-79

The Zhou Family:
Shanghai De Haomen Jiumeng (Old Dreams of the Shanghai Super Rich) by Song Luxia, China Friendship Publishing Co., 2002, pp.306-337
"The Daughter of the No. 1 Car License Plate Owner Zhou Chunqing: Zhou Suqiong" by Song Luxia

Zhenliu Apartments:
A Walker's Guide to Old Western Landmarks in Shanghai Compiled by Shanghai Daily, 2008, pp. 164-168

Zhou Xuan:
baike.baidu.com

Yan Residence:
Famous People, Houses & stories by Huang Guoxin, Tongji University Publisher, 2003, pp. 155-157
Lao Shanghai Huayuan Yangfang (Old Shanghai Garden Villas) by Xue Shunsheng, Tongji Daxue Chubanshe, 2002, pp. 196-197

Yong Quan Fang/Chen Chuxiang:
Lao Shanghai Huayuan Yangfang (Old Shanghai Garden Villa) by Xue Shunsheng, Tongji Daxue Chubashe, 2002, pp. 68-69

Kadoorie Mansion:
A Walker's Guide to Old Western Landmarks in Shanghai
Compiled by Shanghai Daily, 2008, pp. 65-69
Famous People, Houses and Stories by Huang Guoxin,
Tongji University Publisher, 2003, pp. 344-346
Peace and Prosperity: Classical Buildings of Jing'an District, Shanghai, Shanghai Cultural Publishing Co.

The Paramount:
Shanghai Laoyangfang (Shanghai Old Villas) by Song Luxia, Shanghai Science and Technology Cultural Publishing Co., 2004, pp. 126-131

Jing'an Park:
Foreign Devils Have Blue Eyes by Dorothy Carney

Other:
Jing'an District Government, www.jingan.gov.cn

WALK I: A TIME TO DANCE, A TIME TO MOURN

WALK II:
From Huashan Road
To Maoming Road (S)
华山路——茂名南路

True Colors

This walk takes place in the former French Concession. After the first Opium War (1842-43), foreign powers demanded and received land from the imperial court of the Qing Dynasty; the foreigners lived in settlements built on this land. In Shanghai the International Settlement, representing American and British interests, was governed by a municipal council. The French Concession, which consisted mostly of Chinese, Russian, and French people, was under French control. Both had their own laws and regulations. Within both, foreigners were considered to be under foreign jurisdiction, not answerable to Chinese laws.

Foreign Settlements

The British settlement was established in 1845, the American was established in 1848, and the French was established in 1849. In 1863 the British and American combined theirs and called it the International Settlement. Although the settlements ceased to exist in effect during the Japanese occupation, they were formally dissolved in 1943.

Along this walk we will meander through a mostly residential section of the former French Concession, hearing stories of people who overcame personal and social difficulties to make indelible marks on 20th century Chinese history. You will get to know a reform educator who advocated women's rights, the gangster who ruled the underworld, a merchant who treasured antique books, and a singer-turned-restaurateur and communist activist. They all endured many dark periods but believed that the future would be brighter for China.

Subway Line 2—Jing'an Temple Station—Exit 2: Go up the escalator, turn left. Turn left onto Huashan Road, going south. Take the pedestrian bridge over

Cai Yuanpei Residence and Museum 蔡元培故居陈列馆

Yan'an Middle Road. Continue on Huashan Road, until you come to Lane 303.

This villa is in a lane across the street from the Hilton Hotel. It is hard to find, so you will need to look carefully for the sign 303 弄 (Lane 303). At the entrance to the lane, there's a black sculpture of Cai Yuanpei and a plaque in Chinese on the wall with an inscription from Chairman Mao Zedong: 学界泰斗, 人世楷模 ("eminent academic scholar, leading world model"). Just inside the lane, you will see a small sign pointing to the right. Bear right and the museum is on your right, two-thirds of the way down.

Cai Yuanpei (1868-1940) was perhaps the most prominent Chinese educator of the 20th century. Through his progressive efforts, he put China on a new educational path, breaking with the imperial system and advocating learning for the masses.

Although he himself passed the imperial exam and became an editor at the Imperial Academy at age 26 in 1894, he was disappointed to see a weak nation under the Qing Dynasty's rule, and particularly by China's defeat to Japan during the war of 1894-1895. He believed that education was

Cai Yuanpei Residence and Museum 蔡元培故居陈列馆
No. 16, Lane 303 Huashan Rd 华山路303弄16号
(The free museum is closed on Mondays; Museum material is in Chinese and English.)

Cai Yuanpei Residence and Museum 蔡元培故居陈列馆

essential to properly foster talented youth and, through them, change China's destiny.

Twice Cai Yuanpei went abroad, to Germany and France, to study. He came away with the idea of education for the common folk and emphasized studying science, as distinct from the traditional Chinese approach of Confucian teachings and literature. When he was the minister of education under Prime Minister Tang Chaoyi in the provisional government in 1911, he devised five goals for China's education system: national military education, materialism education, morality education, worldview education, and aesthetics education. He thought a well-rounded education would save China from the internal chaos and external aggression of the time.

He became chancellor of Peking University from 1917 to 1923 and is noted for being the first chancellor to allow women to listen to lectures given at the university. Under his leadership, the university established several research centers in areas such as chemistry, calligraphy, philosophy, music, and martial arts. Later he opened the

National Conservatory of Music, which became the Shanghai Music Conservatory, a prestigious music school to this date.

In 1928 Cai resigned from all his posts to concentrate on his job as president of the Academia Sinica located in Shanghai. He held this title until his death in 1940. Because of his leadership, the Academia Sinica established nine research institutes and one museum of natural history. The History Research Institute sponsored archeological digs and discovered the Ruins of Yin, the capital of the latter half of China's second dynasty, the Shang Dynasty, which spanned from 1600 to 1046 B.C. Another achievement was establishing the Zijinshan (Purple Mountain) Observatory in Nanjing. It is still one of the best-known observatories in China.

Cai was also a progressive thinker with regard to marriage. When his first wife died, people tried to match-make for him. So Cai set out several conditions for his next potential marriage, including these three: (1) if either spouse was unhappy, they could separate; (2) the woman would not have bound feet; and (3) the man would not have concubines. You will see in the museum materials that on his wedding night to his second wife in Hangzhou in 1902, instead of the traditional celebration of eating, drinking, and singing in the newlyweds' chamber, he held a lecture, presumably on education and politics!

He briefly lived in this house in 1937, mainly because it was away from a main street and therefore a safer location for him during the Japanese occupation of Shanghai. It was his last residence in the city before he left for Hong Kong, where he died a few short years later. His wife and children came back to live in this house after Cai's death.

During the Cultural Revolution, Red Guards

stormed into the house and took away correspon-dence from Sun Yat-sen 孙中山, the founder of the Republic of China. They left letters from the fa-mous writer Lu Xun 鲁迅 because Lu had signed using his official name, Zhou Shuren, which the Red Guards did not know. They wrote "useless" on the letters and left them behind. That's how some important history was preserved, according to Cai Yuanpei's youngest daughter, Cai Sui'ang 蔡睟盎, a successful scientist in her own right who still lives upstairs.

Walk back onto Huashan Road and turn left. At the next street corner, turn left onto Julu Road, heading east.

Lu Xun

A short-story writer, essayist, translator, and poet, Lu Xun (1881-1936) wrote in both the vernacular and classical style. He was considered a major writer of the 20th century in every style except the novel. Educated in Japan and trained as a medical doctor, Lu Xun chose to be a writer. He was heavily influenced by the May Fourth Movement, the student-led protests of 1919 against the Chinese Government's acceptance of the Treaty of Versailles. After Germany's defeat in World War I, the Treaty transferred the German concessions in Shandong Province to Japan, rather than return-ing them to China. Throughout his career, Lu Xun's writing boldly criticized China's social problems and weaknesses. His former home and museum are located in the Hongkou District and are open to the public.

Julu Road 巨鹿路

Stroll down a short section until you are near the intersection of Julu and Fumin Road 富民路. Despite their faded appearance, the villas and lane houses on this narrow street still show how they used to be desirable places to live. While they served as individual residences in the old days prior to 1949, now several middle-class families may share a villa or lane house.

Bamboo Alley
803 Julu Rd, close to the intersection of Julu and Fumin Road, right side

Here is a charming little path of bamboo trees that passers-by might miss easily. Guess what is at the end of the path – a house? A garden? Well, it's a Japanese restaurant, and very reputable according to general reviews. The door slides open automatically as you approach, and the interior is noted for its warehouse look – spacious, bare, and with a monochrome color scheme. Combined with the little bamboo alley, the restaurant is undoubtedly in an interesting setting.

Go back to Julu Road and turn left, going west. Turn left when you come to Lane 889.

Bamboo Alley

889 Julu Road

In 1903 the English company, Shell Transport, and the Netherlands company, Royal Dutch, formed Asiatic Petroleum Company, Ltd. Originally built for Asiatic Petroleum executives in Old Shanghai, these villas now belong to the government.

The villas facing you have been turned into restaurants in recent years. Go up to the villas, turn left, and walk to the end to a set of gates. Called the Garden Villas, 苑园, the elegant houses inside the gates have been recently renovated and turned into a government boutique hotel. While it does not advertise publicly, its rooms are available for rent when they are not used for official functions.

Turn around and walk back past the restaurants on your left and continue walking straight to the T-intersection ahead. The main street is Changshu Road 常熟路. Turn left to go south.

889 Julu Road

At the intersection of Changshu Road and Changle Road, head straight across at the lights and then turn left to walk east along Changle Road 长乐路.

Changle Road, Julu Road, and many other streets in this area were quiet residential places before Shanghai's recent rapid economic expansion. You will be walking down what's now a noisy, narrow street with traffic jams – yet the lane houses, town-houses, and villas behind garden walls remain.

Cross Huating Road 华亭路 where a subway station for Line 1 is located, and continue on Changle Road.

Shanghai Lan-Lan Chinese Hand Printed Blue Nankeen Co., Ltd.
No. 24, Lane 637 Changle Rd, right side

Walking to the end of the lane, you may have to walk under laundry hanging on poles. Pass through the iron gates, turn immediately right, and walk through the narrow side passage. As you emerge, a garden unfolds in front of you, where you will see blue-and-white fabrics blowing in the wind. In the spring when the flowers and trees are budding, it is an especially pretty scene to come upon.

You have arrived at the place where the traditional Chinese hand-printed blue and white fabrics are made. There is a small museum and shop inside the villa on your left. Feel free to wander around inside. The museum shows the process of making the fabric. This fabric, coming in different patterns

Shanghai Lan-Lan Chinese Hand Printed Blue Nankeen Co., Ltd.

from the lower Yangtze Delta area, is a symbol of the rural look on women's clothes and household items such as quilts. In the shop you can either buy products ready-made or custom order.

Retracing your steps, go back out of the lane and turn right back onto Changle Road.

Blue Nankeen

The blue comes from the indigo plant grown in the mountains of Anhui Province. A process of block-cut, paste and dip-and-dye results in this distinctive look. The paste is made with powders of glutinous rice, plaster, and yellow beans. The process starts in Anhui Province where the paste is applied, then the fabric is transported here, where the paste is scraped off and the fabric washed and dried. The patterns are based on folklore – they are never random. The 1,800 year old tradition of making the blue-and-white fabric is a dying art in China, as most young people are no longer interested in learning it.

752-764 Changle Road, left side

Further along Changle Road, across the street near the upcoming corner, is a bunch of attractive and neat-looking townhouses with patios. Two years ago, the end unit, near Fumin Road, was sold for 10 million RMB. Real estate in desirable areas of Shanghai has risen sharply in value, especially in the last five years, though the world financial crisis has put a damper on the market in general.

From Changle Road, turn right onto Donghu Road 东湖路. At the next corner, Yanqing Road 延庆路, note the blue apartment building at **No. 2 Yanqing Road**. This building housed Russian Jews, including Rena Krasno's family. Krasno has written several books, chronicling her life in Old Shanghai and Japan during World War II. The lane next to the blue apartment building, **Lane 4 Yanqing Road**,

Dong Hu Hotel 东湖宾馆

has a winding stairway in front of the landing of each house, leading up to the front door, and is a relatively unusual style of lane house.

Now, cross Yanqing Road and continue south on Donghu, and our next destination is across the street on Donghu Road.

Dong Hu Hotel
东湖宾馆
70 Donghu Rd, corner of Xinle Road and Donghu Road, marked by a pagoda with a blue tiled roof on top of a rockery inside a glassed-in area

The hotel entrance is on your left side, just a few paces ahead.

Du Yuesheng 杜月笙, nicknamed Big-Ear Du because of his Dumbo-like ears, was a key figure in politics, commerce, and society from the 1920s to the 1940s. He was called the Godfather of Shanghai because he was the leader of the infamous Green Gang that controlled the city's underground world.

Du received this building as a gift. Although he never lived in it, he helped design and install the garden's rockery, with its charming pagoda on top. The garden was used by Du for ancestor worship and as a quiet place for drinking tea and resting. Today the interior of the huge building behind the pagoda has been altered significantly to make it into a hotel.

Du (1881-1951) was born in Pudong to poor

parents. His mother died after giving birth to Du's younger sister. Unable to feed the family, Du's father gave his new daughter to a Ningbo merchant, and, though he searched his whole life, Du was never able to find her. Du's father was soon remarried, but he died when Du was five. One day Du's stepmother, a kind woman, disappeared, mostly likely having been kidnapped, and Du went to live with his grandmother for the next five years. At 13, he moved across the river to work as an apprentice in a Shanghai fruit shop. Before long he joined the Green Gang, a gang of thieves, extortionists, and thugs. When Du was introduced to Huang Jinrong 黄金荣, the gang boss of the time, Huang's wife Guisheng Jie 桂生姐 realized Du's potential and made him their assistant. In 1925 the Huangs opened a company called Sanxin 三鑫 Corporation, trading in opium. Du was made a partner.

Huang held the highest title among the Chinese in the French Concession police force. Along with another gangster, Zhang Xiaolin 张啸林, Du and Huang ran the Concession's underworld businesses: opium dens, brothels, trade unions, kidnapping, hired killers, trade protection rackets, and smuggling. Du employed 16 to 24 White Russian body guards. White Russians were preferred body guards because often they had training in firearms, they were tall, and they did not speak Chinese so there was no danger of the boss being sold out to a competing gang.

Although he was illiterate, Du had others read the Chinese classic novels to him. From books like *The Romance of the Three Kingdoms*, he learned to use military strategies for his personal dealings with politicians. At his most successful, Du had titles in over seventy companies including clubs, gambling parlors, banks, shipping businesses, and factories.

He even founded a bank. He supported Chiang Kai-shek 蒋介石, especially during the Kuomintang massacre of communists in 1927. But he did not co-operate with the Japanese during World War II. Du also organized and donated to good causes such as natural disaster relief.

Despite his ruthless reputation, Du was known to be charismatic and generous to his friends. Du enjoyed Peking opera, so it was no surprise that the last two of his five wives were opera singers. He left Shanghai in 1949 and died in Hong Kong in 1951.

Back outside the Dong Hu Hotel, turn right onto Donghu Road. At the street corner, turn right again onto Xinle Road 新乐路, going east.

Xinle Road has several restaurants that serve Japanese, Chinese, and Western food, and expensive boutiques that are popular with foreigners. Nicknamed Mistress Street, the road is reputedly where rich men buy clothes for their mistresses.

Du's Legacy

In the late 1970s, my parents and I attended the wedding of Du's grandson, Du Gonghao 杜公浩, when he married the granddaughter of Shi Liangcai 史良才, a newspaper magnate in Old Shanghai. The Kuomintang assassinated Shi, whose story and former house are visited in Walk III, "Money and Trouble".

63 Xinle Road, right side

Half way to the next intersection, there is a large yellow apartment building. In the center of the building is a long, narrow, vertical window. Buildings with such interesting architectural details give the French Concession a distinctive style. Throughout the French Concession there are platane trees planted by the French. The branches of these resilient trees on both sides of the street bend together in the middle to make a shaded path underneath.

Former Russian Orthodox Mission Church
55 Xinle Road, corner of Xinle and Xiangyang Rd
襄阳路

The church was built between 1932 and 1934 to serve the thousands of Russians living in the French Concession at the time. More recently, it was a bar and a restaurant. It has recently been renovated, but what its next use will be is still unclear. Several local people in their seventies have pointed out to me that the gray-blue color of the domes is not the original color – in the old days, they were a brilliant blue.

Little Russia

In Old Shanghai, many Russians called the French Concession home. Many were Russian aristocrats – "White Russians" – who had escaped after the deadly Revolution of 1917. Often arriving in Shanghai with little money, they worked as doormen, bodyguards, dancers, and governesses. They accounted for the second-largest population in the French Concession, next to the Chinese.

Mansion Hotel
82 Xinle Rd, opposite the Russian Orthodox Church

Built in 1932, the hotel's lobby is beautifully decorated in period furniture, and there are pictures of Du Yuesheng and souvenirs from Old Shanghai. The hotel brochure claims this was the Sanxin Corporation's headquarters and clubhouse, both run by the three gangsters, Huang Jinrong, Du Yuesheng, and Zhang Xiaolin, as discussed above. Today the hotel has a rooftop restaurant. On a warm day it is delightful to sit on the balcony – also part of the restaurant – having a drink and watching the quaint neighborhood below.

Outside the hotel, retrace your steps onto Xinle Road. At the intersection, turn right onto Fumin Road **富民路** .

The statue you see in the green space on your left side is Tian Han **田汉**, who wrote the words to

WALK II: TRUE COLORS

Liu Yuan 柳园

Liu Yuan
柳园
672 Changle Rd
长乐路
left side

the Chinese National Anthem.

Turn right again onto Changle Road, going east.

Liu Yutang 柳钰堂 came from Ningbo, Zhejiang Province and made his fortune in the shipping business. This lane of houses belonged to his family. He had three sons – the elder died, and the other two were not interested in shipping. Their names were Liu Zhonghao 柳中浩 and Liu Zhongliang 柳中亮, and they liked movies. They eventually owned three popular theaters and three movie production companies. During the 1930s, as an anti-Japanese fever was sweeping through Shanghai, the Liu brothers declared they would show Chinese movies only.

The next generation produced three actors, Liu Hegang 柳和纲, Liu Heqing 柳和清, and Liu Heqiang 柳和锵. Actresses Fenghuang 凤凰 and Wang Danfeng 王丹凤 were daughters-in-law.

The wife of Liu Zhonghao, Li Meizhen 柳梅箴, was a movie buff. In 1934 she saw actress Zhou Xuan 周璇 perform and, impressed by her singing, she invited Zhou to visit at home. When Li heard about Zhou's sad childhood and her unsuccessful search for her birth parents, Li made Zhou her goddaughter. From then on, whatever clothes and jewelry she and her husband bought for their own daughter, they also bought a set for Zhou. Zhou's tragic story is told in Walk I, "A Time to Dance, A Time to Mourn".

During the anti-Japanese Resistance Movement, the Liu production company decided to make a movie based on the famous Qing Dynasty prostitute, Sai Jinhua 赛金花, who married a German man. The Liu movie was a political satire, criticizing Chiang Kai-shek for not fighting the Japanese with the idea that Chiang, like Sai, had sold out China. One actress who auditioned for the part of Sai was Lan Ping 蓝苹. She did not get the part. Decades later, she was known as Comrade Jiang Qing 江青同志, Chairman Mao's wife, officially the prime villain of the Cultural Revolution. One day, probably in the early 1950s, she passed a Liu theater and commented on it still being open for business. Soon after, three movies from the Liu production companies were denied the requisite government approval. Was it a coincidence?

Pan Mingxun
潘明训
Residence
666 Changle Rd
长乐路
next to the Liu Yuan

This yellow villa was built in the late 1920s and is now a hospital. The original owner, Pan Mingxun, came up from Guangdong Province in 1919. He started as a clerk in a foreign bank, learned to speak English, became a salesman, and eventually held a senior position in the Shanghai Municipal Council – the International Settlement's highest authority. Pan had a passion for collecting books from the Song (960-1279) and Yuan (1279-1368) Dynasties.

There once was a man by the name of Yuan Kewen 袁克文, a man particularly fond of partying and spending money. He was the second son of the famous general, president, and self-proclaimed emperor, Yuan Shikai 袁世凱. In order to live well and continue to party, Yuan Kewen decided to sell his family's collections from the Song and Yuan Dynasties, so he came to see Pan. Pan paid 10,000 taels (1 tael = 1 1/3 ounces) of silver for the first set, and from then on Yuan sold one-of-a-kind books in mint condition to Pan. Pan stored his collection in

Yuan Shikai

Yuan Kewen was the son of Yuan Shikai, or Yuan Shih-K'ai (1859-1916), one of the most important politicians in recent Chinese history. Yuan Shikai spent twelve years in Korea in charge of the Chinese military's mission to prevent Japanese dominance there. After leaving shortly before the war between China and Japan over Korea in 1894, in which China was badly defeated, Yuan was assigned to modernize the military for the Qing Dynasty. He was dismissed after his patron, Empress Dowager Cixi 慈西, died in 1908. But he was called back by the imperial court to deal with the Xinhai Revolution of 1911, in which reformers overthrew the Qing Dynasty. Yuan was slow to agree, and acquiesced only after he was assured the office of prime minister. He entered into negotiations with the revolutionaries, and even temporarily sided with them in calling for the emperor to abdicate. By March 12, 1912 when the dynasty fell, Yuan had secured himself the position of President of the Republic, opposing Sun Yat-sen's idealist principles. In 1915, Japan demanded the control of formerly German territory in Shandong and Manchuria, presenting Yuan with what came to be known as the Twenty-One Demands, which Yuan gave in to. Further, he dissolved the parliament and proclaimed himself emperor. But there was much opposition to his scheming, and his empire lasted only three months until March 1916. He died that year in June.

this villa, which he named Baolitang 宝礼堂 (these three characters can mean either "Precious Ceremony House" or "Precious Gift House").

By 1941 Pan had died and his son, Pan Shizi 潘世兹, inherited his father's estate. Fearing the Japanese would come to destroy it, he asked a British organization to help. They put the collection on a British military craft and shipped it to Hong Kong for safe-keeping in the vaults of HSBC. In 1951 the collection returned to China, but this time it did not come to Changle Road but to the Beijing Library, to which Pan Shizi had donated the collection of 104 books from the Song Dynasty and seven books from the Yuan Dynasty. Today the collection bears the words "Donated by Pan". Pan Shizi also donated the villa to the government.

Pan Shizi was known as a gentleman and a scholar who was educated in America and spoke excellent English. He was the last president of the St. John's University before the school was dissolved in 1952 and its various departments combined with other universities. Pan is still remembered fondly by his students, my own father being one of them. Afterwards he became a professor at Fudan University.

After his wife and son moved to the United States, Pan remained in Shanghai. His last years were lonely ones, being taken care of by a maid after suffering a stroke. However, he finished a major translation called *Sanzi Jing* 三字经 ("Canon in Three Characters"), a 13th century compilation of Confucian thoughts to teach young children in couplets of three characters. It was required reading for children in Singapore, by order of President Lee Kuan Yew. Pan died in 1992 at age 84.

Continuing east along Changle Road, cross Xiangyang Road (N) 襄阳北路.

St. John's University

St. John's University, by the banks of the Suzhou Creek on the west side of Shanghai, was an Anglican college established in 1879 by Bishop Samuel Isaac Joseph Schereschewsky. The architect of the quadrangle on campus was William Halsey Wood of Newark, New Jersey, U.S.A. St. John's started with 39 students, and instruction was initially in Chinese, though it changed to English in 1891. In 1905 it became St. John's University. Having been registered in Washington, DC, the school enjoyed the status of a U.S. domestic college; thus, graduates could go directly to graduate schools in the U.S. The school had a reputation as an excellent educational institution, and its students tended to come from wealthy families who loved Western ways of life. In 1952, when the school was split up, most professors went to Fudan University and the East China Normal University. The St. John's campus became the East China University of Politics and Law 华东政法大学, and remains so to this day. The campus has preserved many of the original buildings and is worth a visit. The school offers a short course, conducted in English, introducing Chinese laws and regulations. East China University of Politics and Law, 1575 Wanhangdu Road 万航度路, Subway Lines 2, 3 and 4, Zhongshan Park Station.

Shanghai First Maternity and Infant Health Hospital
上海第一妇女婴儿保键医院
536 Changle Rd, left side

One of the best maternity hospitals in the city, it has a swimming program for infants as young as three days. If you go at the right time in the morning (9.30) or afternoon (1.30), you can see babies soaking in little tubs. But please note, things in Shanghai change quickly, so the swimming program and/or the times may have changed.

In many places across Shanghai, and indeed in most of China, shops selling similar products are located on the same street. Around this hospital are stores selling maternity wear and infant products.

337-329 Block of Changle Road 长乐路337–329号

337-329 Block of Changle Road, right side, immediately across from the hospital

This stretch of the street used to flood, so it was raised. That is why the first-floor doors and windows on these buildings appear to be so low.

This two-story bookstore is one of the few bookstores in Shanghai carrying English books. Yummy

Garden Books & Coffee and Ice Cream
325 Changle Rd, right side

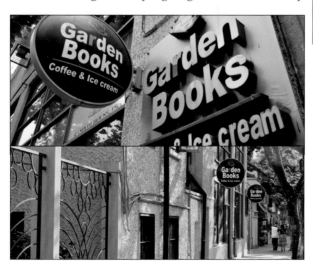

Garden Books & Coffee and Ice Cream

WALK II: TRUE COLORS

Changle Cun 长乐村

ice cream is sold on the ground floor, and there is an area to sit and read.

Outside the bookstore, turn right. Go straight on through the intersection of Changle Road and Shaanxi Road (S) **陕西南路**.

Changle Cun 长乐村 (Changle Village)
197 Changle Rd, right side

The number "197" is marked on the first building on the right side inside the lane.

You can get a good sense of what a local community is like by taking a peek down these lanes of charming townhouses with little gardens. laundry hang on poles, and old people sit in the back alley, cleaning vegetables or chatting to neighbors.

Back outside the village, turn right and continue along Changle Road to the next intersection.

Lyceum Theatre 兰心剧院
corner of Changle Rd and Maoming Rd (S) 茂名南路

Originally built in 1866 on Yuanmingyuan Road near the Suzhou Creek, after being destroyed in a fire the theater was rebuilt here in 1931 by the British Consul for the Amateur Dramatic Society. Once the British prima ballerina assoluta Margot Fonteyn danced here. It is one of the best-known theaters in Shanghai. In recent years, the International Festival Chorus performed Handel's *Messiah* here

Lyceum Theatre 兰心剧院

in December. The IFC is an amateur choral group composed of many foreigners and some local Chinese people, and is one of the very few truly

Margot Fonteyn

Margot Fonteyn (1919-1991), born to an English father and Brazilian mother, was considered one of the greatest ballerinas of the 20th century. Her performance as Aurora in Tchaikovsky's Sleeping Beauty stood out especially, and she formed a life-long partnership with Rudolf Nureyev, who had defected to the West. She also had a colorful personal life. She was married to a Panamanian diplomat and playboy, Dr. Roberto Arias. Fonteyn was arrested when Arias tried a coup to overthrow the government. In 1965 a rival politician shot Arias, which left him a quadriplegic. She stayed with him partly because she was very close to his children from a previous marriage. His burdensome medical bills, which caused her to continue to work, drained her money, so the Royal Ballet held a special gala in 1990 for her benefit. Shortly after her husband's death, she was diagnosed with cancer, and she died in Panama, where she had lived on a cattle farm.

Okura Garden Hotel 花园饭店

cross-cultural gatherings in Shanghai.

Turn right onto Maoming Road (S), heading south.

Flanked by two landmark hotels, the Okura Garden Hotel and the Jin Jiang Hotel, this stretch of Maoming Road is at the heart of the former French Concession. It is one of the very few commercial streets in Shanghai that have not changed much since the recent economic development. Because my parents' home was a stone's throw away, I used to love walking down this short block. Even today, it is still my favorite commercial street in the city because it is a clean, elegant, and stylish street. There are also many boutiques on Maoming Road, both north and south of this section.

Okura Garden Hotel
花园饭店
58 Maoming Rd (S)
茂名南路
right side

Using the east entrance (swing doors) on Maoming Road, you may go inside the former French Club to admire the perfectly preserved original architecture and design. Climb the broad circular stairway, and observe the classic Art Deco style of Old Shanghai. The nude figures on the landing were covered during the Cultural Revolution. If the banquet hall is open, take a look inside. Look up at the rich colors of the oval stained glass in the center of the ceiling.

Jin Jiang Hotel 锦江饭店

Designed by Paul Veysseyre, an architect responsible for many buildings in the French Concession, this two-story structure was built in 1926. Members played croquet on the lawn, and there were twenty tennis courts. Today the garden often hosts weddings.

It was the first club to admit Chinese as members. My own grandfather, He Gonghua 何公华 (a.k.a. He Xianhua 何显华), the chief engineer in a French company called Longhai Railway Co. 陇海铁路, liked to entertain his friends at the club as he spoke French. The club was also the first to allow women, though they were limited to forty at a time. Tea dances on Sunday afternoons were a favorite activity with the younger set.

American soldiers occupied the building during the 1940s, and after 1949 the hotel was used as a club for elite government officials. In the early 1980s this was a gathering place for foreign diplomats. In 1985 the hotel was turned into the Okura, with work completed in 1989 when the high-rise wing was added.

Jin Jiang Hotel
锦江饭店
59 Maoming Rd (S), across the street from the Okura Garden Hotel

The Old Jin Jiang Hotel was originally called Cathay Mansions, being the tallest building in Shanghai in 1929 and belonging to Victor Sassoon, whom we met briefly on Walk I, "A Time to Dance, A Time to Mourn".

Before Cathay Mansions, Victor Sassoon had built the Cathay Hotel, also known as Sassoon House (today's Peace Hotel), on the Bund. That created a sensation because it was the tallest building in Shanghai at the time, boldly built on reclaimed swamp land. Somehow, the ground did not sink under its weight.

On the same grounds as Cathay Mansions is an apartment building called Grosvenor House, but it has always been known as Eighteen Floors 十八层楼 to the locals. It was built after the Cathay Mansions had been completed, and also belonged to Victor Sassoon. In those days Grosvenor House was considered to be first-class apartments in Shanghai, and even today the location of this building is extremely desirable.

It was in the Jin Jiang Hotel that Chinese Premier Zhou Enlai 周恩来 and U.S. President Richard Nixon signed the Shanghai Communiqué in 1972. This Sino-U.S. agreement paved the way for the first diplomatic relations between the two countries since 1949. Along with Deng Xiaoping's 邓小平 1978 Four Modernizations, the communiqué led to today's tide of expatriates coming to China to live and to trade.

According to a business directory of the time, a woman named Marie Logan was the manager – a rare occurrence back then. Interestingly, in the post-1949 New China the first manger was also a woman. The following is the story of Dong Zhujun 董竹君, the Jin Jiang Hotel's general manager after 1949, and how the current name of the hotel came about:

Dong Zhujun (1900-1997) was born in Shanghai to a poor family. Her father pulled a rickshaw, and her mother was a cleaning woman. When she was 13 years of age, her father fell ill and could no longer work to support the family. So, Dong was sold to a brothel – to sing though, not to sell her body. She had a nice voice and was a quick learner, and she soon became a favorite singer. In this brothel, she met Xia Zhishi 夏之时, who had followed Sun Yatsen's revolution while studying in Japan. He became a soldier and fought bravely in the Xinhai Revolution of 1911. He was appointed the vice-governor of Sichuan at age 24. But Yuan Shikai soon seized power and considered Xia an enemy because of his allegiance to Sun, so Xia needed to escape to Japan. He asked Dong to come along, and she agreed on three conditions: She was to go not as a mistress but as a wife; Xia would send her to school in Japan; and when they returned to China, Xia would be a politician, and Dong would be a homemaker and assistant to him. Xia agreed, and the couple married in 1914. Xia was 27, and Dong 14.

Upon their return to China, they lived in Chongqing with Xia's old-fashioned family, in which boys were more important than girls. She bore him four daughters and one son. Meanwhile Xia never regained his political position, became depressed, started smoking opium, and was unhappy about having four daughters. He forbade his daughters to go to school and became abusive towards his family. Once he kicked Dong with his boots and tried to chase her down the street with a knife.

Dong escaped her terrible marriage by moving to Shanghai with her daughters in 1929, but she paid a heavy price by leaving her three-year-old son behind: they would not see each other again for over ten years. In Shanghai in 1930, she opened a textile factory with the help of an uncle and friends, but the factory was bombed by the Japanese on

January 28, 1932. She was then thrown in jail by the Kuomintang, suspected of being a Communist Party member after she refused to pay a bribe.

One day a merchant from Sichuan who had heard of her plight offered her 2,000 yuan. With this money she opened a Sichuan-style restaurant in Shanghai in 1935. It was called Jin Jiang 锦江 (King Kong) Restaurant, the name meaning "Shining River" or "Lustrous Silk Washed in the River". The decor was a fusion of Chinese and Western style, and the plates had a signature design of sprigs of bamboo. She used Japanese lanterns, birdcages, and fresh flowers to create a special atmosphere, and the restaurant was a huge success from the start. One frequent customer was Du Yuesheng, the gangster boss, and he even helped her expand her restaurant. A year later, Dong opened a Jin Jiang Tea House.

During this time, Dong was deeply involved in social work. She sponsored college students with tuition payments, established a magazine called *Shanghai Women* 上海妇女, and financially supported some Communist Party members who were on the run. Her restaurant became a meeting place and a contact post for the underground communists. Dong was able to help protect communists being sought by the Kuomintang by sending advance warnings to them, and rescue others in prison through her friendships with KMT officials. From 1941 to 1945 she lived in Manila to avoid the Japanese because she had refused to cooperate with or support them.

In 1951 the Communist Party government decided to establish a luxury hotel to host high-ranking officials and foreign visitors. They chose the Cathay Mansions building, and Dong was asked to be the general manager. Ever the shrewd businesswoman, she both took the job and moved her restaurant and teahouse there. Hence the Jin Jiang Hotel was born.

During the Cultural Revolution, Dong was accused of being a double agent and was imprisoned from 1967 to 1972. In all those five years, she wore the same t-shirt and spent only 20 RMB to buy soap, toilet paper, and toothpaste from her prison warden.

Later, Dong wrote an autobiography called *My Century* 我的一世, and one of her daughters became a filmmaker and made a documentary about her.

I met Dong Zhujun at her Siheyuan (ancient shared-courtyard houses) home in Beijing in 1979 because she was a family friend. At that time, I was too young to appreciate her incredible history. Only when I heard her name mentioned on the radio in early 2007 did I realize that her story would be worth telling. At that time I decided to devise a walk with the story of Dong Zhujun as the highlight and the Jin Jiang Hotel as the final stop.

Just ahead at the intersection of Maoming Road (S) and Huaihai Road (M), there is a subway station for Line 1. Formerly Avenue Joffre, Huaihai Road is today famous once again for its many shops and restaurants.

Further Reading:
Cai Yuanpei:
Cai, *My Father's Generation and Beijing University,* Peking University Press, 2006

Du Yuesheng:
Du, the godfather of Shanghai, chinadaily.com.cn
Gangster Remembered for Culture and Blood, chinaview.cn
Shen Ji, *Shanghai Da Hang (Shanghai's Big Shots),* Xuelin Publishing House, 2007
Du Yuesheng, Tales of Old China, www.talesofoldchina.com/shanghai/people/t-peop01.htm

Mansion Hotel:
Hotel brochure (available inside)

The Liu Brothers:
Song Luxia, *Shanghai De Haomen Jiumeng (Old Dreams of Shanghai's Super Rich),* China Friendship Publishing Co., 2002, pp.338-371

The Pans:
Song Luxia, *Shanghai Lao Yangfang (Shanghai Old Villas),* Shanghai Science and Technology Culture Publishing Co., 2004, pp. 100-101
Lao Shanghai Huayuan Yangfang (Old Shanghai Garden Villas) by Xue Shunsheng, Tongji Daxue Chubanshe (Tongji University Publisher), 2002, pp. 40-41
A Walker's Guide to Old Western Landmarks in Shanghai, Compiled by Shanghai Daily, 2008, pp. 87-90

The French Club:
Okura Garden Hotel pamphlet
Stone-Paper-Scissors Shanghai 1921-45 by the Stead

Sisters, Oxon Publishing, 1991

Frenchtown: Shanghai Western Architecture in Shanghai's Old French Concession by Tess Johnston and Deke Erh, Old China Hand Press, 2000, pp. 101-107

Dong Zhujun:

Dong Zhujun by Dong Guoying (Dong Guoying is Dong's granddaughter)

My Century by Dong Zhujun, SDX Joint Publishing Co., 2008

A Walker's Guide to Old Western Landmarks in Shanghai, Compiled by Shanghai Daily, 2008, pp. 78-82

Victor Sassoon and Cathay Mansion:

China Hong List 1934, "A Business and Residential Directory of all Foreigners and the Leading Chinese in the Principal Ports and Cities of China," Printed and published at the offices of the *North China Daily News Herald*, Ltd., p.47

Old Shanghai's best address, Shanghai Daily

"Sassoon's Shanghai," by Anne Warr

www.walkshanghai.com

WALK III:
From Nanjing Road (W)
To Shaanxi Road (N)
南京西路——陕西北路
Money and Trouble

This walk encompasses an area of the former International Settlement dense with famous villas, close to the shopping and restaurants of the Nanjing Road (W) commercial area.

On this walk, you will learn how a venerable department store was founded and how a shrewd Jewish businessman and his Buddhist wife built their opulent estate. You will hear about an assassination, a double suicide, a colorful multi-generational family and a political marriage between the two families who ruled China from 1920s to 1940s. You will also see a large villa where priests lived and a treasure house where the earliest Chinese writings were collected. Although they all played crucial roles in the first half of the 20th century in China, most of these people's efforts died along with them. Yet, they left intriguing stories for future generations to learn from and be entertained.

Subway Line 2—Jing'an Temple Station—Exit 3: Turn left onto Nanjing Road (W) 南京西路, going east. Cross Changde Road 常德路, continue on Nanjing Road (W), and cross Tongren Road 铜仁路. The Ritz Carlton Portman Hotel/Shanghai Center 上海商城 is coming up on your left side.

Standing on Nanjing Road (W) in front of the Portman, you may look across the street at the extensive, yellow building and the grounds around it.

Shanghai Exhibition Center
上海展览馆
1000 Yan'an Rd (M)
延安中路

You are looking at the Exhibition Center's façade on Nanjing Road (W).

Built in 1955 by the Soviet Union, this became the first exhibition hall and main conference facility in Shanghai. The center was completely renovated in 2001. It has nine entrances, 93,000 square meters of floor space, 42 multi-function rooms, over 100 conference rooms, a movie theatre, and a water fountain with music and lights. The main entrances

WALK III: MONEY AND TROUBLE

Shanghai Exhibition Center 上海展览馆

are on Yan'an Road (M) and Nanjing Road (W).

This was the location of the estate of Silas Aaron Hardoon (1851-1931), a British Jew born in Baghdad, Mesopotamia. His father was a bank clerk and moved the family to India when Silas was five. They relied on the patronage of the eminent Jewish merchant David Sassoon in India. After six years in Hong Kong, Hardoon came to Shanghai in 1874, starting as a watchman. He worked his way up in David Sassoon & Sons by being an efficient rent collector and securing good real estate deals. He later became the managing partner of E.D. Sassoon & Co., the company owned by David Sassoon's son, Elias David. One main business interest was the importing of opium.

Possessing a frugal and shrewd nature, Hardoon used his savings to buy real estate properties. With the rents, he invested in more land. In 1883, when the Sino-French War started, many foreigners left Shanghai to return home. This afforded Hardoon an opportunity to purchase houses and land at very low prices along Nanjing Road. When China was defeated in April of 1885 and the foreigners returned to Shanghai, Nanjing Road became a commercial street, and land prices skyrocketed.

Because Hardoon stayed calm and did not retreat during unsettling times, he was considered to have made a significant contribution to the city's development and order. He was invited to be a director of the governing boards in the French Concession in 1887 and the International Settlement in 1898.

When the International Settlement expanded in 1899 into the Jing'an Temple area, his holdings in the area became more valuable. In 1901, Hardoon established his own real estate company. He bought some land between Henan Road and Xizang Road. Due to the lack of transportation, the land was not valuable at the time, but Hardoon used 600,000 taels of his own silver to pave the road and the area became far more desirable. Eventually he owned forty-four percent of Nanjing Road. Lanes and buildings owned by him had the character 慈 ("mercy") in their names, possibly because Hardoon was keenly interested in Buddhist concepts in Chinese culture. He was also called the King of "Tu" 土, a Chinese character meaning both opium and land because those were his main concerns.

There was a folk song that went like this:

"Hardoon, Hardoon, different from the rest,
哈同哈同，与众不同，
A night watchman, simple eater and frugal spender,
看守门户，省吃俭用，
Earning money to pave roads, benefiting the public,
攒钱铺路，造福大众，
Build road, build road, endless flow of riches.
筑路筑路，财源亨通。"

In 1886 Hardoon married a woman born in Shanghai to a Chinese mother; the parentage of her father was in dispute, whether it was French or Chinese. Her name was Luo Jialing 罗迦陵, or Lisa Roos. A devout Buddhist, she asked a famous monk, Huang Zongyang 黄宗仰, also known as Wu-mushanseng 乌目山僧 (the "Monk from the Wumu Mountain"), to design their garden at this location. The construction of Shanghai's most opulent estate began in 1904 and finished in 1910. It was called "Ailiyuan" 爱俪园, taking Chinese characters from the couple's names. (Silas Aaron Hardoon's middle name used the Chinese character 爱, "love", while the Chinese transliteration of "Lisa" starts with 俪. The latter can also mean "wife", so the name 爱俪园 may in fact be the "Garden of Silas Aaron's Loving Wife".) The locals called it simply the Hardoon Garden. It covered 200 mu (33.4 acres), and it had many pavilions, rockeries and ponds. The Western-looking villas co-existed with the traditional lattice-covered Chinese-style hallways. Supposedly the Hardoons were inspired by the fictional grand villa and garden from the *Dream of the Red Chamber*, one of China's four great classical novels.

The Hardoons hosted some notable artists and politicians at Ailiyuan, such as Sun Yat-sen 孙中山, who stayed here in 1912. They also held charitable auction galas such as the ones in 1910 and 1917 to aid flood victims in Jiangsu and Henan Provinces. On such occasions, lights were hung everywhere in the garden, and musical bands played. The Hardoons donated money to establish Cai Yuanpei's 蔡元培 school, and Cai, whose residence is featured in Walk II "True Colors," went on to become the chancellor of Peking University and, among other achievements, found the Shanghai Music Conservatory.

In 1914 the Hardoons sponsored the establishment of the first modern Buddhist institute in China, called Huayan College 华严大学. Luo was the principal of the school, and Wumushanseng was in charge of admissions. He recruited 30 monks and another 90 children from poor, illegitimate and other disadvantaged family backgrounds. Also offered at the school were history, geography, and science curriculums from Cai Yuanpei's school. In 1915 the Hardoons established a school called Cangsheng Mingzhi Daxue 仓圣明智大学, named after the mythical creator of Chinese characters, Shengjie 圣颉. The school consisted of grade school, middle school, college prepatory, and girls' school. In 1916 Guangcang Xuetang 广仓学堂 was established, and it contributed to the study of oracle-bone inscriptions (the earliest Chinese writing) and published Buddhist canons. The famous Chinese painter, Xu Beihong 徐悲鸿, was a teacher here.

The Hardoons had no children of their own but adopted two dozen, both Chinese and Caucasian. Some took the name Hardoon, while others took the name Luo. At Hardoon's funeral the Jewish community was shocked to see chanting Buddhist and Taoist monks. When Lisa died in 1941, the children began disputing inheritance rights, as Hardoon and Lisa's wills left contradictory instructions as to who should inherit what. The Hardoon estate became neglected, and in the early 1940s the Japanese camped here. By 1945 only a few rooms remained due to fires caused by faulty wires and neglect. The Hardoon children's court battle lasted 16 years, becoming the most famous inheritance contest in Shanghai. By 1949 the children had all left Shanghai for foreign shores. When the Communist government took power, it also took control of all Hardoon real estate properties.

From the Portman, turn right onto Nanjing Road (W), going west. Walk past the small park next to the Portman and you will be standing in front of two big cream villas; the former Guo Mansions.

Guo Mansion
郭家故居
1418 Nanjing Rd (W)

Today these two imposing cream colored mansions are governmental offices. Before 1949 they were the private residences of two brothers, Guo Le 郭乐 (Gocklock Kwok) and Guo Shun 郭顺 (Gockson Kwok), Cantonese Chinese from Australia. The Guos started with vegetable shops and went on to have a banana plantation. They established a department store in Hong Kong called Wing On 永安 in 1907. The Guo brothers came to Shanghai to open another Wing On department store in 1918 (the characters are written 'Yong An' in Pinyin), which still stands on the Nanjing Road (E) pedestrian street. They were also in the textiles business. The Guos used the Cantonese spelling of their last name, Kwok, and continued to do so until the Cultural Revolution when the old was to make way for the new, and Pinyin spellings were enforced.

The Guos used an unusually simple but effective method to decide on the location of their Shanghai department store: two people stood on Nanjing Road, at the east and west ends, handing out beans to passersby. At the end of the day, it was discovered that more people passed by the east end, and those people seemed richer because more carried packages as they passed. So the Guos decided to build their department store on Nanjing Road (E) 南京东路. Silas Hardoon owned the land where the department store was to be built, so the Guos signed a lease for 50,000 taels of silver (1 tael equaled roughly 1 1/3 ounces) each year for 30 years. In 1932, a new Wing On building was constructed on neighboring land that the Guos had bought at a higher-than-market price, and connected with the original department store via a pedestrian bridge.

Guo Mansions

The new Wing On was mainly a hotel, with restaurants and entertainment facilities like a dance hall. By 1933, the 37-year-old Guo Linshuang 郭琳爽, son of Guo Quan 郭泉, another one of the brothers, had taken control as general manager. Guo Linshuang had gone to the U.S., Germany, England, and Japan between 1923 and 1927 to buy products and to learn how foreign companies operated. He expanded the sales of China-made products and used advertising broadly. He later negotiated with George Hardoon, Silas Hardoon's adopted son, and bought the land of the original Wing On for US$1.12 million in 1946. On May 25, 1949, Wing On's roof sported the first Communist flag on Nanjing Road. The department store became a joint effort with the government in 1955, and Guo continued as the general manager. He died in 1974 at age 78 in Shanghai.

Guo Biao 郭标 (Bew George Kwok), also a founder of Wing On who supported Sun Yat-sen, had a socialite daughter, Daisy. Like many young women from wealthy and educated families – such as the Soong Sisters and my own mother – she attended the McTyeire School for Girls, or Shixi Nüshu 市西 女塾. Today the school is the prestigious Shanghai Number 3 Girls Middle School, the only all-girls school in the city, located at 155 Jiangsu Road.

Daisy refused to marry the man arranged by her father. Instead she married a handsome, tall man who had attended Tsinghua University and MIT, but who turned out to be a playboy. His business was importing scientific instruments from Germany. In the early years of the People's Republic of China, when the government called on citizens to openly make criticisms of the government and society, he voiced his opinion and was branded a rightist and sent to Ti Lan Qiao Prison in 1957. He died there three years later. Daisy said his head looked like an apple on a stick; she suspected he had died of starvation, despite the food packets she had sent.

When her husband was in jail in 1957, Daisy's bank account was seized to pay a fine for her husband. She was ordered to clean chamber pots, was later in a factory doing iron smelting, and worked in building and road construction. In 1963 she was assigned to teach an evening English class to the staff of the Shanghai Foreign Trade Department. However, in 1967, she was sent to Chongming 崇明岛, an island in the Yangtze near Shanghai, to once again be reformed-through-labor. In the 1970s, she was an advisor to the Foreign Trade Department and was also a private tutor of English. For most of those years she lived in a tiny room with her son, who later moved to the U.S. She also had a daughter who was a ballerina in Beijing. Despite her advancing age, she went abroad six times to

The McTyeire School

The McTyeire School for Girls was established in 1892 by American Methodist missionary, Young J. Allen, with Laura Askew Haywood as its first principal. The school was named after Bishop Holand N. McTyeire, head of the Southern Methodist Mission in China. Bishop McTyeire had also helped his distant cousin by marriage, Commodore Vanderbilt, in selecting the land, supervising the building, and choosing faculty for the Vanderbilt University in Nashville, Tennessee. Originally located at the Methodist Moore Memorial Church 沐恩堂 on Hankou Road, McTyeire moved to the Jiangsu Road location in 1917, set in 13 acres and known as the Jin Family Flower Garden. A former 4-story family mansion became the main building for the school and was named Wuyi 五一 ("May First"). In 1935, Hungarian architect L.E. Hudec designed the new main building named the Richardson Hall, named after headmistress Helen Richardson who had died a year earlier. The building is also called Wusi 五 四 ("May Fourth"). Today, this stately white mansion still stands, facing a vast expanse of green lawn. The entry hall of the building features a large stained glass window, intact. The McTyeire was known for fostering social conscience and self-reliance in young ladies.

Bishop McTyeire had an interesting connection with China. At age 9 a young man by the name of Charlie Soong left his home on Hainan Island 海南 島 to work in his uncle's shop in Boston. There he met two Chinese college students who convinced him to get an education instead of selling tea in the shop. Because Charlie's family did not agree, he ran away and became a stowaway on a boat. Through a captain of the ship, Charlie went to the School of Religion at Vanderbilt, where he met Bishop McTyeire in 1882. It was Bishop McTyeire who allowed Charlie to be ordained as a minister in 1885. Charlie returned to China and married the following year. He became a Sunday school teacher and soon made a fortune in printing the Bible and other materials, but he was best known as the father of the Soong Sisters and T.V. Soong. Charlie's Sunday school was part of the Moore Memorial Church where the McTyeire School for Girls started.

visit relatives. She died in Shanghai, at age 90, in 1998.

Most of the Guos left Shanghai before 1949, but a few remained, including Daisy, her sister's family, and Guo Linshuang. Stories of personal struggle and resilience like Daisy's were common among elderly people in Shanghai during the Cultural Revolution.

Shi Liangcai
史良才
Residence
257 Tongren Rd
铜仁路
left side

At the intersection ahead, turn right onto Tongren Road, going north.

This 1922 French Colonial villa now belongs to the Shanghai Municipal Foreign Affairs Office. Over seventy years ago it was the private residence of

Shi Liangcai 史良才

Shi Liangcai (1880-1934). Shi was a social progressive thinker. He viewed the Qing Dynasty as corrupt, and later bought *Shen Bao* 申报, a newspaper, through which he could express his views. "Shen" 申 is another name for Shanghai, but *"Shen Bao"* not only means *"Shanghai Report"* – it can also refer to reporting to a higher body.

Shen Bao was the longest-running and one of the most influential newspapers in Old Shanghai, and Shi used his paper to comment on social problems and support the anti-Japanese resistance movement in 1931. He dared to publish "The China Human Rights Defense Alliance Act" called for by Soong Ching-ling 宋庆龄 (Madame Sun Yat-sen), Cai Yuanpei, and other patriots. From 1931 to 1934 Shi allowed *Shen Bao* and its monthly magazine and subsidiary, *Free Talk,* to publish articles written by left-leaning authors such as Mao Dun and Lu Xun, often accusing Chiang Kai-shek of dictatorial style and criticizing his government's policies. Predictably, this enraged Chiang's Kuomintang Party. On his way back from

Hangzhou with his family on November 13, 1934, a Kuomintang intelligence squad stopped Shi's car and assassinated him, along with his chauffeur and his son's young friend.

His widow auctioned off this villa, along with its furniture, and their vacation home elsewhere. She donated the proceeds to the fight against the Japanese. Today, this building belongs to the government.

Continue walking north on Tongren Road.

An Enduring Friendship

Shi was a protégé of my great grandfather, Di Pingzi 狄平子, *an art collector and owner of a publishing company and reading room/tea house on Fuzhou Road. Di and Shi had a falling out, but upon Shi's death, Di sent a quilt made with symbols of Buddhism, as a sign of reconciliation, to cover Shi's body at his funeral. Shi's daughter became a family friend of Di's descendants for many years.*

Wu Tongwen
吴同文
Residence
333 Tongren Rd, left side, corner of Tongren Road and Beijing Rd (W)
北京西路

Wu Tongwen made a fortune in the business of selling green paint. In 1932 when the Japanese invasion of China became imminent, Wu realized the value of the green paint for military use and stocked up enough for supplies. Because the green color brought him wealth, he considered it his lucky

Wu Tongwen 吴同文 *Residence*

color. His father-in-law, a wealthy paint merchant who owned the famous Lion Grove Garden 狮子林 in Suzhou, gave him 3.33 mu of land (0.56 acres) at this location for him to build a house. Wu bought the house number 333 and had the house built in 333 days between 1936 and 1937. The color, of course, was green, and it is still called Green House today.

Hungarian architect L.E. Hudec designed the house, with its signature simple, curved lines. Hudec guaranteed that it would still be considered modern after 50 years, and it was the first house in Shanghai to have an elevator. It also had air conditioning, heated floors, a furnace room, and a billiard room..

Wu believed the round shape to be a good *fengshui* omen. However in 1966, during the Cultural Revolution, Wu and his second wife committed suicide here, fearing there would be rough times ahead for capitalists like themselves. In 1999 a Taiwanese architect passed by and fell in love with the house. He leased it from the government and is sub-leasing part of it to a restaurant and bar. His own firm and residence are upstairs.

Across from Wu's house is **314-320-330 Tongren Road,** three rows of five-story buildings also designed by Hudec, built in 1932.

Next, head east on Beijing Road (W).

314-320-330 Tongren Road

Henry Lester Institute of Medical Education

Henry Lester Institute of Medical Education and Research
北京西路
1320 Beijing Rd (W), left side

This black-and-tan, Art Deco-looking building on the left side of the street was built in 1932. Henry Lester, an American architect, lived in Shanghai for over 50 years. When he died in 1926, he left his entire estate to charitable endeavors in Shanghai for education and medical research. Today this building is a medical research center belonging to Jiaotong University.

Bei Zuyi
贝祖诒
Residence
1301 Beijing Rd (W), right side

Built in 1934, this was the private residence of a descendant of the prominent Bei family, Bei Zuyi. He was the director of the Bank of China and the governor of the Central Bank of China. The Bei family owned an opulent garden in Suzhou called Lion Grove Garden 狮子林, now a World Heritage Site.

Bei Zuyi was also the father of the Pritzker Prize-winning American-Chinese architect, I.M. Pei. (His full name is Ieoh Ming Pei, the latter being an alternate spelling of the family name Bei.) Pei is considered the master of Modernist architecture. His latest design is the Suzhou Museum, opened in 2006.

Bei Zuyi 贝祖诒

You are looking at the back side of the villa, which housed the servant quarters. Note the unique windows, shaped like traditional Chinese coins. The patterns on the stones around the door frame are the stylized character 寿 ("Shou", meaning "long life"); there are supposedly one hundred of them altogether around the villa. The front entrance to the villa is at 170 Nanyang Road.

Continue east on Beijing Road (W). At the intersection, cross both Xikang Road 西康路 and Beijing Road (W), then continue along Beijing Road (W).

Avondale House

No. 2, Lane 1222 Beijing Rd (W), first house on the right inside the lane

This imposing, Spanish-style villa was built in 1930. Priests of the Augustinian Procuration lived here. Today it houses lower-middle-class families – "72 lodgers", meaning many families sharing the same house.

Then retrace your steps back onto Beijing Road (W). Turn left, and continue east.

At the next intersection, Beijing Road (W) and Shaanxi Road (N) 陕西北路, turn left into Shaanxi Road (N).

440-446-454-462 Shaanxi Road (N)

440-446-454-462 Shaanxi Road (N) 陕西北路,
right side
This row of townhouses has stairways from both
sides of the front entrance, reminiscent of New
York's Brooklyn townhouses.

The Mansion
457 Shaanxi Rd
(N), left side

Stand in front of the wide entrance to 457 Shaanxi
Road (N); you will see the villa inside.

It shares grounds with the the Shanghai Dic-
tionary Publishing Co, 上海辞书出版社. The villa,
which bears a heritage plaque, is an office building now. You may be able to walk up to the villa,
turn left, and look at the broad balcony and patio to
know the grandeur of the villa in its former times.
Or sometimes a strict guard may stop you.

Built in 1919 by L. E. Hudec, this was the home
of Sir Robert Ho-tung 何启东 (1862-1956), a businessman from Hong Kong. Born to a Cantonese
mother and European father, possibly English of
Dutch and Jewish descent, Ho-tung became an assistant in the comprador department (liaison) for
the British-owned trading company Jardine Matheson, and married the daughter of a director. With

his bilingual language skills and business acumen, Ho-tung rose quickly and became the head comprador. Making his money in commodities trading and real estate, he financially supported Sun Yat-sen's revolution to overthrow the Qing Dynasty and later befriended Chiang Kai-shek 蒋介石.

Robert Ho-tung had two Eurasian wives. His first wife was unable to bear children so, following Chinese tradition, Ho-tung adopted his brother's son. Later Ho-tung's second wife bore him three sons and seven daughters. One of the sons, Robert Ho Shai-lai became a Kuomintang general and an ambassador to Japan from 1952 to 1956. Other descendants of Sir Robert, including Edward and Eric, were successful businessmen and philanthropists.

Ho-tung funded many parks and schools in Hong Kong. He was the first Chinese to be allowed to live in Victoria Park, an exclusive enclave of wealthy homes. His son, Edward, and his grandson, Eric, married Caucasians, and Eric was made a Commander of the British Empire (CBE) in 2001. The Ho-tung family is one of the very few Chinese families in which different generations received honorary titles of the British Empire and in which racially mixed marriages are common.

A grandnephew, Stanley Ho 何鸿燊, owns the biggest Chinese casino in Macao. He speaks four languages, owns many properties, and has interests in transport, banking, and tourism, among others. Stanley Ho is a colorful character with four wives, two of whom he married after Hong Kong instituted the monogamy policy, and he has 17 children.

Ohel Rachel Synagogue
500 Shaanxi Rd (N), right side, across the street, near the intersection

Currently the synagogue is on the grounds of the Shanghai Education Bureau Education Research Center. It is not open to the public, and a special

WALK III: MONEY AND TROUBLE

Ohel Rachel Synagogue *Liu Huizhi 刘晦之 Residence*

permit is required to enter. A Sephardic Jew, Jacob Elias Sassoon, commissioned the synagogue as a memorial to his wife. Unfortunately he died a few months before it was completed in 1920. It was a center of religious studies and the earliest Jewish synagogue in Shanghai. It is in the Greek Revival style and thirty 19th-century Torahs were kept here. As in all synagogues, the altar faces Jerusalem.

This area was an active Jewish community in the 1910s and 1920s; the Shanghai Jewish School was to the left of the synagogue. During World War II the Japanese used the synagogue as a stable. In 1952 synagogue member Aba Toeg sent the Torahs that he had helped store to Israel and handed the building over to the government. It was then used as a warehouse and office space until 1998, when the government restored it. The façade you see on Shaanxi Road (N) is the back side of the synagogue.

At the upcoming intersection of Shaanxi Road (N) and Xinzha Road 新闸路, turn left onto Xinzha Road, heading west.

Liu Huizhi
刘晦之
Residence
1321 Xinzha Rd
新闸路
*a little way
down the
street on your
left side*

Liu Huizhi (1879-1962) was a bank president. His father was the governor of Sichuan Province and a favored general and friend of Viceroy Li Hongzhang 李鸿章 in the Qing Dynasty. It is believed Li gave the Liu Family the magnolia trees at the entrance of the garden. Liu Huizhi hated foreigners and missionaries, and he feared foreigners buying up Chinese land. Yet he made a lot of money selling antiques to the Prince of Sweden.

Go inside the gate, through the arch on the right and you will see a pagoda on your left. It was here that Liu housed his priceless collections of early Chinese writings – oracle-bone inscriptions and other inks, weapons, musical instruments from the Tang Dynasty, etc. This private library had over 10,000 scrolls and manuscripts. During the Japanese occupation, he refused to cooperate and escaped to Hong Kong. He donated some of his collections to the Shanghai Museum and also shared his library materials with the eminent Chinese oracle-bone scholar Guo Moruo 郭沫若. His two Tang Dynasty musical instruments, made in 781 A.D., now belong to the Beijing Palace Museum. Unfortunately, the pagoda itself has long been converted to living quarters. No aura of scholarly research or collection remains.

Liu's son, Liu Yongling 刘永龄, a school friend of my father, went to Hong Kong in 1973 and worked his way up from a technician/engineer to own dozens of factories in high technology and exports in the 1980s. Liu Yongling has established scholarships at Jiaotong University and other colleges. He donated this villa and garden to the government, and multiple families now live here.

Now retrace your steps, turn right onto Shaanxi Road (N) and continue south, crossing Beijing Road (W).

Shanghai Grace Church 怀恩堂

The Soong Mansion

Shanghai Grace Church 怀恩堂
375 Shaanxi Rd (N), right side, at the intersection of Shannxi and Beijing Rd (W)

This church has been here since 1942 and was built by the American Baptist missionary Dr. R. Bryan. Today this church, like all Protestant churches in China, is non-denominational. Most of its services are in Chinese, except for the 9am Sunday service, where simultaneous English translation is available. You may ask to go in and look at the sanctuary, which is beautifully restored.

The Soong Mansion
369 Shaanxi Rd (N), next door to the church

This is now the clubhouse of the Soong Ching Ling Foundation, which concentrates on women and children's welfare issues. It is open to members only, and the black gate is usually closed. However, tours by advance arrangement may be possible.

Built in 1908 with a peaceful garden, this villa was bought by Charlie Soong's wife after his death in 1918 because their former home reminded her too much of her husband. A descendant of the famous Chinese scientist Xu Guangqi 徐光启, she was a devout Christian. Every morning she led her children to pray in the prayer room off to the side of the living room.

Soong May-ling 宋美龄 and Chiang Kai-shek

held their marriage ceremony in the front room in 1927. In the large adjoining room Soong May-ling had entertained her celebrity guests. In a corner is the piano that the three Soong Sisters played. Upstairs was Soong May-ling's bedroom, where her slippers are still in the closet.

Go south on Shaanxi Road, and the upcoming main street will be Nanjing Road (W). You are in the middle of two subway stations for Line 2, with each about a ten-minute walk in either direction along Nanjing Road. To the left is the Nanjing Road (W) Station, and on the right is the Jing'an Temple Station. There are many restaurants nearby.

The Soong Sisters

The elder Soongs encouraged their children – three daughters and three sons – to express their thoughts freely but at the same time observe traditions, requiring, for example, the daughters to wear their hair in a traditional bun. The Soong children, three daughters and one son, were an important part of 20th-century Chinese history. The eldest daughter, Soong Ai-ling 宋藹齡, married a wealthy merchant, H. H. Kung 孔祥西, who held various posts in Chiang Kaishek's government. The second daughter, Soong Ching-ling 宋庆龄, married Sun Yat-sen, who is widely credited for providing the impetus to overthrow the Qing Dynasty. The third daughter, Soong May-ling, married Chiang Kai-shek, leader of the Kuomintang Party, the party in charge of China until 1949 and on Taiwan thereafter. Their brother, T. V. Soong 宋子文, held various posts in the Chiang government.

Having been educated in America, the Soong siblings spoke English as their first language, Shanghainese as their second, and Mandarin as their third.

Further Reading:
Hardoon:
Shanghai Daban Hatong Waizhuan by Shen Ji, Xueling
Publishing Co.
thehardoons.com
Shanghai Jewish Center, www.chinajewish.org
The Scribe www.dangoor.com
Nehardea Magazine,
  www.babylonjewry.org.il/new/English/
nehardea

Guos:
Famous People, Houses & Stories by Huang Guoxin
  and Shen Publisher, 2003, pp. 122-124
Wing On's Changing Fortunes, Shanghai Star,
  starnews.com.cn
Lao Shanghai Huayuan Yangfang (Old Shanghai Garden Villas) by Xue Shunsheng and Lou Chenghao, Tongji Daxue Chubanshe, 2002, pp. 22-23

Shi:
Famous People, Houses & Stories by Huang Guoxin
  and Shen Fuxuan, Tongji University Publisher,
  2003, pp. 236-239
Center for World Chinese Media Studies,
  www.cmc.pku.edu.cn

Wu:
Famous People, Houses & Stories by Huang Guoxin
  and Shen Fuxuan, Tongji University Publisher,
  2003, pp. 126-128
Lao Shanghai Huayuan Yangfang (Old Shanghai Garden Villas) by Xue Shunsheng and Lou Chenghao, Tongji Daxue Chubanshe, 2002, pp. 136-137
Jing'an District Government, www.jingan.gov.cn
Six More Shanghai Walks by Barbara Green, Tess

Johnston, et al., Old China Hand Press, 2008, p. 45

Bei Zuyi:
Lao Shanghai Huayuan Yangfang (Old Shanghai Garden Villas) by Xue Shunsheng and Lou Chenghao, Tongji Daxue Chubanshe, 2002, pp. 128-129.

Avondale House:
Six More Shanghai Walks by Barbara Green, Tess Johnston, et al., Old China Hand Press, 2008, p. 37

The Mansion/Robert Ho-tung:
The Mansion brochure pp. 38-40
Six More Shanghai Walks by Barbara Green, Tess Johnston, et al., Old China Hand Press, 2008

Ohel Rachel Synagogue:
Shanghai Jewish Center, www.chinajewish.org
A Walker's Guide to Old Western Landmarks in Shanghai compiled by Shanghai Daily, 2008, pp. 60-64

Liu Huizhi:
Shanghai De Haomen Jiumeng (Old Dreams of the Shanghai Super Rich), China Friendship Publishing Co., pp. 266-302

The Soong Mansion:
Soong Ching Ling Foundation material (inside the villa)
Famous People, Houses, and & Stories by Huang Guoxin and Shen Fuxuan, Tongji University Publisher, 2003, pp. 79-83

WALK IV:
From Xingguo Road To Huaihai Road (M)
兴国路——淮海中路
Murder is Easy

This walk covers a western section of the former French Concession. Half of the streets are broken into short blocks. The area has been one of the most desirable living quarters in both Old Shanghai and New Shanghai,

You will walk by beautiful gardens and hear the stories of the colorful people who owned them. You will see where a former Chinese prime minister's murder was carried out with ease, and learn how a street frequented by expatriates got its name. You will encounter romances, love affairs, business acumen, and political disasters, In short, this is an easy walk steeped in history.

Subway Line 2—Jiangsu Road Station—Exit 4: Turn left, then left again at Jiangsu Road 江苏路, going south. Stay on Jiangsu and take the pedestrian bridge over Yan'an Road (W) 延安西路. Ahead is a T-intersection where Jiangsu ends. Turn left onto Huashan Road 华山路, and right at the traffic lights just ahead. You should now be on Xingguo Road 兴国路; the hotel entrance is coming up on your right side.

Xingguo Guest House
兴国宾馆
(the Radisson Plaza)
72 Xingguo Rd
兴国路

Start at the lobby entrance. Although the Radisson high-rise is relatively new, it sits on the grounds of the Xingguo Guest House that existed before the Shanghai development of recent years. There are several villas here which, sixty years ago, were private residences for foreigners. No. 6 housed an American merchant; No. 7 was the home of a doctor.

Today, these villas belong to the government. Some are leased to companies or private citizens, while others may still host official meetings. (If it looks like there is an official event, please do not go near. The villas in the back are private, and there is no public admittance.)

Xingguo Guest House 兴国宾馆

Out of the Radisson lobby, turn right, and walk in a counter-clockwise direction past Villa 2, Villa 3 and another building. Villa 6 is the cream-colored house ahead, behind a sign that shows the directions of the villas. Bear left of Villa 6, walk past the serene gardens, and you will come out by Villa No. 1.

Villa No. 1 is the biggest and most distinguished of all the villas in this group. It was built in 1934 for George Swire, the taipan 大班 (big boss) of the But-terfield and Swire Company, merchants and steam-ship agents. Supposedly Swire wanted a grand mansion because his rival, Henry Keswick of Jar-dine Matheson, had built a great mansion on Hon-gqiao Road 虹桥路 (Hongqiao District) in what was then considered the countryside. When the house was finished, Swire showed up for the completion ceremony, but inexplicably he never returned to

The Imperial Color

Yellow is a common color for repainting of old houses around Shanghai. The Chinese have always favored yellow: it was an imperial color and it is associated with birthdays for the elderly, representing long life.

Shanghai again.

A Welsh architect (who never set foot in China) designed the house; his name was Clough Williams-Ellis. Photos accompanied the monthly progress reports that were sent to him. He later wrote that although Butterfield and Swire sent him a roundtrip ticket to come to Shanghai, he thought he was too busy to come.

Because the roof is made of copper, this house was known as the "Copper House". At one time it was rented to the head of a company that made the Hazelwood Ice Cream, so the house was known to foreigners as the "Ice Cream Man's House".

After the founding of the People's Republic in 1949, residents of all private houses had to pay property taxes. A few years later, the trustees of Swire felt the taxes were becoming too onerous, so they offered to give the house to the government in lieu of paying taxes. The first mayor of Shanghai, Chen Yi, stayed here for a while. Chairman Mao also stayed here.

Villa No. 1 is close to the hotel entrance on Xingguo Road. Outside of the hotel turn left, going north. Note the lovely house in pale yellow across the street at 67 Xingguo Road.

At the Xingguo-Huashan intersection, turn right onto Huashan Road and keep walking east, past the many villas on both sides of the road. Some villas have been converted for commercial use as a company office, restaurant, or art gallery. Other more run-down villas still house many families, each possessing just one or two rooms.

Guo Dihuo
郭棣活
Residence 9
893 Huashan Rd
华山路
right side

Guo (or Kwok as in Cantonese spelling) was assistant general manager of the Wing On Department Store, and his family lived in this villa built in 1947. Guo donated it to the government, just as he had done with another villa, in 1958. That other villa, set on 15 mu (2.5 acres), is now known as No. 5 on the grounds of the Xi Jiao State Guest House on Hongqiao Road on the west side of the city.

Wing On was a family business. Two of Guo Dihuo's relatives lived side-by-side in the mansions near the Portman Ritz Carlton Hotel on Nanjing Road (W), as detailed in Walk III, "Money and Trouble".

Ahead, cross Fuxing Road (W) 复兴西路 and continue walking on Huashan Road.

Ding Xiang Garden
丁香花园
849 Huashan Rd, right side

This is one of the most famous and largest gardens in Shanghai. The cream-colored building with the red trim, opposite the water fountain, on your right hand side, is the original and main building. It faces a huge, lush Chinese-style garden with a pagoda and accentuated by a wall topped by a twisting dragon. Ding Xiang is now a club for retired elite government officials. The garden and the villa are solely for their enjoyment; the public may not enter. But there is a Cantonese restaurant in a newer building at the end of the driveway, and because of this we can come here.

Ding Xiang Garden 丁香花园

Although popular belief holds that the powerful Qing Dynasty Viceroy, Li Hongzhang 李鸿章, built this villa, the heritage plaque and books written by recent scholars all agree that the villa was actually built by Li's youngest son, Li Jingmai 李经迈. Since the dragon was a symbol belonging to the emperor, and Li Hongzhang was a servant of the imperial court, it is most unlikely that he would have built a dragon in his own garden.

Head out of Ding Xiang Garden and turn right back onto Huashan Road. This stretch of Huashan Road was at the western edge of the city in the late 1800s and early 1900s. The traffic and noise of today make it hard to believe this was once "the suburbs".

At the next intersection cross Wukang Road 武康路 and continue on Huashan Road.

Apartment Villas
823-825-827 Huashan Rd, right side

After heading in to this compound, you will find three buildings. Each has a neatly arranged three stories with two units on each floor. Each unit has two bedrooms, two living rooms, two bathrooms, and one kitchen. Notice how much quieter it is here compared to outside on the street. My family knew two families who lived here. When I was in junior high, I used to come here to the home of my pediatrician, Dr. Dai, because his son and I were taking calligraphy lessons together from a private tutor. I always thought they were very lucky to live in a quiet and attractive apartment. At that time my own home, a traditional lane house, was already occupied by many families and lacked the privacy of Dr. Dai's apartment. Another family we visited was that of the daughter of the newspaper publisher, Shi Liangcai, who was featured in Walk III, "Money and Trouble".

Outside the compound turn left and backtrack onto Huashan Road.

831 Huashan Road
left side, corner of Huashan Rd and Wukang Rd
武康路

Built in 1918, this villa supposedly belonged to an owner of flour factories, Fufeng 阜丰, whose grand-uncle, Sun Jianai 孙家鼐, was a tutor to Qing Emperor Guangxu 光绪. The villa owner was also a relative of Li Hongzhang and bought the land from the Li family. This villa underwent extensive renovation in 2008 and changed from a dilapidated, small villa into a clean-looking and much bigger villa. It is not clear how faithfully the renovation has followed the house's original design.

Turn left onto Wukang Road.

Mo Shangqing
莫觞清
Residence
2 Wukang Rd, at the corner of Huashan and Wukang Roads, right side

This was the former home of silk merchant Mo Shangqing. He had more than ten silk factories, including the biggest silk factory in Shanghai. He sold to domestic and international buyers, and was the basis for the main character in *Zi Ye* 子夜, written by the famous playwright Mao Dun 茅盾. One day during a dance party at home, Mo was kidnapped – a common occurrence in Old Shanghai. Gangs did this to extract money. Kidnapping was a main business concern of the Green Gang, under the leadership of Du Yuesheng, the Godfather of Shanghai, whom we encounter on Walk II, "True Colors". Mo was later freed, but he never recovered from the shock and died shortly afterwards in 1938. His son-in-law had already taken over the business, and Mo's family moved out of the large villa and into the smaller house next door.

Continue on Wukang Road.

Residences of Chen Lifu
陈立夫
67 Wukang Rd, and
Chen Guofu
陈果夫
Lane 107 (further ahead beyond Fuxing Rd (W)
复兴西路

Residences of Chen Lifu 陈立夫, 67 Wukang Road, and **Chen Guofu** 陈果夫, Lane 107 (further ahead beyond Fuxing Road (W) 复兴西路 intersection, hidden behind a storefront with only the second floor partially visible as it juts into Wukang – grey

Residences of Chen Lifu 67 Wukang Road

with red bricks in Tudor style), both left side

The two Chen brothers bore one of the four dynastic family surnames in pre-Communist China. The other three families were the Soong family, Chiang Kai-shek and his sons, and Kong Xiangxi (a.k.a. H. H. Kung), who had married the eldest Soong sister. Together, these families ruled China's non-communist political world from the 1920s to the 1940s.

Chen Guofu and Chiang Kai-shek worked together at Whampoa Military Academy. Chen Guofu was at one time the president of the Agricultural Bank of China, but he contracted hepatitis and was sometimes confined to bed. He left Shanghai for Taiwan in December, 1948, and he died of lung disease in 1951.

His brother, Chen Lifu, was Chiang's secretary and the secretary of education in 1938. He also went to Taiwan. In the U.S., Chen borrowed US$20,000 from H. H. Kung and started a chicken farm in New Jersey. He moved back to Taiwan in 1969 and wrote books on Chinese medicine and philosophy. He supported the idea that the world should reach out to Mainland China, even before it began to open up. In his personal life, Chen Lifu was married for

Tang Chaoyi Residence No. 1, Lane 40 Wukang Road

63 years, and he and his wife supposedly never argued. His long-time habits were to shower at 5.30am and walk 1,000 steps after breakfast.

Our next stop is directly across the street from Chen Lifu's house. Go inside Lane 40, and look for the first large, yellow villa on your right.

Tang Chaoyi
武康路
Residence
No. 1, Lane 40
Wukang Rd,
right side

Educated at Columbia University, Tang Chaoyi (1862-1938) was the first prime minister of the Chinese Republic under Yuan Shikai 袁世凯, though he supported Yuan's rival, Sun Yat-sen 孙中山. In 1938 it was rumored that he was collaborating with the Japanese. His friends, including gangster boss Du Yuesheng 杜月笙, tried to persuade him to go to Hong Kong, but he would not go. Suspecting Tang of being a traitor, Chiang Kai-shek's Kuomintang sent over secret assassins.

The assassins included a man by the last name of Xie, who was from the same village as Tang in Guangdong Province. They were in fact friends. The assassins came to this house under the pretense of showing Tang precious antiques, which he enjoyed collecting. The men carried a chest; in it were a sword and some porcelain. Seeing Xie, the guard allowed them into the house.

Tang received his guests and sent his servant out of the room. While Tang was bent over examining one of the antiques with his back turned, the assassins brought out an axe and hit him in the back of the head. The men left the villa before the servant returned and discovered his body.

Tang's death stirred the political world and caused many older Kuomintang leaders to ask about the true nature of his death. To quell dissatisfaction, Chiang Kai-shek ordered his government to pay funeral expenses and to include Tang's name in the official government archives of history.

After the murder, assassin Xie became paranoid and was checked into a mental hospital. He even suspected the doctors of spying on him and kept a pistol ready. The doctors reported this to the police, who sent over an investigator. Xie brought out his pistol, but the investigator fired and killed him first.

After 1949, government officials lived in this villa. As of April, 2009, the house was under renovation.

Back outside the lane, turn right and continue on Wukang Road. Cross Fuxing Road.

Calbeck, Macgregor & Co. President's Residence
99 Wukang Rd, left side

This villa was built in 1928 for the boss of the wine and spirit merchants, Calbeck, Macgregor & Co. In the early 1930s, a man by the name of Tang Hai'an 唐海安 lived here. He was in charge of the Shanghai Customs, and he was a crony of Song Ziwen 宋子文, also known as T.V. Soong, brother of the Soong Sisters and a powerful member of Chiang Kai-shek's government. As a sign of his respect for Soong, Tang went to the train station to greet him when Soong returned from Nanjing on weekends. Tang was once captured by the Japanese but was later released. He died in Hong Kong.

Calbeck, Macgregor & Co. President's Residence, 99 Wukang Road

After the founding of the People's Republic, Liu Jingji 刘靖基 lived here. Liu was a prominent antique collector who donated forty pieces to the Shanghai Museum, including a Song Dynasty calligraphy.

Cross Fuxing Road (W) and continue south on Wukang Road.

Chen Guofu's Lane 107 house is ahead on the left side

This villa was built in 1923. It was at one time home to Ba Jin, one of the most celebrated contemporary writers of China. He wrote and translated over 13 million words. His trilogy, *Spring*, *Autumn*, and *Family*, examining feudal families in old Chinese society, won him fame and repute.

Ba Jin
巴金
Residence
113 Wukang Rd, left side

Midget Apartments, 115 Wukang Road, intersection of Wukang and Hunan, left side
This apartment building was built in 1931 in a modern style; all efforts to trace the source of the apartment name have been unsuccessful.

Hunan Villa
湖南别墅
262 Hunan Rd
湖南路
right side, corner of Wukang and Hunan Rds, across from Midget Apartments

This villa, hidden behind high yellow walls with black bamboo on top, was bought by Zhou Haifu 周海佛 in 1943. Zhou was the treasury secretary under Wang Jingwei 汪精卫, leader of the pro-

Japanese puppet government during the Japanese occupation. Zhou changed the name of the road from Ju'erdian Road 居尔典路 to Hunan Road because he was from Hunan Province. Three years later, Zhou died in prison in Nanjing, and his son joined the Communists.

Shanghai's first post-1949 mayor, Chen Yi 陈毅, lived here for a short time, as did He Zizhen 贺子珍, Chairman Mao's second wife. He Zizhen joined the Communist Party in its early stages, and she was considered an outstanding female revolutionary. She married Mao in 1928. They had three sons and three daughters, but only one survived to adulthood. Some simply died in childhood, and others were given to peasants to take care during the Long March and were never found again. He Zizhen lived until 1984.

Cross Hunan Road; continue on Wukang Road.

Zhou Zuomin
周作民
Residence
Nos. 1 and 2, Lane 117 Wukang Rd, left side

Designed by a Shanghainese architect, the villas share a Chinese garden with rockery, bridge, creek, and many types of trees such as osmanthus and plum.

Both villas belonged to a banker, Zhou Zuomin (1884-1955). He was a poor man from Jiangsu

Zhou Zuomin Residence, Nos. 1 and 2, Lane 117 Wukang Road

Province who, with financial aid from a friend, studied in Japan and became an official in the treasury department in the northeast of China. By 1915 he held a key position in the Communications Bank of China, and in 1917 he founded his own bank called Jincheng Yinhang 金城银行. Many warlords of the north invested in the bank, and Zhou, in turn, invested in transportation, mines, and trade. The bank became one of China's four largest banks and was the number one privately owned bank by 1936.

One day, after World War II, the police came to arrest Zhou because he was said to have supported the Japanese. He tried to escape through the back door of his house but was caught. He was later released, perhaps due to lack of evidence. He went to Hong Kong in 1948, but in 1951 he became the first big boss in the banking business to return to Mainland China. His businesses thereafter became jointly owned with the government. He died in 1955.

After 1949, high-ranking city officials lived here. These officials were not in favor during the Cultural Revolution, and Red Guards frequented the premises to put up confrontational posters. Neighbors said that these villas did not have good *fengshui* because several times in their history great disturbances had happened there.

At the next intersection, cross Tai'an Road 泰安路 and continue on Wukang Road.

**390
Wukang Rd**
right side

Built in 1932, this lovely villa is in the Mediterranean style. Formerly the residence of the Italian Consul-General, it now houses the Shanghai Automotive Industry Corp. and the Shanghai Automotive Industry Sales Co., Ltd.

Here we may pause to hear about an important foreigner in China, John Calvin Ferguson, and his connection with this street.

390 Wukang Road

Ferguson (1866-1945) was born into a preacher's family in Ontario, Canada. He attended Boston University. He spent nearly 60 years in China, starting as a missionary, and became involved in politics and cultural affairs. Believing in the "Social Gospel" that advocated education, social responsibility, and political reform, Ferguson assisted in founding a Methodist school that eventually became Nanking University. In Shanghai when Sheng Xuanhuai 盛宣怀 established Nanyang 南洋, the predecessor of the prestigious Jiaotong University 交通大学, Ferguson was its first president, serving from 1897-1902. My paternal grandfather, He Gonghua 何公华, was among the first graduating class of Jiaotong.

When the Qing Dynasty was overthrown, Ferguson was the only foreigner on a committee that examined the art treasures of the imperial palace for the Beijing Palace Museum in 1912. Ferguson bought a newspaper from a Briton called *Shanghai News Daily* 新闻报. It was best known for its coverage on financial matters and competed against *Shen Bao* 申报. He ran the paper for thirty years.

Several sources say today's Wukang Road was

called Ferguson Road in Old Shanghai, because of his contribution to Chinese society. Recognizing his assistance, the French Concession authorities named a street after him.

Huang Xing
黄兴
Residence
393 Wukang Rd, across the street from 390 Wukang Rd

The south wing, in English country style, was built in 1912, and the Art Deco north wing in 1930. Note the strange, narrow, pointy corner on the right side of the Art Deco building, as you face it.

Huang Xing (1874-1916) lived here briefly in 1916. He was noted as a revolutionary leader, army commander and statesman who worked with Sun Yat-sen.

Meite Gongyu
美特公寓
(Normandie Apartments)
1850 Huaihai Rd (M)
淮海中路
corner of Wukang and Huaihai, left side

This striking apartment building is eight stories high, the first two floors in dark grey and the rest in red brick. It was designed by Ladislaus (Laszlo) Hudec and built in the 1920s in the shape of a ship. (Please see Walk III, "Money and Trouble", for more information about Hudec.)

Cross to the opposite side of Huaihai Road (M) and turn left, going east. Just ahead is our next destination.

Meite Gongyu 美特公寓

Soong Ching-ling Residence
宋庆龄故居
1843 Huaihai Road (M), right side

Built in 1920 for a shipping magnate, this villa changed hands several times before Chiang Kai-shek's second son, Chiang Wei-kuo 蒋纬国, moved in. When Soong Ching-ling returned from Chongqing in 1945, she donated the villa she had shared with her husband, Sun Yat-sen – the "Father of the Chinese Republic" – on Xiangshan Road 香山路 to the government as a memorial. Under pressure from politicians to find her a suitable place to live, the Kuomintang Party transferred the deed title from Chiang Wei-kuo to Soong Ching-ling. This became her residence whenever she was in Shanghai, until her death. Soong (1890-1981) received many world leaders here.

There is a serene garden in the back and there is also a museum on the grounds, where can be found correspondence between her and her siblings in English. Eldest daughter Ai-ling and second daughter Ching-ling studied at Wesleyan College in Macon, Georgia, U.S.A., while the youngest daughter, May-ling, graduated from Wellesley College in Wellesley, Massachusetts.

Bao Yugang 包玉刚 Residence

Ai-ling worked as Sun Yat-sen's English secretary. When she got married, her sister, Ching-ling, took her place. Ching-ling fell in love with Sun, and they married in Japan in 1915, despite Soong's parents' objection. Her parents felt Sun was too old and was of an inappropriate generation because Sun and Charlie Soong, Ching-ling's father, were friends. Also, at the time Sun was still married to his first wife. Her bedroom furniture was a belated wedding gift from her parents, who had initially opposed her marriage to Sun.

As Sun's widow following his death in 1925, Ching-ling was active in the anti-Japanese resistance movement and supported a KMT alliance with the Communist Party. Although she had no children of her own, the Communist government called her the "Mother of the Country". She founded the Children's Palace on Yan'an Road (formerly the Kadoorie estate and explored in Walk I, "A Time to Dance, A Time to Mourn"), and held honorary titles in the Communist Party until she was finally inducted as a party member shortly before her death. More about the Soong family may be found on Walk III.

The next lane is almost straight across the street from the Soong Ching-ling Museum. Cross Huaihai Road (M) and continue east.

Bao Yugang
包玉刚
Residence
No. 1, Lane 1818 Huaihai Rd (M), left side

Bao, better known as Y.K. Pao, was born in 1918 in Ningbo. He studied in Shanghai and worked in banking. He eventually left for Hong Kong with his father, and in 1955 he decided to go into the shipping business. He borrowed US$770,000 from a Japanese bank and bought a ship from England. He named it Jin An Hao 金安号, meaning "Prosperity and Peace". His method was to lease the ship long-term at a low monthly rate, contrary to the common practice of that time of short-term leasing. That's why during the 1957 shipping downturn, Bao's business did not suffer. In 1963 HSBC started investing in his business, and by 1980 he had over 200 vessels.

In the 1970s Bao invested in real estate, hotels, and transportation in Hong Kong. He also made donations to build a library at the Jiaotong University and to establish a college in his hometown, Ningbo, China. A dance fan, Bao sponsored dance competitions and even danced at a TV appearance for charity. He was knighted by Queen Elizabeth II before he died in 1991 at age 73.

His family continued in the shipping business and has had controlling shares in the Norwegian company now known as BW Gas. Bao's eldest daughter founded a school in 2007 called the Y.K. Pao School on the grounds of the Shanghai No. 3 Girls' Middle School on Jiangsu Road, which was formerly the McTyeire School for Girls in Old Shanghai mentioned in Walk III, "Money and Trouble".

Shao Xunmei
邵洵美
Residence
*No. 17, Lane
1754 Huaihai Rd
(M), left side*

Poet Shao Xunmei (1906-1968) lived here, but his lane house, one of a lane of charming houses according to pictures, was torn down in recent years; in their place are fancy villas. Only a heritage plaque on the right of the black gates designates the location of the old lane houses.

Shao was a grandson of Qing Dynasty officials and was educated at Cambridge University. He left college one year before graduation when he was called back home under the excuse of family finance reduction – really it was because his grandmother wanted him to marry so she could have a great-grandchild. While abroad, he befriended several prominent artists such as the painter Liu Haisu 刘海粟 and Xu Zhimo 徐志摩. Back in Shanghai, Shao published many weekly and monthly magazines from the 1920s through the 1940s. He translated

English books into Chinese in the 1950s, such as *The Adventures of Tom Sawyer*.

Before Shao left Shanghai for Cambridge, he had become engaged to his cousin, Sheng Peiyu 盛佩玉, granddaughter of powerful Qing Dynasty official and merchant, Sheng Xuanhuai 盛宣怀. As a going-away gift, she knitted him a white woolen vest. Shao wrote her a poem, based on that vest, as an engagement gift and had the poem published in the newspaper, *Shen Bao*. Later in her autobiography, *The Sheng Family – Xunmei and Me*, Sheng Peiyu said she had kept that newspaper clipping for over sixty years.

When they got engaged, Sheng had three conditions stemming from the vices she had seen her own family suffer under: 1. Shao would not have lovers; 2. He would not smoke (opium); and 3. He would not gamble. Shao agreed to her conditions and they had nine children together, but as she would later discover, he broke his promises.

An American freelance reporter, Emily Hahn, came to Shanghai in 1935. She was writing for *The New Yorker*. Widely known to have had a love affair with her, Shao gave her the name "Xiang Meili" 项美丽 (Beautiful Hahn). It is believed Hahn once lived at No. 6 in Lane 1754. Shao's wife, Sheng, described her rival as speaking in a soft voice and having straight facial features but a big bottom! Sheng also said that Hahn kept her pet monkey in order to get attention. Through Shao, Hahn got to know the Soong Sisters, whom she later wrote about in a biography.

During the anti-Japanese resistance movement, Shao's own publication company was destroyed, so he used Hahn's name to publish a Chinese and an English monthly magazine, criticizing the Japanese. In May, 1938 the Communist Party decided to publish Mao Zedong's anti-Japanese speech abroad. Being supporters and sympathizers, Hahn and Shao were made responsible for the printing and distribution of the book. At night, Shao drove his car up and down Huaihai Road and Hongqiao Road, stuffing the book into the mail slots of foreigners' homes.

Emily Hahn

Emily Hahn (1905-1997) graduated from the University of Wisconsin with a degree in mining engineering. (She had no intention of working in mining; she did mining engineering because she wanted a course with a chemistry class.) While working after graduation, realizing her employer treated her more as a clerk than an engineer, she quit and went traveling. After a spell as a research assistant to a writer in London, she spent time in Africa and later came to China. While in China, she smoked opium and reportedly kept company with Victor Sassoon before she met Shao. After she left China, she had an illegitimate daughter with the head of the British Secret Service in Hong Kong. He divorced his wife to marry Hahn; however, they eventually split up. Emily Hahn continued to write, authoring a total of 52 books and 181 pieces for The New Yorker. In her later years she wrote about wildlife preservation and monkeys. Her autobiography, Times and Places, a Memoir, was published in 1970. Her bestsellers were The Soong Sisters and China to Me.

In the 1950s the Shaos' lane house here was turned into a cafeteria. From 1958-1961, Shao was imprisoned. After his release, he lived in his son's apartment, while his wife lived in Nanjing with a daughter's family. Shao suffered from heart problems and died in 1968 at age 62, a pauper. Through the years, Shao's business endeavors made no money, instead they drained the family resources

Chiang Ching-kuo 蒋经国 Residence

inherited from his prominent grandfathers. When he died, his wife could only afford to buy him a new pair of shoes to send him off.

Continue on Huaihai Road (M), crossing Hunan Road 湖南路.

Chiang Ching-kuo (1910-1988) was born to Chiang Kai-shek and his first wife. Chiang spent his youth in Shanghai and attended university in Russia. He held various posts in the Kuomintang Party, before he succeeded his father as the party president (by which time the party's territory was restricted to Taiwan). He held that position until his death.

When Chiang came with his family to live here in August, 1948, the Kuomintang was rapidly losing the war to the Communists. Chinese society was chaotic, and inflation was rampant; the elder Chiang commanded his son to stabilize the economy. There were two fronts to Chiang Ching-kuo's approach: 1.) forcing people to hand in their gold, silver, and foreign currencies in exchange for newly minted paper money; and 2) freezing prices on

Chiang Ching-kuo 蒋经国 Residence
No. 2, Lane 1610 Huaihai Rd (M), across the street from the Shanghai Library, left side

goods. Chiang Ching-kuo dubbed this policy "hunt the tiger" because he promised to deal harshly with offenders, no matter how powerful they were. Chiang put Du Yuesheng's son in jail for his refusal to cooperate. This infuriated Du, who spread word that a son of H. H. Kung (Chiang Kai-shek's brother-in-law) was evading taxes. Chiang Ching-kuo ordered Kung's company to be closed. In turn, Kung sent his sister-in-law, Madame Chiang Kai-shek (Soong May-ling), to deal with Chiang Ching-kuo, her step-son. Since Kung, Soong and her husband Chiang Kai-shek were all intimately related, Chiang Ching-kuo found himself at a disadvantage.

Further, both prongs of Chiang's policy backfired. The price freeze forced merchants to withhold their products from the open market and caused the rapid rise of a black market. The paper money was rendered useless when the Kuomintang's control of Mainland China collapsed a few short months later; many middle-class people lost much of their money through this scheme. Thus, by the time they left for Taiwan, the Kuomintang had lost a large portion of their base of support from the people.

Chiang Ching-kuo married a Russian, Faina (1916-2004). She was an orphan; her parents were aristocrats chased out of their home by the Russian revolutionaries. A private person, Faina was rarely seen or heard by the public other than necessary official occasions, and she refused the invitation by the KMT to orally state her history for the official archives. She and Chiang had four children, three sons and one daughter. All three sons had died before her own death on Taiwan in 2004.

While Chiang was already married, he had an affair with his secretary, who bore him twin sons in 1942. The boys took their mother's last name. The woman died suddenly under mysterious

Sheng Chongyi Residence, 1517 Huaihai Road

circumstances before her babies were one year old. One of the sons is still alive on Taiwan and, in 2005 he officially changed his and his deceased brother's last name to Chiang.

Built in 1900, the mansion boasts eight Roman pillars at the front entrance. It was built for a German and was later occupied by Sheng Chongyi, the fifth son of Sheng Xuanhuai, the powerful official and merchant of the Qing Dynasty mentioned earlier on this walk. Commonly called Sheng No. 5 because he was the fifth child, Sheng Chongyi was smart and shrewd in business dealings. But according to his niece Sheng Peiyu's autobiography, his wife was foul-tempered: she beat her maids and made them kneel on steel ash trays as a punishment. Sheng No. 5 and his wife's only son died at birth, and they had a daughter who was very spoiled. Sadly she died at 12 of lung disease, and her father named the nearby Weeping Gem Lane 鸣玉坊 after her. In 1948 Sheng No. 5 sold this villa to another industrialist for one million U.S. dollars.

An interesting fact about Sheng's family involved the court battle between his unmarried sisters and his brothers. When Sheng Xuanhuai, the patriarch, died, the estate passed to his wife. And

Sheng Chongyi
盛重颐
Residence
1517 Huaihai Rd (M), right side, now the Consul-General of Japan's residence

when she died and the estate was finally divided in 1928, the sons and eldest grandson each got a share, but not the daughters. Encouraged by the Soong sisters, the two unmarried daughters went to court and sued under the KMT's equal rights amendment. This was an unprecedented act of defiance of old traditions. Although the women won a partial victory, they paid nearly all of their inheritance in court-related fees.

Here is another story: After returning from his studies in America, T.V. Soong worked as an English secretary to the general manager of a big company. Sheng No. 5's older brother, Sheng No. 4, headed that company. Because T.V. Soong often went to the Sheng's house to report on business, he met Sheng's younger sister, known as Miss Sheng No. 7. They fell in love, but Sheng's mother disapproved of their relationship because at the time the Sheng family name was very famous but the Soongs' was not. T.V. Soong decided to join Sun Yat-sen's revolution and defer marriage. When he came back to Shanghai, he was already married, and Miss Sheng No. 7 was heartbroken. Later, when she was 32, she married a cousin. One day with Sheng No. 5's help, T.V. Soong came to this mansion on Huaihai Road (M) to meet and to explain himself to Miss Sheng No. 7. She was not expecting him, and when she saw T.V. Soong she left right away, saying: "My husband is waiting for me." However, after World War II, when a beloved nephew was arrested by the Kuomintang on suspicion of working for the Japanese, Miss Sheng No. 7 had to call on T.V. Soong, who was now brother-in-law to Chiang Kai-shek, to get the nephew released. "I want to have lunch with my nephew," she said.

"You will, tomorrow," Soong replied. Sheng's

nephew was indeed released by the KMT the next morning.

This is the current consulate of the United States.

Rong Hongyuan 荣鸿元 Residence
1469 Huaihai Rd (M), right side, corner of Wulumuqi Rd 乌鲁木齐路

Built in 1921 in the French Renaissance style, this villa belonged to Jardine, Matheson & Co., the largest British trading firm in Asia at the time. During World War II a Japanese businessman and his family lived here. Later, the Consul-General of Switzerland made his home here. In 1946 Rong Hongyuan, a son of a wealthy textile family, bought the building. He spent a great deal of money on remodeling but did not live here long. In 1948 the KMT arrested Rong, accusing him of illegally exchanging money, and he was sentenced to six months in jail. The second day after his release from jail, Rong left for Hong Kong and, eventually, Brazil. He never returned to Shanghai, living out the rest of his days believing he had been wrongfully accused. After 1949, the house was used by the All China Women's Federation. It became the center for political education during the Cultural Revolution and later a government guesthouse before the U.S. leased it as its consulate in 1980. The estate underwent extensive renovation in 1997 and 2003-2005 to preserve its beauty and to make it more suitable as a consulate. Today the Consul-General hosts receptions on the ground floor, while the second floor is office space. The American Women's Club holds its yearly summary wrap-up for its members here with the Consul-General.

We have ended the walk at the consulate district in the former French Concession. Across from the U.S. Consulate is the short Taojiang Road 桃江路. There are a few restaurants here, and nearby is Hengshan Road 衡山路, with lots of restaurants, bars, and boutiques popular with foreigners. There is also a subway station for Line 1.

Further Reading:
Xingguo Hotel:
A Walker's Guide to Old Western Landmarks in Shanghai, compiled by Shanghai Daily, 2008, pp. 188-194
Frenchtown: Shanghai Western Architecture in Shanghai's Old French Concession by Tess Johnston and Deke Erh, Old China Hand Press, 2000, pp. 64-67

Guo Dihuo:
Lao Shanghai Huayuan Yangfang (Old Shanghai Garden Villas) by Xue Shunsheng and Lou Chenghao, Tongji Daxue Chubanshe, 2002, pp. 138-139
Shanghai Lao Yangfang (Shanghai Old Villas) by Song Luxia, Shanghai Science and Technology Cultural Publisher, 2004, pp. 40-41

Dingxiang Garden:
Shanghai De Haomen Jiumeng (Old Dreams of Shanghai's Super Rich) by Song Luxia, China Friendship Publishing Co., 2002, pp. 1-41
Shanghai Lao Yangfang (Shanghai Old Villas) by Song Luxia, Shanghai Science and Technology Cultural Publisher, 2004, pp. 115-117
"Fantasy and Reality: Dingxiang Garden" by Wang Weiqiu, B13 *Xinmin Evening News*, September 2, 2007
Heritage plaque

Mo Shangqing:
Shanghai Lao Yangfang (Shanghai Old Villas) by Song Luxia, Shanghai Science and Technology Cultural Publisher, 2004, pp. 36-37

Chen Lifu and Chen Guofu:
Famous People, Houses & Stories by Huang Guoxin

and Shen Fuxu, Tongji University Publisher, 2003, pp. 91-94

Lao Shanghai Huayuan Yangfang (Old Shanghai Garden Villas) by Xue Shusheng and Lou Chenghao, Tongji Daxue Chubanshe, 2002, pp. 54-55

Tang Chaoyi:
Shanghai Lao Yangfang (Shanghai Old Villas) by Song Luxia, Shanghai Science and Technology Cultural Publisher, 2004, pp. 30-33

Lao Shanghai Huayuan Yangfang (Old Shanghai Garden Villas) by Xue Shusheng and Lou Chenghao, Tongji Daxue Chubanshe, 2002, pp. 82-83

Calbeck, Macgregor, & Co.:
Shanghai Lao Yangfang (Shanghai Old Villas) by Song Luxia, Shanghai Science and Technology Cultural Publisher, 2004, pp. 28-29

Zhou Zuomin:
Shanghai Lao Yangfang (Shanghai Old Villas) by Song Luxia, Shanghai Science and Technology Cultural Publisher, 2004, pp. 34-35

Lao Shanghai Huayuan Yangfang (Old Shanghai Garden Villas) by Xue Shusheng and Lou Chenghao, Tongji Daxue Chubanshe, 2002, pp. 108-109

Shanghai Archives Online, www.archives.sh.cn/hshrw

Hunan Villa:
Shanghai Lao Yangfang (Shanghai Old Villas) by Song Luxia, Shanghai Science and Technology Cultural Publisher, 2004, pp. 62-62

Famous People, Houses & Stories by Huang Guoxin and Shen Fuxu, Tongji University Publisher, 2003, pp. 69-70

WALK IV: MURDER IS EASY

John Calvin Ferguson and 390 Wukang Road:
Lao Shanghai Huayuan Yangfang (Old Shanghai Garden Villas) by Xue Shusheng and Lou Chenghao, Tongji Daxue Chubanshe, 2002, pp. 154-155
Shanghai Lao Yangfang (Shanghai Old Villas) by Song Luxia, Shanghai Science and Technology Cultural Publisher, 2004, pp. 62-63
www.shtong.gov.cn
www.gmw.cn

Huang Xing:
www.baike.baidu.com/view/43318.htm
www.csonline.com.cn/information

Normandie Apartments:
Heritage plaque

YK Pao:
baike.baidu.com
Shao Xunmei:
Shanghai Lao Yangfang (Shanghai Old Villas) by Song Luxia, Shanghai Science and Technology Cultural Publisher, 2004, pp. 12-13
Shanghai De Haomen Jiumeng (Od Dreams of Shanghai's Super Rich) by Song Luxia, China Friendship Publishing Co., 2002, pp. 254-258
A Walker's Guide to Old Western Landmarks in Shanghai, compiled by Shanghai Daily, 2008, pp. 141-146
Sheng Beiyu's autobiography, *The Sheng Family – Xunmei and Me*, Renmin Wenxue Chubanshe, 2004

Emily Hahn:
www.engr.wisc.edu/alumni/perspective
www.todayinliterature.com

Chiang Jingguo:
Shanghai Lao Yangfang (Shanghai Old Villas) by Song Luxia, Shanghai Science and Technology Cultural Publisher, 2004, pp. 14-15
Famous People, Houses, and Stories by Huang Guoxin and Shen Fuxu, Tongji University Publisher, 2003, pp. 75-77
A Walker's Guide to Old Western Landmarks in Shanghai, compiled by Shanghai Daily, 2008, pp. 137-140

Rong Hongyuan:
Shanghai Lao Yangfang (Shanghai Old Villas) by Song Luxia, Shanghai Science and Technology Cultural Publisher, 2004, pp. 8-9

Sheng Family:
Shanghai De Haomen Jiumeng (Od Dreams of Shanghai's Super Rich) by Song Luxia, China Friendship Publishing Co., 2002, pp. 42-83

Sheng Chongyi:
Shanghai Lao Yangfang (Shanghai Old Villas) by Song Luxia, Shanghai Science and Technology Cultural Publisher, 2004, pp. 10-11
Famous People, Houses & Stories by Huang Guoxin and Shen Fuxu, Tongji University Publisher, 2003, pp. 136-139
Sheng Beiyu's autobiography, *The Sheng Family – Xunmei and Me*, Renmin Wenxue Chubanshe, 2004

WALK V:
From Huaihai Road (M)
To Shaoxing Road
淮海中路——绍兴路
Spheres of Influence

This walk takes place in the heart of the former French Concession, south of Huaihai Road (M), where lovely villas and large gardens abound. You will hear about a scholar of oracle-bone inscriptions and his love life, two generals and their sacrifices to save China from the Japanese in 1936, and how the jazz craze of the 1930s possessed a family and their friends. One local artisan became famous for his lanterns in the shape of animals such as the dragon. Another foreigner, who lived in a beautiful, large mansion, was an avid racer of dogs and horses.

Subway Line 1—South Shaanxi Road Station—Exit 1: out of the subway station, turn right and turn right again at Huaihai Road (M) 淮海中路

To get your bearings, turn right immediately past the Starbuck's, 935 Huaihai Road (M), and walk into the neighborhood.

Huaihai Fang
淮海坊
Lane 927
Huaihai Rd
淮海中路

Called Joffre Terrace in the olden days, this long lane of tidy townhouses with patios was built in the 1920s. It was considered a good place to live because of its convenient location, and several well-known writers, artists, and even one diplomat lived here. Almost all the houses are identical, but I recommend exploring the second-last laneway on the left. As you head down this laneway, No. 87 is on your right side, and No. 47 is on your left side. Looking at No. 47, you should be facing the front gates of the townhouses. Looking at No. 87, you should see the back doors of the townhouses. (Once you are standing there it will make sense.)

No. 52 was home to **Zhang Xianglin** 张祥麟 (1891-1976). He graduated from St. John's University and got his master's degree from Columbia University. From 1927 to 1929 he was the Chinese Consul-General in New York and was the secretary-general of

Huaihai Fang 淮海坊

the HSBC between 1943 and 1953. During the Cultural Revolution he was a patient of my mother at the hospital nearby on Huaihai Road (M), Xuhui Central Hospital. She did not know about his history until his daughter told her about it many years later. Some things from the past were not talked about during the Cultural Revolution.

No. 59, down the laneway, was the home of the prolific writer, **Ba Jin** 巴金 (1904-2005). Ba studied in France and Japan and wrote and/or translated over 13 million words. While living here, he wrote the best-sellers, *Spring* 春 and *Autumn* 秋, which are still in print. They were part of a trilogy, including the epic, *Family* 家, which portrays a large feudal family, focusing on how young people were stifled by old traditions.

No. 64 was home to **Xu Guangping** 徐广平 (1889-1968), a former student and wife of writer Lu Xun 鲁迅. She lived here from 1936 to 1948, during which time she edited *The Complete Works of Lu Xun*. After 1949, she held various governmental posts in the People's Republic, including vice-chair of the

All China Women's Federation. (Please see Walk II, entitled "True Colors", for more information on Lu Xun.)

No. 33 was home to actress, **Hu Die 胡蝶** (1908-1989), who portrayed teachers, prostitutes, dancers, older women, younger women – just about every type of role – in the 1930s and 1940s. In 1959 she won the best actress award at the Asia Film Festival. She eventually migrated to Canada, where she lived out the rest of her days.

No. 99 was home to **Xu Beihong 徐悲鸿** (1895-1953). A giant in the contemporary Chinese art world, Xu specialized in oil painting. During World War II, he donated his paintings for war causes. His Chinese ink drawings of horses are easily recognizable.

At the end of the laneway, turn right onto a tiny, narrow alley. At the end of this short alley, turn left and exit through the other main gates of this lane community; you will come out on an entirely different street from the one you entered on. Some of Shanghai's lanes allow for this kind of short cut.

Astrid Apartments
corner of Maoming Rd (S)
茂名南路
and Nanchang Rd
南昌路
across the street from where you are standing

An eight-story apartment building built in 1933 in the Art Deco style, the Astrid building has a façade of orange-green tiles.

Astrid Apartments

Cross Maoming Road (S) and Nanchang Road, then walk east on Nanchang.

Nanchang Road consists of short blocks. There are many boutiques along the road, located in what used to be ground floor residences. Continue down Nanchang to Lane 127. If you reach the Ruijin (No.2) Road 瑞金二路 intersection, you have gone too far.

He Keming 何克明 Residence
No.4, Lane 127 Nanchang Rd, right side

Inside the lane, take the first right. Number 4 will be on your right side. He Keming (1894-1989) was a Chinese lantern craftsman. He started with a booth in Shanghai's Yu Garden 豫园 when he was 16. He invented the method of using lead wire for structure instead of the traditional bamboo. He used silk for covers, and he accented the lanterns with gold and silver threads and a variety of colors. Shaping them into animals considered lucky in Chinese folklore, such as the dragon, his lanterns were exhibited in the U.S., Australia, Japan, and other countries.

Outside the lane turn right onto Nanchang and continue across Ruijin (No.2) Road.

Castle-like Villa
79 Nanchang Rd, right side, half way down the block

Down an ordinary-looking lane, Lane 79, and past a yellow house with a garden and a large fruit tree, you will come to an interesting villa with a half-rounded front. I met a resident who said his grandfather had the house built seventy years ago, and that now he and his two uncles shared the house.

Townhouses
212 Nanchang Rd, diagonally across from 79 Nanchang Rd, left side

Very old and tired-looking, these townhouses look like they came from Charles Dickens' era. Tall trees line a narrow path, making the lane look melancholy, but here is a neighborhood full of action – a farmer's market, mahjong players, and steaming bun vendors all set up shop inside this lane.

Outside 212 Nanchang Road, turn left but stay on this side of the road.

WALK V: SPHERES OF INFLUENCE

He Keming Residence 何克明

Townhouses

Yang Hucheng Residence 杨虎城

Yang Hucheng
杨虎城
Residence
No. 65
Nanchang Rd,
right side, just
before Sinan Rd
思南路
intersection

Yang held various military posts in the Kuomintang government, but he supported Sun Yat-sen's 孙中山 policies of alliances with the Communist Party and Russia. He is best known for his role in the Xi'an Incident of 1936. When the Japanese invaded China, Chiang Kai-shek 蒋介石 was reluctant to fight against them, instead concentrating his efforts against the Communists. Faced with the prospect of the nation being occupied by a foreign power, Yang and another general, Zhang Xueliang 张学良 devised a plan to force Chiang's hand. In Xi'an in December, 1936, armed kidnappers attacked Chiang's lodging, capturing Chiang while he was trying to escape up a nearby hill. (Today that point is marked, and you may go to visit the historical park the lodge is located in.) The two generals put Chiang under house arrest, and, with no alternative, Chiang agreed to cooperate with the Communists to fight the Japanese. Doubtless the Xi'an Affair infuriated Chiang Kai-shek; Yang was shortly sent abroad under the excuse of making a tour of several countries. He was later lured back and spent twelve years in prison. Finally, in 1949, the Kuomintang assassinated Yang, along with his young son, baby daughter, secretary, and his secretary's family. Yang's wife was spared only because she had already died.

Cross Sinan Road and continue on Nanchang Road, going east.

Guo Moruo
郭沫若
Residence
No. 7, Lane 178 Nanchang Rd, left side

The house is the first one in the second row on your left side. If the gate is locked, you can go around through Lane 166.

Guo (1892-1978) was a historian, author, poet, playwright and expert on the earliest examples of Chinese writing, the Jiaguwen 甲骨文, or oracle-bone inscriptions. He wrote volumes on Chinese artifacts and several historical plays, including one on Wu Zetian 武则天, the woman who has been called the only female emperor in China's history.

In 1927 Guo joined the Nanchang Uprising, in which the communist-leaning faction of the KMT tried and failed to take control from the right-leaning faction. He and a group of liberal literary figures then formed a Marxist society. During World War II, Guo worked for the anti-Japanese resistance movement. In the People's Republic he held various governmental positions, including president of the University of Science and Technology China, a position he held for over twenty years.

Guo's first wife was chosen for him by his parents. Five days after the wedding in 1912, Guo left home and never returned to her. She stayed with his family for the rest of her life, for 68 years. Between 1916 and 1937 Guo lived many years in Japan, with a Japanese woman who bore him five children and severed her relationship with her parents for him. However, he left her in 1937 to return to China. Guo married a Chinese woman in 1939, and they had six children. After World War II, Guo's Japanese common-law wife came to China. When she realized that Guo already had another family, she decided to manage on her own.

Guo stayed in this house in 1923, when his poetry anthology, *Xing Kong (Starry Sky)*, was published.

Shanghai Association of Science and Technology (Shanghai Science Hall)
科学会堂
No. 47 Nanchang Rd, across the street

This was formerly a French sports club with a large tennis court. When the French Club moved to the current Okura Garden Hotel address on Maoming Road (S) in 1926, this building became the College Francais, or College Municipal Francais. It was a public school for any child in the French Concession who wished to attend, whether French, Russian, or Chinese. From old pictures we can guess the education probably ranged from elementary to high school.

Retrace your steps back along Nanchang Road, and turn left onto Sinan Road 思南路, going south.

There are several large villas on Sinan Road, such as No. 36, across the street.

When you come to Gaolan Road 皋兰路, the next intersection, turn left.

Zhang Xueliang
张学良
Residence
No. 1 Gaolan Rd, next to the park entrance

Built in 1934, it was rented by Zhang's office for him and his long-time mistress, Zhao Yidi 赵一荻 (known as Miss Zhao No. 4 赵四小姐).

Zhang (1901-2001) was the son of an important warlord who was killed by the Japanese. Zhang himself became a top general under Chiang Kai-shek, but on September 18, 1931 he let the Japanese occupy China's three northeastern provinces without resistance. This was part of what is known as the 9-18 or Mukden Incident and is still regarded as a shameful chapter in Chinese history.

However, Zhang is depicted favorably in history books here because of his role in the Xi'an Incident in December 1936, in which, after two weeks of house arrest and negotiations, Chiang finally agreed to cease his campaign against the Communists and focus on fighting the Japanese. On December 25, General Zhang accompanied Chiang from Xi'an back to the capital, Nanjing.

The Kuomintang court in Nanjing sentenced Zhang to ten years in prison for his role in Chiang's kidnapping, but he received a reprieve and was put under house arrest instead. Zhang asked Chiang to allow him to fight during World War II but was met with silence. In 1947, he again petitioned Chiang for his freedom, and again Chiang rebuffed him. The Kuomintang took Zhang with them to Taiwan in 1949. In 1957 on Chiang's 70th birthday, Zhang sent him a gift of a gold watch. In return, Chiang gave Zhang a walking stick. It was 1959 when Chiang agreed to lift the house arrest order, but Zhang remained under surveillance on Taiwan. He finally became a free man in the late 1970s.

Zhang was already married when he met 16-year-old Miss Zhao No. 4 in 1928. She came from a powerful family and was considered a society beauty. Zhang and Zhao lived together for decades, while in name she served as his secretary. This was convenient because the position allowed her to be constantly by his side. They had one child, a son. In 1956 Zhang converted to Christianity and decided that the status of his relationship with Zhao contradicted Biblical teachings, so he asked for, and received, a divorce from his wife. He married Zhao in 1964 in Taiwan with Soong May-ling 宋美龄, Chiang's wife, among their wedding guests.

After 1949 Zhang and Zhao lived a mostly quiet life, with politics notably absent. They lived their last years in Hawaii – Zhao died in 2000 at age 88, while Zhang died the following year at age 101.

Facing Zhang's residence, turn left, and enter the park.

Fuxing Park 复兴公园

Fuxing Park
复兴公园
at the end of Gaolan Rd
皋兰路

Note: the park has multiple entrances, so please remember how you entered so you may find your way out easily. As with most parks in Shanghai, Fuxing Park is free.

Established in 1909 as the French Park, this park is fun to visit. Stroll along the walkways, and you may see older people dancing. In late May and early June, multitudes of fragrant flowers will greet you.

There are two statues in the park, side by side, of Karl Marx (1818-1883) and Friedrich Engels (1820-1895), the fathers of Communism. Retrace your steps to the park's entrance on Gaolan Road and walk down Gaolan Road away from the park. Cross Sinan Road. Continue on Gaolan Road – it is a short street.

St. Nicholas Russian Orthodox Church
No. 16 Gaolan Rd
right side

In 1932 a Russian general organized a fundraiser to build a church in memory of those who died for the Tsar during the revolution. This church was completed in 1934 and was known as the "society church" because it was rented out to Chinese and others for fancy weddings. It was closed down in

1955, but in more recent years it has enjoyed new life first as a factory that made washing machines and lately as a bar. In 2008 it was closed for remodeling, and as of April, 2009 it had not yet been reopened.

Facing the church, turn left and continue down Gaolan Road.

***No. 23 Gaolan Rd** left side*

This has got to be one of the prettiest villas in Shanghai. The house was built in 1918 for foreigners and in 1945 was bought by a Mr and Mrs Yang, who had nine children. The current owners are a husband from Australia and a wife from China's Miao ethnic minority. With the deed title to the house, the couple searched archive materials and found the original blueprints. They have since painstakingly restored the house to its former glory, and it is often featured in magazines.

The walls are hand-plastered with dark grey pebbles. The top part of each window shutter has the queen of hearts as its design. The owners bought a red carved wooden window in a cut-out

St. Nicholas Russian Orthodox Church

No. 23 Gaolan Rd

Song Hanzhang Residence, No. 28 Gaolan Road

design and installed it on the side wall in the front courtyard.

This house is in a short lane, so wander in a little farther, to the end, so that you may get a full view of the restored villa next door (which belongs to a bank, according to neighbors) and the two hidden lane houses behind No. 23.

Song Hanzhang 宋汉章 Residence
No. 28 Gaolan Rd, right side, at the corner of the intersection of Gaolan and Ruijin (No.2) Rd 瑞金二路

Song (1872-1968) worked in the Daqing Bank, which later became the Bank of China. He was the managing director of the Bank of China in 1935. This building is now a language school that teaches Chinese to foreigners.

Shanghai No. 4 School for the Deaf, No. 31 Gaolan Road, left side

This beautiful, new school is one of four schools for the deaf in Shanghai. The sign language used in Shanghai schools is different from the American sign language. In this school, students also learn to speak Chinese.

At the intersection, turn left onto Ruijin (No.2) Road, and left again at Xiangshan Road 香山路, the next street.

Shanghai Museum of Sun Yat-sen's Former Residence

No. 6 Xiangshan Road 香山路, left side
This large villa was built in the 1920s in the French Renaissance style and was home to Catholic priests called Augustinian Recoletos. This order of priests started in Spain in the 16th century and was accepted by the Vatican in the 19th century. Note the chapel, which is believed to retain some original stained glass.

Cross Sinan Road, continuing along Xiangshan Road.

The first house, No. 9, is a newly established museum about Sun Yat-sen. Number 7, a Spanish villa built at the turn of the century, was the home he lived in with his wife, Soong Ching-ling 宋庆龄, from 1918 to 1924.

Both the Kuomintang and the Communist Party recognize Sun Yat-sen as the founding father of the Republic of China. But after the overthrow of the Qing Dynasty came a chaotic period in Chinese history. Many warlords tried to claim territories, and there was division within the KMT, Sun's own party, as to its direction. On January 26, 1922, Sun and the Soviet envoy, after meeting here, released a

Shanghai Museum of Sun Yat-sen's Former Residence
No. 7 Xiangshan Road, end of T-intersection, open from 9am-4pm everyday, 20 RMB entrance fee

Zhou Enlai's Residence
周公馆

Shanghai Cultural and Historical Research Center 上海文史研究所

joint statement announcing Sun's decision to align with the Soviet Union and with the recently founded Communist Party.

Out of Sun's museum, turn left on Sinan Road, going south.

Shanghai Cultural and Historical Research Center
上海文史研究所
No. 41 Sinan Road, left side

This yellow villa compound, built in the 1930s as a private residence of financier Yuan Zuoliang 袁佐良, was renovated in the spring of 2008 to serve as offices of the city government agency that concentrates on cultural and historical research. The center publishes a magazine called *Century*, which is sold in the shop next door. The shop also sells noteworthy paintings by members of the Center.

Cross Fuxing Road (M) 复兴中路, continuing south on Sinan Road.

Zhou Enlai's Residence
周公馆
No. 73 Sinan Rd left side

Entrance is free to this charming villa with a wooded garden. The garden has a side door that takes you to an identical villa next door. The ground floor of that villa has been converted to a museum about the Communist Party's activities prior to 1949, and it is also free.

Zhou (1898-1976) studied in Japan and France and joined the Communist Party in 1922. He was one of the earliest revolutionaries and held various high posts in the party. In Xi'an in 1936, Zhou met with Kuomintang general Zhang Xueliang, where they agreed on the policy of "ceasing the civil war (between the Communists and Kuomintang) and fighting Japan as one".

This house was built in the 1920s. In June, 1946 it became known as the Zhou Residence, but in reality, it was the offices of the Communist Party in Shanghai. Zhou, his comrade Dong Biwu 董必武, and others held several press briefings and met with American envoy George Marshall here. Zhou left for Yan'an in November, 1946, when negotiations with the Kuomintang failed.

Across the street, from the top window of what used to be the Shanghai Maternity and Children's Hospital, the Kuomintang's intelligence agency set up a look-out to keep an eye on the comings and goings of the Zhou Residence.

After the founding of the People's Republic in 1949, Zhou became the Premier. In 1972 he and U.S. President Nixon signed the Shanghai Communiqué that led to the establishment of diplomatic relations seven years later.

At the front gates of Zhou Enlai's Residence on Sinan Road, turn left. There are a total of twenty-two villas in this area that belong to the local government and have been undergoing renovation, with some completed already.

Villa 87, at the end of the next lane and identical to Zhou's, was the home of Mei Lanfang 梅兰芳 (1894-1961) the name synonymous with Peking Opera. Born into a family of actors, he started learning Peking Opera at age 8 and was on stage by 11. He made significant contributions to Peking

Ruijin Hotel 瑞金宾馆

Opera in costume, makeup, music, dance and singing style. His style of opera became known as the Mei Style.

When the Japanese occupied Shanghai, Mei refused to perform, using his advanced age as an excuse. In October, 1945, after the Japanese were defeated, Mei returned to the stage in both the Lyceum (see Walk II) and Majestic theaters.

Mei lived here between 1933 and 1958. He received many notable visitors, including Charlie Chaplin and his wife. Mei's wives and some of his children were singers and musicians.

Retrace your steps back onto Sinan Road. Turn right to head north. At the intersection of Sinan and Fuxing Road (M), cross Sinan and then turn left onto Fuxing, going west to the next intersection, at Ruijin (No.2) Road. Cross Ruijin and turn left.

Ruijin Hotel
瑞金宾馆
118 Ruijin (No.2) Rd
瑞金二路
right side half way down the block

This government-owned estate includes a hotel and villas on beautiful grounds. You may enter and wander around. There are several restaurants in this peaceful, charming setting, including Jin Yi Xuan Restaurant on the ground floor of No. 1, serving Shanghainese cuisine.

The compound formerly belonged to Irish

businessman H. E. Morriss Jr., whose father founded and owned the influential, English-language *North-China Daily News* from the 1920s to the 1940s. Morriss Jr. loved horses and dogs, so it was very convenient for him that the dog-racing track called Canidrome was close by.

The elder Morriss came to Shanghai in 1867 and bought 109 mu (18.2 acres) from local peasants. He died in 1919. The Morrisses owned many lane houses on Yan'an Road (E), Chongqing Road (N), etc. Their lanes all had the Chinese character "马" – meaning "horse" – in the name, taken from the Chinese transliteration of the Morrisses' surname, 马立斯 (pronounced "Mah-lee-suh").

Harry Morriss Jr., born in 1883, designed and built Villa No. 1 as his own residence in 1920. Note the original marble pillars cut from one piece imported from Europe. In the ground floor lobby are many pictures of Old Shanghai, including one of "Benjamin Maurice", who was not the owner of this villa. If you go up the broad stairway with its intricate wood banisters, you will see a colorful wrought iron screen of flowers, dogs, and a peacock at the second floor landing. But the second floor itself is not open to the public because it has guest rooms.

During World War II the Italian Consulate occupied the villa. The Kuomintang took over the estate in 1945, and Chiang Kai-shek and Soong May-ling stayed here briefly and had offices here. The first mayor of post-1949 Shanghai, Chen Yi, had his office here also, and Chairman Mao Zedong visited. There are signs outside offices and bedroom suites commemorating these occasions.

The grounds around the villa are well-groomed and peaceful. An architecture professor from the Tongji University named this villa Wo Yin Lou 卧茵楼, meaning "Villa Reposing on Green Grass".

Harry's brother Gordon was a partner in a brokerage firm. After 1949 he supposedly lived in the gatehouse to the right of the entrance, until his death in 1952, after the government expropriated his home to use as a state guesthouse.

Chinese sources say during World War II a man known as Sheng Laosan 盛老三 operated Shanghai's largest opium dealership in Villa No. 3. Sheng was a relative of the famous Qing Dynasty official and merchant Sheng Xuanhuai (see Walk IV, "Murder is Easy"). After the war Sheng Laosan was sentenced to death by the Nanjing Supreme Court, and the government confiscated this villa. Today it has a café and has guest rooms on the second floor. The ground floor consists mainly of a large reception area, where the original, beautiful stained glass window of a drinking tiger is the focal point. This space is available for rent for party functions.

Villa No. 4 was built in the 1930s by a Japanese bank, the Mituyi Group, as their office for South China. During World War II, the Japanese high command used the building; after, the Kuomintang took it back. Recently it housed a popular bar and restaurant, but it is under renovation as of April, 2009.

Outside the hotel's main gates, turn right. Cross Yongjia Road 永嘉路, and turn right onto Shaoxing Road 绍兴路. You will now be going west.

Shaoxing Road is known as the "Publishing Street", because there are several publishing houses located here. There are also a number of art galleries.

Zhu Jilin
朱季琳
Residence
No. 5 Shaoxing Rd
绍兴路
left side

Zhu owned the Nanshi Electric Company and Tram Company 南市电力公司和电车公司. A devout Catholic, he had a chapel included when his house was built in 1933. With a large brood of children – some of whom received a Catholic education in France – the Zhus could have their own church service, complete with their own priest, choir, and musical accompaniment, all members of the family.

Among the hired help in this household were electricians, carpenters, and hair stylists. At dinner the family sat around a long table, with a servant standing behind each chair. During the Cultural Revolution, those of the family that remained in Shanghai were chased out of their grand mansion to live in the garage.

In the 1930s and 1940s, jazz was a newly imported fashion from America, and some of the Zhus formed their own family band that performed at parties. The Zhus rehearsed in their dance hall on the second floor every Saturday morning and invited guest conductors from Ciro's Club and Club Ramstron. On Sundays they welcomed friends to listen, and cars, motorbikes, bicycles, and rickshaws would line the front of the house. At one point the Zhu orchestra performed live every Friday for two hours at a radio station called XMHA, and they once won top prize in a competition against three professional bands.

One organizer of the band was Zhu's grandson, Zhu Zhaohe 朱兆和, who played piano, guitar, cello, and saxophone. After 1949 he worked in a factory and got into trouble for performing Latin dance music at a show. During the Cultural Revolution, thousands of records were taken away, and Zhu relied on his memory to write down the scores. He compiled over ten such music booklets, gave some to friends, and still keeps five of them.

Today the huge building is the Shanghai News Agency Publishing Company.

Du Yuesheng
杜月笙
Residence
No. 54
Shaoxing Rd
right side

Du Yuesheng (1881-1951), Huang Jinrong and Zhang Xiaolin were known as the three big gangster bosses of Old Shanghai.

Shaoxing Park

The three of them supported Chiang Kai-shek in his massacre of communists in 1927. Du was a consultant to Chiang's military, yet it is believed he also shielded Communist Party official Zhou Enlai's cousin.

Du was in charge of an underground world of opium dens, kidnapping, and brothels in the French Concession. He could also be very kind; in 1937 he collected large quantities of towels, cigarettes, and canned goods for the soldiers in the anti-Japanese resistance. He donated 1,000 imported gas masks. Du died in Hong Kong in 1951; he was 70 years old. (Please see Walk II: True Colors for more about Du.)

This house, one of several he owned, was home to his fourth wife. Today, the building houses the Shanghai Business Newspaper Agency.

Shaoxing Park
62 Shaoxing Rd

Built in 1951, this little park attracts elderly people who enjoy playing card games and Chinese checkers. Children are welcome too, of course.

Ruan Lingyu
阮玲玉
Residence
*Lane 96
Shaoxing Rd
right side*

An actress, Ruan (1910-1935) appeared in nearly twenty films, often depicting the dark side of society and the suffering of poor and hungry lower-class women. The characters she played included dancers, peasant women, prostitutes, artists, and factory workers. Her sad personal life matched the tragic heroines she portrayed: she lost her father when she was six, her mother left to find work when she was seven, and she had a tumultuous marriage. After she committed suicide at age 25, a huge crowd turned out to mourn her death.

Lots of clean clothing dangles from poles around these three-story, red-brick lane houses and their semicircular balconies, making it a good place for laundry photos as you will see.

Turn right on Shaanxi Road (S) 陕西南路.

Luwan District Library
卢湾区图书馆
235 Shaanxi Road (S)
陕西南路
corner of Shaoxing Rd

There is a statue of a man named Hu Mingfu 胡明复 on the library's grounds. Hu (1891-1927) was from Wuxi, and in 1916 he was the first Chinese student to receive a Ph.D in mathematics from Harvard. In 1915, he founded the *Science* magazine and became one of the founders of the China Science Society. He worked as a professor in Shanghai and wrote several mathematical books. Tragically, he drowned in Wuxi when he was only 36. In 1929, educator Cai Yuanpei and others suggested a library be named after Hu. It was established here in 1930 as the Mingfu Library, and today it is the Luwan District Library.

This concludes our walk. Go north on Shaanxi Road (S) to find many lifestyle shops that sell flowers and household goods. In ten minutes, you will come to the intersection of Shaanxi and Huaihai, where the subway station is for Line 1.

Further Reading:
Huaihai Fang/Hu Die:
Meili Ruijin (Enchanting Ruijin) by Sha Hailin,
Ruijin Er Road Neighborhood Party Committee

Hu Die:
www.culture.people.com.cn

Zhang Xianglin:
Meili Ruijin (Enchanting Ruijin) by Sha Hailin,
Ruijin Er Road Neighborhood Party Committee

Ba Jin:
www.new.xinhuanet.com/ziliao/2002-01/24
/content-252296.htm
www.baike.baidu.com/view/1717.htm

Xu Guangping:
Heritage plaque
Lu Xun Museum, Hangout

Xu Beihong:
www.artchinanet.com/artlife/xubeihong/main.
htm
www.cnart.biz/cnart/xian_dai/xubeihong
/new_page_1.htm

He Keming:
Shanghai Mass Art Center: www.dfwyzd.org
lit.eastday.com

Yang Hucheng:
www.netor.com/m/box200102

Guo Moruo:
www.hoodong.com/wiki/guomoruo

Shanghai Association of Science and Technology (Shanghai Science Hall):
http://seville.oo.nu/blog/2007/03/029/old_shanghai_hall_college_francais
Frenchtown: Shanghai Western Architecture in Shanghai's French Concession by Tess Johnston and Deke Erh, Old China Hand Press, 2000, pp. 113, 120-125

Zhang Xueliang:
Famous People, Houses, and Stories by Huang Guoxin and Shen Fuxu, Tongjin University Publisher, 2003, pp. 105-107
Shanghai Lao Yangfang (Shanghai Old Villas) by Song Luxia, Shanghai Science and Technology Cultural Publishing Co., 2004, pp. 84-85
Lao Shanghai Huayuan Yangfang (Old Shanghai Garden Villas) by Xue Shunsheng and Lou Chenghao, Tongji University, pp. 78-79
news.bbc.co.uk/2/hi/asia-pacific/1602017.stm
www.zxl.chinaspirit.net.cn
www.baike.baidu.com/view/4095.htm

St. Nicholas Church:
orthodox.cn/localchurch/shanghai/nikolaitsar_en.htm
Frenchtown Shanghai Western Architecture in Shanghai's French Concession by Tess Johnston and Deke Erh, Old China Hand Press, 2000, p. 113

Song Hanzang:
Meili Ruijin (Enchanting Ruijin) by Sha Hailin, Ruijin Er Road Neighborhood Party Committee

Sun Yat-sen:
Shanghai Lao Yangfang (Shanghai Old Villas) by Song Luxia, Shanghai Science and Technology Cul-

WALK V: SPHERES OF INFLUENCE

tural Publishing Co., 2004, pp. 82-83
Six Shanghai Walks by Barbara Green, Tess Johnston, et al., Old China Hand Press, 2007, pp.
71-74

Zhou Enlai Residence:
Famous People, Houses, and Stories by Huang Guoxin
and Shen Fuxu, Tongji University Publisher,
2003, pp. 13-16
*Lao Shanghai Huayuan Yangfang (Old Shanghai Gar-
den Villas)* by Xue Shunsheng and Lou Chenghao, Tongji University, pp. 182-183
Shanghai Lao Yangfang (Shanghai Old Villas) by Song
Luxia, Shanghai Science and Technology Cultural Publishing Co., 2004, pp. 80-81

Mei Lanfang:
www.chinaopera.net
www.history.xikao.com/person
www.news.xinhuanet.com/ziliao/2003-12/04/
content
www.book.sina.com.cn/nzt/1095391565

Ruijin Hotel:
Famous People, Houses, and Stories by Huang Guoxin
and Shen Fuxu, Tongjin University Publisher,
2003, pp. 31-35
*Lao Shanghai Huayuan Yangfang (Old Shanghai Gar-
den Villas)* by Xue Shunsheng and Lou Chenghao, Tongji University, pp. 18-19
*A Walker's Guide to Old Western Landmarks in Shang-
hai* compiled by Shanghai Daily, 2008, pp. 100-
107
www.ruijinhotelsh.com
The Old Villa Hotels of Shanghai photos by Deke Erh,
Old China Hand Press, 2001, pp. 18-19

Shaoxing Park
Meili Ruijin (Enchanting Ruijin) by Sha Hailin,
　　Ruijin Er Road Neighborhood Party Committee

Ruan Lingyu:
Meili Ruijin (Enchanting Ruijin) by Sha Hailin,
　　Ruijin Er Road Neighborhood Party Committee
　　www.culture.people.com.cn
　　www.talesofoldchina/shanghai/people/t-peo-
　　ple06.htm

Hu Mingfu:
　　www.gmw.cn/content/2005-06/07/content_24427.
　　html
　　http://baike.baidu.com/view/529399.html

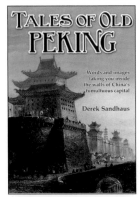
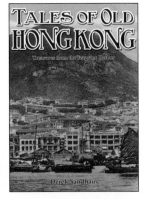
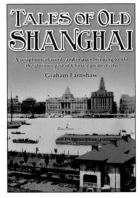
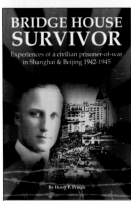

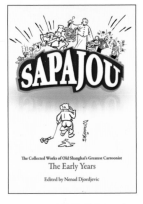
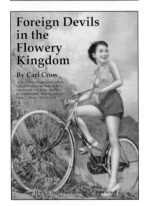

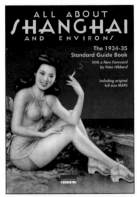

"Strategy for women alone."*

The Love Crisis

"Examines the wide variety of male behavior...the frustration and anxiety that develops between men and women using the endless trial-and-error tactics that underlie many relationships."

The New York Times *

"Botwin's appraisal is singleminded and done with a stiletto. It's bound to cause tears of recognition in women. It could be a cure for heartache if it weren't so sobering and devastatingly accurate."

—Nena O'Neill, co-author of *Open Marriage*

"Early warning signs that can tell you he's not worth your affections."

—*Cosmopolitan*

"This is a really neat book. It's lively, readable, sensible, and most important, *usable*. It's a book to be left on one's shelf for reference and re-reading, a book to give to a friend or a daughter. It should be on the best-seller list."

—*West Coast Review of Books*

The Love Crisis

HIT-AND-RUN LOVERS, JUGGLERS, SEXUAL STINGIES, UNRELIABLES, KINKIES, AND OTHER TYPICAL MEN TODAY

Carol Botwin

with Jerome L. Fine, Ph.D.

BANTAM BOOKS
Toronto / New York / London

THE LOVE CRISIS:
HIT-AND-RUN LOVERS, JUGGLERS,
SEXUAL STINGIES, UNRELIABLES, KINKIES,
AND OTHER TYPICAL MEN OF TODAY

*A Bantam Book published by arrangement with
Doubleday & Company, Inc.*

PRINTING HISTORY

*Doubleday edition published August 1979
2nd printing .... September 1979
Serialized in Cosmopolitan, February 1979;
The National Star, February 1979;
New Woman, November/December 1979;
Beauty Digest, March 1980;
Talk, May 1980; and* Glamour

*Bantam edition / October 1980
2nd printing .... June 1981*

Bantam Books are published by Bantam Books, Inc., Its trademark, consisting of the words "Bantam Books" and the por-
trayal of a bantam, is Registered in U.S. Patent and Trademark
Office and in other countries. Marca Registrada. Bantam
Books, Inc., 666 Fifth Avenue, New York, New York 10103.

To Alexandra and William

...and to all the men who have contributed to this book in one way or another:

H.B., J.M., H.P., M.A., S.C., E.G., R.L., V.L., P.T., S.W., G.P.,
E.R., S.L., W.R., L.G., C.L., P.L., F.J., D.D., M.K., N.P., R.S.D.,
H.G., L.P., O.R.L., D.W., B.C., T.W., K.M., M.L., F.G., T.D.O.,
S.N., D.A., E.L., N.C.P., J.N., W.L., I.C., L.M., L.K., F.J., J.A.,
C.L., R.T., A.N., F.G., M.E., L.I., O.Z., T.S., P.O., E.F., D.L.C.,
H.R., F.D., P.R., V.G., V.P., D.L., E.F., J.G., S.A., Q.R., M.N.,
S.T., W.N., C.A., B.L., C.P., N.A., A.F., G.J., S.R., M.C., R.L.,
T.Y., D.L., B.A., M.M., O.E., D.L., P.O., S.N., N.F., S.T., D.E.,
B.D., V.S., N.M., J.N., B.W., G.O., D.G., M.B., G.O., S.V., L.M.,
E.W., M.D., R.B., J.L., H.J., R.P., D.T., B.A., H.C., G.L., C.S.,
S.B., P.R., P.S., D.W., G.P., P.N., A.V., A.S., L.B., B.G., E.B.,
F.H., C.L., W.R., T.U., F.P., A.T., B.F., R.deB., N.A., L.P., H.O.,
H.G., L.S., F.K., B.L., C.P., M.W., E.W., J.P., Y.L., J.W., D.M.,
B.G., G.V., M.H., A.J., I.G., D.S., E.B., J.G., J.B., D.C., R.T., D.O.,
S.C., K.S., J.O., J.B., F.H., R.F., A.C., J.C., C.H., D.I., T.P., D.G.,
P.C., M.A., C.M., B.W., D.L., E.F., J.G., C.P., A.S., J.N., H.M.,
C.C., H.K., J.E., S.K., A.H., B.R., L.I., L.A., J.C., M.P., D.C., J.U.,
K.O., M.P., T.O., R.W., CMcK., J.S., M.W., S.S., C.G., R.G., S.P.,
G.G., M.N., C.O., D.R., J.B., S.S., V.A., A.B., P.D., M.W., S.B.,
C.D., W.F., M.T., M.M., N.P., M.D., E.D., N.G., S.K., M.N., L.S.,
S.Y., T.T., V.N., S.B., H.O'N., P.K., S.T., B.D., G.M., P.D., E.H.,
P.C., R.B., P.H., W.Z., I.P., P.G., E.B., T.Q., P.L., P.McG., H.D.,
R.G., H.G., A.K., J.S., A.H., A.T., R.L., D.S., P.F., R.A., W.B.,
A.T., R.W., R.R., R.B., S.R., J.S., J.C., E.B., M.J., E.F., T.A.,
P.B., V.B., M.W., A.H., G.N., J.Q., W.K., P.L., A.R., K.B., P.B.,
M.B., W.G., D.S., J.M., S.S., N.A., W.T., M.C., J.K., H.H., J.J.,
K.P., D.R., E.W., T.K., I.B., B.M., C.M., M.K., S.B., K.M., E.L.,
F.N., N.O., D.F., M.F., T.P., K.D., A.L., T.P., T.R., O.R., L.W.,
P.W., P.B., R.V., M.B., L.W., L.J., E.B., T.W., J.K., J.G., K.B.,
A.K., R.B., X.P., N.R., S.G., D.H., J.S., D.D., R.E., R.L., T.H.,
J.N., E.S., E.M., M.K., L.R., M.C., J.D., P.P., B.P., S.F., K.G.,
K.J., S.F., P.B., H.G., J.S., D.V., L.B., C.C., C.S., L.D., B.A., N.H.,
G.W., R.S., M.H., K.F., R.S., F.P., A.G., M.R., E.C., K.F., F.S.,
D.M., S.D., L.D., L.C., B.H., E.M., C.S., A.B., W.R., C.C., W.C.,
E.F., O.T., J.P., L.W., T.A., J.R., H.K., W.H., R.R., G.W., C.D.,
O.T., S.B., A.C., T.A., E.L., A.J., K.A., K.H., P.M., T.C., W.J.,
T.R., T.S., D.Y., N.L., H.W., C.W., G.R., G.A., J.G., R.H., W.K.,

G.S., D.J., F.C., H.G., M.N., E.M., S.B., J.C., O.G., G.G., W.H.,
J.T., H.M., A.P., P.O., W.H., R.G., F.Y., P.S., H.E., I.P., D.B.,
L.S., R.N., E.N., J.K., T.P., L.S., M.N., T.R., T.P., M.J., H.S.,
L.B., A.L., T.G., O.P., S.W., F.H., P.Y., M.P., H.L., J.P., G.M.,
W.W., E.S., B.W., M.B., M.W., K.H., T.W., H.H., J.L., S.C., J.W.,
J.B., G.G., M.H., R.S., C.M., W.I., W.Y., P.D., R.W., A.D., C.B.,
J.L., T.P., S.M., T.A., L.R., H.L., S.S., M.L., D.C., K.G., C.K.,
A.D., B.S., D.L., F.A., S.A., B.S., S.H., V.S., N.G., B.D., A.L.,
R.N., D.M., G.F., A.H., G.F., P.N., E.W., B.G., E.J., D.E., B.R.,
R.M., A.L., J.K., F.R., F.P., L.W., E.W., E.B., B.P., C.G., J.P.,
J.A., J.J., O.W., R.C., G.W., R.W., M.K., F.C., N.K., I.C., A.W.,
G.W., G.G., M.F., W.T., Y.R., M.B., P.W., C.R., T.L., J.B., E.R.,
G.Y., J.M., M.K., T.M., P.W., C.T., M.F., F.P., I.L., J.B., M.T.,
S.G., F.D., R.H., J.O., W.K., P.V., O.X., N.Z., G.C., H.L., C.C.,
H.D., T.O., S.G., R.E., T.R., T.L., P.F., A.B., E.L., A.N., A.M.,
S.I., T.A., J.W., P.R., T.N., S.D., E.D., B.D., S.P., C.T., D.N., W.O.,
E.P., R.S., T.M., T.P., D.E., S.W., C.W., F.T., B.Y., A.M., A.W.,
P.T., R.T., D.M., B.A.

CONTENTS

Acknowledgments

I am grateful to Dr. Jerome L. Fine, who supplied me with the technical psychological information I needed to write about the inner lives of men. He was always wise, generous, and good-humored.

I want to give very special thanks also to Dr. Berta Anagnoste, who kept me going with her encouragement and added her wisdom to sections of this book. Jeannette Hopkins helped me immeasurably with her suggestions about the manuscript. In addition, my gratitude goes to the following, for their insights, in interviews, when I first thought of writing a book about men's love lives six years ago: Dr. Otto Ehrenberg, Dr. John O'Connor, Dr. Maj-Britt Rosenbaum, Dr. Bennett Rosner, Dr. Clifford Sager. Edward Botwin did me many favors as I was finishing the book, adding to his consistent kindness over the years.

Michael Waful also did me favors that helped the book progress. Henriette Gray lived through the final days of typing the manuscript with fortitude and patience.

Preface

When Carol Botwin first talked to me three years ago about *The Love Crisis*, it was a happy meeting of minds. She, as a journalist and a woman, had been observing discernible patterns in men's interactions with women, and wanted to write a book about them. I, as a clinical psychologist, psychoanalyst, and a man, had been aware of these same patterns and had been thinking about the state of men in our culture, in general.

Preliminary discussions between us quickly established the fact that we shared many attitudes and had, independently, come to many similar conclusions about American men. Although Carol Botwin had already done considerable research on the subject by the time we met, she felt that *The Love Crisis* would benefit from a consultant in the field of psychology. I agreed to share my knowledge, opinions, and experiences with her.

The male patterns described in this book are accurate renderings of behavior I have observed over the past nineteen years while treating patients in over 35,000 hours of clinical practice as a psychotherapist, and as a supervisor [in the Department of Psychiatry at the Mt. Sinai School of Medicine and the William Alanson White Psychoanalytic Institute in New York City.] The underlying theories that form the basis for much of the material in *The Love Crisis* are based on the psychoanalytic doctrines of Sigmund Freud as well as some of the more contemporary formulations of interpersonal, developmental, and ego psychologies and from various theories of family therapy. In addition, the book incorporates anecdotes, observations, and quotations derived from more than one hundred interviews with men and women conducted by Carol Botwin over the past few years, as well as recent thinking in the fields of sociology and social psychology.

Although the tone of *The Love Crisis* is sometimes light, the psychological insights in it are meant to help you develop a process of thinking and understanding about behavior that goes beyond surface appearances. Hopefully, these insights will take some of the mystery out of male behavior for women, and shed some light on their own behavior for men.

Jerome L. Fine, Ph.D.
New York City, 1979

The Love Crisis

Chapter 1
Introduction

The Love Crisis

I am sitting in a restaurant in Los Angeles with a twenty-eight-year-old screenwriter, a twice-divorced woman in her late thirties, and a thirty-two-year-old pretty, blonde secretary who works for the county museum. We are all attractive, lively women, but what are we talking about with such animation and despair? The Man Situation. Everyone at the table is complaining about "what's out there."

"Out there," as women all over the country know, means the mating scene; and wherever women gather today—whether in California, Chicago, Boston, Dallas, San Francisco, or New York—the talk is the same: complaints and horror stories about men. These conversations may be witty as well as sorrowful or bitter, but they always end up with one exasperated question: "What is wrong with men today?"

There are 27 million single women in the United States, a number that is fast increasing as marriages split at ever more rapid rates, and as women find themselves

reluctantly alone—unable to connect, unable to find partners for long-term, committed relationships.

Inevitably one hears words like "crazies," "schmucks,"
"bastards," "jerks," "losers" used to describe the men they
meet—men who are elusive, men who have sex and disappear, men who dole out sex as if it is rationed by the
government. One hears of hostile men, impotent men,
men who never make passes, men who only make passes,
men with whom you can't communicate, men who think
loving is dangerous and commitment a venereal disease.

But married women tell equally sad tales about the
men they live with—husbands who have given up sex as
a way of life, husbands who tyrannize over them, husbands who are impotent, husbands who love work or tennis or TV more than they love their wives or children.

Behind all of the bitching, however, there is one
heart-breaking truth: the women of this country still
yearn for that special man to share their lives with. They
may have satisfying jobs and good friends, and many do;
they may be lively, bright, and fun, and many are; but,
without a man in a meaningful relationship, something
is still terribly missing—and most women, liberated or
not, are willing to admit this.

So the current mood among females is one of despair,
exasperation, puzzlement. I am beginning to hear more
and more, from very desirable women, a recurring statement: "I have resigned myself to being alone." Women
realize we are in a Love Crisis in this country. Never has
such suspicion and mutual distrust existed between the
sexes. Women find men erratic, elusive, devious, skittish,
self-centered, alienated, subtly (or not so subtly) hostile,
sexually troubled, and unable to love in a rational, giving,
ongoing, way. And they want to know why.

What makes the men they meet, have sex with, and
perhaps live with so frustrating to deal with?

The answer, lies, for the most part, in the neuroses
of men that compel them to follow destructive patterns in
their relationships. An explanation of the typical game
plans of men with women make up the heart of this book.
This doesn't mean that nice, normal men capable of good
relationships don't exist. Indeed, they do (see chapter 13),
but a good man is harder than ever to find. Important in
this respect is the fact that single women far outnumber

single men in every age group above the twenties. There are 1,321,000 more unattached females than males between the ages of 30 and 54 in this country. The number of available men is further decreased by the homosexual population. It is estimated that 13 percent of the male population is gay. The man shortage means that men can and do get away with all sorts of objectionable behavior because it's a buyer's market. If the current woman won't put up with a man's unfulfilling way of relating he can always find another woman who will—at least for a while.

Another important answer to complaints about men lies in social pressures that shape men's characters in certain ways and promote tendencies to instability and fear of commitment. And increasingly, the answer lies in the fast changes in relationships between the sexes because of female and sexual liberation.

Sex used to be linked to love and commitment. People who slept together generally had a chance to know each other beforehand. Courtship preceded consummation, and sex was a marking stone in a relationship. A woman gave in to a man as a sign of her devotion and trust. He felt obligated to her when she did. Marriage was often the price that men—and women—paid for a steady source of sexual pleasure.

Now, in the aftermath of the sexual revolution, women sleep with men promptly and freely, and men feel no obligation to them. As a result, relationships have become devalued and sex is overburdened.

Sex is so heavily advertised by the media in our culture that it has come to represent to many the bluebird of happiness. No longer signifying love or commitment, it has assumed other symbolic meanings. It has become a "fix" for a variety of problems, an evasion of central issues in one's life. Sex has become a panacea. It is used to counteract boredom and anxiety, to dispel loneliness, to give you a "lift" when you are blue, to verify that you are attractive when you are doubting it. It even serves to end an evening gracefully. After all, the other person expects it, so why hassle?

If men and women in the past had love affairs before marriage, they were usually limited—a few courtships or sexual entanglements, then marriage. Now premarital sex often starts in the early adolescent years; people

marry at later ages or not at all; divorce recycles husbands
and wives at dizzying rates.

Men and women come to each other these days
haunted by their pasts. Most of us can look back upon a
stream of failed relationships. Our disappointments and
hurts progressively toughen us, make us slightly more
cynical, and, if they don't embitter us, at least make us
cautious with one another. The faith, trust, emotional investment, and exuberance that marked our first affairs
are no longer possible the nth time around, but pessi-
mism is. We despair. Can relationships ever turn out well?
we ask ourselves, and each other.

Men and women eye each other speculatively, criti-
cally. We get together gingerly. The sense of adventure
and promise we originally had with one another has given
way to foreboding, the feeling of risk. Consciously or unconsciously, we hold back our emotions. We are afraid to
invest. We don't want to be hurt again.

Feigned or real indifference, the feeling that a relationship is doomed before it starts, fault-finding that
starts early because it's better to find out what's wrong
with *them* before they find out what's wrong with *us*, the
ability to end relationships faster and with less regret or
effort because we are accustomed to endings—all of these
things make our relationships fragile and tentative, permeated with an aura of impermanence.

Many of us are angry that relationships never work
out, angry at being constantly rejected and wounded, angry at not being loved, angry that this new person wants
something we don't seem able to supply, angry that life
has not turned out the way it is supposed to. We all still
dream about love. We just never seem able to find it.

The Collapse of Chivalry

The eclipse of the feminine mystique—which allowed
men to put women on pedestals and defer to them while
treating them as inferiors—has added to our tentativeness
with one another. We are confused. Should a man help a
woman with her coat? Should he shake hands with her?
Should he pay for her meal? Many men feel acutely uncomfortable without traditional formulas to draw upon,
especially when women themselves are so inconsistent.
Some women expect a man to pay for dinner, others are

insulted if he wants to; still others decide according to the man: if he makes more money than she does, he pays; if he doesn't, they share. Very few women are liberated enough to decide that if they make more money than the man, they should pick up the whole tab. This may make a man angry. He remembers that he has borne the economic burden of dating for too many years, able or not.

Linked to the confusion is sex. Many men feel they are entitled to a little action if they pay—precisely why some women now refuse to let them pick up the whole check. One thirty-three-year-old sociologist, unnerved by the current upsetting social climate, finally worked out a system he thought would work. If a woman allowed him to pay for a meal, he figured it meant she was willing to sleep with him; if she didn't, she wasn't interested. He became furious recently when a conventional woman allowed him to pick up the entire check and then refused to go with him to his apartment. He felt she had acted unfairly. Not realizing she had violated his code, she could not understand why he was suddenly surly after dinner, and why he never called again.

Some men react to the death of chivalry with a release of hidden hostility. They feel absolved from all social obligations to women. Many men today call a woman for a date *only* at the last minute. Others have intercourse at their apartment, and then, in the wee hours of the morning, if the woman has to return home, don't even bother to get up to bid her goodnight, let alone accompany her downstairs to see her safely into her car or a taxi. Men rationalize. They think they are treating women as equals, but the way they choose to let a woman take care of herself sometimes seems like an insult—and I'm not sure that isn't what is intended. Intentional or not, women often feel humiliated by what they regard as, not equality, but lack of consideration.

Many men today find themselves disturbed by women who make their preferences known and even initiate sex. In the days when women didn't "put out," men used to dream of highly sexual and willing women. Now that such women have become a reality, they scare men to death.

Some men, of course, do find joy in the sexually assertive woman; they discover that they are more virile with her. But to those whose male egos are threatened, the sexually aggressive woman can seem demanding, castrating, unfeminine.

There is a hidden regret among many men for the good old days when it took some doing to get a woman into bed. They liked the feeling of conquest. It gave a boost to masculine pride. Some of the kick seems to be missing when women tumble into bed all too easily.

The collapse of convention, therefore, has created anxiety and resentment in both sexes. Although chivalry and courtly manners may have been a hidden tactic to dominate women by treating them as frail incompetents, so far tension alone has replaced the old code, and tension breeds anxiety, irritability, anger—emotions that do nothing to help men and women relate in a friendly or loving way.

The challenge to male supremacy and dominance is a frightening one to many men. They feel that something is being taken away from them. Because they are on the defensive for the first time in history, men are often hostile, quick to call a woman with spunk a "libber," or to label a "libber" a dyke. A woman who believes in liberation is, to them, unfeminine or castrating.

The women's liberation movement is the latest blow to men, who were already feeling increasingly helpless and powerless in our culture. Competition in school, then on the job, is often ruthless; politics seems beyond individual control; inflation erodes hard-earned salaries; clogged highways are frustrating; one's own children don't listen with respect any more and can't be counted on in old age. And hanging like a mushroom cloud above all of us is the pervasive threat of nuclear extinction. Men used to look to women for solace in fearful times, for relief from competition in the man's world. Now wives and girlfriends are competitive, abrasive, and frightening too. Men feel increasingly alone and lost, increasingly alienated and sad. Depression is epidemic in our society.

Women feel they are gaining something from liberation. Men feel they are losing what they have had.

Sexual Restlessness and Discontent

Sex has become a restless activity. One never quite gets what one wants from the experience. Loneliness returns and boredom reasserts itself even while the bed is still warm. A sexual conquest will make you feel like a king or queen for a day or night only. Sex used like a handshake, to say "hello" or "goodnight," can be a flat experience. Still, one tries it again the next time and hopes for something better.

The vague sense of dissatisfaction that results when sex is used as a panacea, is often pinned onto the other person. She/he did not provide you with enough.

Although women are as inclined as men to use sex as a "fix," they are also, by conditioning or biology, apt to find themselves bound to a sexual partner, nevertheless. Sex, for the majority of women, still has unconscious strings attached, strings tied to their psyches, to their need for security, intimacy, love.

Women may have sex because they are lonely, or to feel desirable, or because it is expected of them, but, once in bed, they find themselves wanting something more emotionally—they begin to want the man, not just the experience. Women feel dissatisfied because he isn't giving them enough.

Women want the same old things, in the end, even in this era of sexual liberation. They want love, commitment, marriage or at least "living together," and these desires begin to assert themselves, to everyone's surprise, even in relationships that start coolly and casually, with sexual pleasure the only object. Women find themselves "hooked" by their "fixes." Sex, by itself, does not create the same bonding desire in men. Their penises are not automatic transmitters to the heart. If they feel that something is missing, if sex is not all that great, or even if it is, restlessness overtakes them. Maybe someone else will satisfy them more. And today, freed from any sense of obligation to a sex partner, they resist blandishments, pressures, pleas for more intimacy or commitment, more righteously and more easily than before. She has no right to expect that from me. It isn't what I promised.

Men feel freer to move on when commitment or love becomes an issue or even a possibility. There is always more, or different, sex around the corner.

This is a crucial facet of today's Love Crisis. Sex for most women, leads to a desire for something more. For the majority of men, it doesn't.

Confusing and Escalating Demands

Yesterday's woman may have been satisfied with a man who was successful, a man who took her out, well, a man who was strong, assertive, and protective. The last three things were very important. She wanted a macho man. It may surprise you, but today's woman wants many of the same things. Despite liberation, women still respond emotionally to the dominant, macho man, although they want him to be tender and sensitive as well.

Men have also increased their demands upon women. It used to be enough that a woman was pleasant and pretty, looked up to him, and was willing to build her life around him. He still wants these things, but added to that, he may want his woman to be independent, able to handle responsibility on her own.

New demands superimposed on old create contradictions. The macho, domineering, strong man is rarely capable of tenderness and sensitivity. He associates these traits with femininity. Women who are capable of being independent and making decisions on their own will rarely defer to a man on a continual basis. They have opinions of their own.

By requiring a combination of qualities impossible to find in one person, men and women guarantee failure in their relationships.

Jealousy still survives as another complication in the age of sexual liberation. Although men often feel, intellectually, that they have no right to be jealous, that women today are free to sleep with whomever they wish, it is the rare man who can stand a rival or even a hint of one in a woman's life. Jealousy has, if anything, become an even bigger green-eyed monster than in the past. Men are more uptight because they can no longer rely on women being faithful simply because that's the way women are.

Men still want women to be true to them, while they are free to sample other goods. The double standard has a new twist—women often want men to be monogamous while they are free to play around a little. Just think of the implications, and complications, when such men and women get together.

The double standard is alive and well in other ways too; it has simply gone underground. Men are loath to admit it, but they—and women, also—still tend to look down on a woman who sleeps with too many men too casually. As in the past, there are no social penalties for the promiscuous male, who is not above deliberately exploiting the "liberated" woman by sleeping with her and then scorning her for it.

Much of the lip service paid to sexual liberation these days conflicts with the way men and women really feel in their hidden selves.

Men and women are confusing each other mostly because they are a mass of contradictions inside. Women want to be independent and strong, and on good days they feel that they are. On other days, they revert to how they have been brought up to feel—weak, in need of protection. As a result, they sometimes put out vibes that say the man must treat them as equal and capable; and at other times they send out messages that say they want him to be protective. The man is confused by these changing moods and demands.

A man, too, may want to be catered to one day, because that is what he is comfortable with, and the next day complain that the woman is too clinging and not self-reliant.

Although some strict traditionalists of both sexes survive, most of us are a chaotic mix of old and new. Because of our own inconsistencies, we send out contradictory signals to each other. Marriages and affairs, alike, are infused with the same sense of confusion and impermanence. Men and women marry with a clear understanding, even if they never talk about it, that, if things don't work out, they can always get a divorce. Divorce, now, is too often considered the first solution—not the last. Impermanence as even a possibility necessarily dilutes the commitment that partners bring to a marriage, and conflicting, changing demands add to the sense of instability.

It used to be men who devalued the homemaker's role. "What does she do with her time all day?" they would ask themselves. "Why is she so tired and irritable?" Men had little understanding and no empathy for the time and patience required for the tasks of combined homemaking and motherhood. Wives, however, used to take pride in their accomplishments. Being good homemakers meant they were fulfilling their roles as women.

Today the emphasis on careers for women has affected them. Homemakers contrast themselves to working women and tend to denigrate their roles. They feel inferior. They are not accomplishing anything important in life. Discontented with themselves, they sometimes transpose their unhappiness into demands on husbands. He must make me happy. He must make me worthwhile with his love, attention, sex, understanding, and accomplishment. He must help out more in the home.

Many men today feel overwhelmed by the needs and the escalating emotional demands of their wives. It no longer is enough for them to bring home the paycheck and be kind. No matter how much they do for her, she always seems to want more.

Many discontented housewives have seized upon women's liberation themes to express the unhappiness they feel about themselves. They accuse husbands of not helping out enough, not understanding women's plight. Sometimes they are right, sometimes not. Many is the well-meaning husband who has tried to understand and help, but finds, no matter what he does, that he is unable to make his wife happy. No man can make up to a woman for her own bad feelings about herself.

This is not meant to denigrate the arguments of feminists, but simply to make the point that malcontents sometimes use legitimate political issues to express their own inner agonies, instead of coming to grips with the real causes of their frustration or unhappiness.

If a wife returns to work, the marriage experiences another kind of strain. The husband may pitch in more but secretly resent it, convinced that a job as mother's helper is not a man's proper role, no matter what he says about equality to the world. Old lessons about masculinity are hard to shake.

His wife often feels put upon by her new role as well. Not used to the stresses and pressures of the business world, she may expect her husband to pat her on the back for the mere fact that she is working, to ease her way with constant moral support and guidance. Her expectations may rankle him. He's been working all these years, he feels, and nobody has had to hold his hand along the way. Little does he know that someone has.

The husband of a working wife may be afflicted also with jealousy. He is afraid she will find someone at work to have an affair with. He projects. He knows all too well how men have been carrying on for years.

The husband may have legitimate cause for his jealousy. Affairs among married women have been increasing since the sixties, according to post-Kinsey studies. Dissatisfied housewives who feel rotten can reassure themselves by an affair, and working wives are in a position to be tempted if they are inclined to dally. It is easier to find a lover out in the world than in a suburban backyard, or in an apartment house lobby.

Loss of control is another subliminal issue. A husband is often very grateful for the second paycheck in the family, but her income means less power for him in the relationship. A working wife is no longer entirely dependent on her husband for money. Again, an old lesson about masculinity comes to the fore. Men are supposed to be in charge. Even if husbands espouse equality outwardly, underneath they frequently feel that their role as a man is challenged or undermined by a wife's economic independence. Many a marriage disintegrates today when a wife starts to earn as much as, or more than, her husband. She has, in effect, emasculated him.

Additional strains in marriage can come from increasing sexual demands. The wife who may have put up with a husband's premature ejaculation, impotence, or sexual incompetence for years, may wake up these days to demand her right to fulfillment. Two husbands I spoke to were in shambles when they learned from their wives that they had been faking orgasms for years. These wives now want authentic sexual experiences and had pressured their husbands to improve their techniques as lovers. Both husbands were in a state of shock, but they tried. Neither marriage, however, lasted for long afterward. The husbands' egos had been dealt irreparable blows.

Insufficient sex can cause as much trouble as inefficient sex. As I point out later, frequency falls off for many husbands soon after marriage, or babies, or in their middle years. Wives used to accept this as their lot. They no longer are willing to. Many middle-aged wives feel sexier than ever before, and they are not willing to remain frustrated. If their husband fails to give them what they want, nowadays they may resort to divorce or find a lover.

And men aren't getting what they want from women

either. On the singles scene they chase after sexual experiences that will give a sense of peace to their lives—something sex cannot deliver—or sex without strings. They think, sometimes angrily, Why do women always want more? Wasn't the point of sexual liberation to be free?

Men want no demands on their emotions, yet discover they can't handle it if the woman turns out to be as cool as they are.

One magazine editor flipped out not long ago when his secretary, who invited him to her apartment because he was unhappy, slept with him, and then promptly announced: "Listen, just because you've slept with me doesn't mean you own me." "That's not what she was supposed to say," he complained. "That was what *I* was supposed to say."

Another man who had been courting a woman he liked for a few weeks last summer ended up in bed with her when she announced, "I feel like getting laid, but that's all I want." Although he had been very attracted to her sexually, he was unable to reach a climax. "It was so cut and dried, so unemotional," he complained.

When men say they want sex without entanglements, the entanglements they are referring to are their own. No matter how much they deny it intellectually and verbally—and they do these days—underneath it all, men feel cheated if a woman who sleeps with them doesn't care for them. They object to being reduced to a sex object just as much as women do. For men, however, the experience of being "used" is new.

The sexual revolution has led to performance anxiety, particularly among men. Most men are tinged with it to some degree. When strangers or near-strangers couple with little feelings or no commitment to one another, of course performance becomes all-important. Men and women become anxious about their ability to please sexually, since they have little desire to please otherwise. With no affection or tenderness, what is left to give except an orgasm?

Performance anxiety plagues women as well as men, but men feel under more pressure because of changed female attitudes. Both feminism and effective contraception have created women who seek their own pleasure more actively. Women no longer routinely "service" men.

They expect gratification. Some threatened men see this as a "demand." Unless a man gives a woman what is expected—orgasm—he is, in his own eyes, a failed lover. A man no longer measures sex experiences by his own pleasure alone, but by hers as well.

Since women are now more sexually experienced, it frightens some men, too, to think that their performance is apt to be measured against someone else's. There is also the threatening knowledge that women are capable of multiple orgasms; they can go on until exhaustion, according to Masters and Johnson. Many men are no longer content to win a single orgasm from their partners, but strive to produce a whole string of them. If they don't, they often feel inadequate.

Men used to complain that women aren't interested in sex. Now they complain when they are. It is one of the many ironies between the sexes in the Love Crisis.

"I'm sorry they ever found out they can have orgasms too," says Slocum in Joseph Heller's book *Something Happened*. Men approach women today as if they are critics. It is hard to relate to someone you fear.

Fear, created by confusion and threats to male dominance, is always worse for the neurotic, who is insecure and fearful to begin with, and some studies indicate that the unattached men who are raising such cries of anguish from women are a psychologically troubled lot, indeed.

Statistics assembled by sociologist Jesse Bernard in *The Future of Marriage* point to the plight of single men: Unmarried men are seven times more likely to exhibit "severe neurotic symptoms" than single women. Bachelors are more depressed and passive and show more antisocial tendencies. They feel more prone to nervous breakdowns and are more likely to spend sleepless, troubled nights because of insomnia or nightmares. According to George Gilder in *Naked Nomads,* a book that documents the sad shape of single men, more than 60 percent of the men in mental institutions have never been married.

One study in Manhattan by Leo Srole and associates indicates that about twice as many single men as unmarried women between the ages of twenty and fifty-nine suffer from impaired mental health. Psychological problems grow worse with age. By the time the Big Apple's swinging bachelors hit fifty, a whopping 46.1 percent of them are troubled human beings.

Divorced men seem to be in even worse shape than bachelors. They are three and a half times more likely to commit suicide than divorced women, and three times more likely to die from cirrhosis of the liver—a byproduct of alcholism.

When women who are looking for a man to connect with in a decent, meaningful relationship complain, they apparently know what they are talking about!

Every woman has her private collection of horror stories about men these days, and among friends they are often traded. Over and over again, when women finish telling each other their latest tale of woe, they cast their eyes toward the ceiling and ask, "What's *wrong* with him?" and then, flooded with memories of past disappointments, "What's wrong with them all?"

It is the purpose of this book to answer those questions—to illuminate the inner workings of twenty-one typical lovers whom women tangle with today, in and out of marriage. No one man fits the complete description in any chapter, of course. These are meant to be generalized composites. Men will exhibit some of the symptoms, not all. They may also cross over, showing symptoms from several categories. For example, a tendency toward perfectionism, as it is described in the chapters *Hit-and-Run Lovers* and *Jugglers,* is common in many other lovers as well. A Hit-and-Run Lover may turn into a sexually Stingy Lover in a close relationship. A Romantic may have one-night stands in between his true loves. A man may move from one category to another at different ages or stages in his life.

Because I have chosen to concentrate on men does not mean I don't recognize that women fall into similar patterns. There is The Nurse, who has no identity of her own so she gains one by dedicating herself selflessly to others. There is The Martyr, who gives and gives and gives in order to take, take, take. There is the Ball Breaker—nobody is good enough for her, so she avoids possible rejection by turning suitors into unsuitables. There is The Princess, who expects all of her wishes and needs to be anticipated and fulfilled by a man whose life must revolve around hers. And dozens more. But to describe them would take another book.

For the moment I am addressing myself to the Love Crisis as women see it. I am trying to answer that repeated question, the product of despair: "What is wrong with men today?"

I am aware that many men are going to hate this book. I have tried to be humane, but men will recognize themselves somewhere—the truth often hurts. Every man that every woman knows, or has known, shares *some* of the characteristics of the lovers described, whether it is dread of intimacy, perfectionism, a feeling of being oppressed or crowded by women they are close to, declining sexual interest in love affairs, a tendency toward multiple relationships, an inability to enter long-term relationships or to end affairs decently.

The knowledge this book supplies about men should lead to compassion rather than contempt. Atrocious as some of their behavior is, these men don't deliberately set out to hurt or harm. They cannot help themselves. Their psychological problems control them rather than the other way around. These men make themselves just as unhappy as the women they get involved with.

Women also play a role in their own unhappiness. They allow themselves to be victimized. Just because women have affairs more easily these days doesn't mean they know how or when to get out of them. The final purpose of this book, then, is to help women solve their own personal Love Crises.

Chapter 2

Hit-And-Run Lovers

They met at an art gallery opening. He saw that she was alone. First he noticed her pink silk dress. Pretty. Then he checked out her figure—slim, breasts protruding against the soft fabric. Long legs. Nice.

From across the room she realized that he was looking at her. He was attractive, she thought. Distinguished with his silvery gray hair, his well-cut suit, his tan in the middle of winter.

When he started a conversation with a comment about the painting behind her, she was glad. He looked like somebody with possibilities. She had been divorced for a year and hadn't met any interesting men, just losers. She longed for a nice, warm, close, sexy, ongoing relationship with a man. Maybe he was the one. He certainly looked good. And sexy, too, she thought as he stared into her eyes directly, measuring and flattering her at the same time. As they talked he seemed intelligent, understanding.

He liked her looks and felt her responding. He offered to get her another glass of wine to replace the empty one she was holding. Somewhere in the conversation he let her know that she was "a beautiful woman." To punctuate his remarks he touched her arm. After a while he suggested: "If you have nothing to do, would you like to have dinner with me?"

She had nothing better to do. God, what could be better, she thought, than the beginning of a relationship with this handsome, suave man?

They talked and drank more wine over dinner, and as they were preparing to leave the small French restaurant he suggested that she come to his place for a drink: "It's nearby."

She hesitated, wondering whether she was prepared to sleep with him, or at least to hassle with him about it, if she accepted his invitation. But then she looked into his tanned face. His blue eyes were crinkled from the smile that accompanied his invitation.

She could see those eyes peering at her over more lovely dinners like this in the future, and so she said, "I'd love a drink."

At his apartment he opened another bottle of wine and put an album on the stereo—Donna Summer having musical orgasms. As they talked he moved closer to her on the couch and then he kissed her. His hands moved quickly. They opened buttons and hooks deftly. He pulled up her skirt with expertise. She wondered if she should let this happen so quickly, but she found him really attractive and so she let herself respond. The sex with him was wonderful. "You were great," she whispered afterward, snuggling her head on his shoulder.

Her mind raced ahead to all the terrific sex she was going to have with this wonderful man.

"And so are you," he answered, moving slightly, suddenly feeling restless, bored. He wondered how soon it would be before he could get her out of his apartment so that he could watch a little TV in peace and go to sleep.

An hour and a half later they were in front of his house and she was getting into a cab. As she rode off waving and smiling, he said, "Speak to you soon." The next day she waited for his call. And the next day. And the day after. She never heard from him again.

Almost every woman today has such a tale. One young lawyer told me about a man she had met at a party who kept calling her every day for two weeks before she would go out with him. When she finally said yes, they drove to his country home and spent a romantic day by the fireside, and a nice night in his bed. Because he had pursued her so diligently and because the day and evening had been so fine, she was sure that she would see him again. "Speak to you next week," he said as they parted. He never called again either.

A married woman told this story about a young actor: "I met him when I was having lunch at the counter of a health food place near my office. He was on the stool next to mine and he started a conversation. We exchanged names and he asked where I worked. We parted pleasantly and I didn't think any more about him. I hadn't given him my telephone number or any hint that I was interested in him as a man. At that point I wasn't. The next day I received a phone call from him at my office. He wanted to know if I would have a drink with him after work. I told him, 'No.' Lunch? I said, 'No' again. He insisted he wanted to see me. I told him I was married and I didn't want to see him. He hung up, but the next morning he called me again. I told him 'No' once more. He kept calling me for two weeks, being as funny and charming as possible, and finally I said I'd have lunch with him. He was very witty at lunch, and a sense of humor always gets to me. He kept inviting me to have drinks, more lunches. Once even breakfast. This went on for a month. All the time he was telling me how much he liked me and kept pressuring me about sex. Finally, we made a rendezvous. We had all those long conversations over lunch and on the phone. I felt we had a real relationship going. We slept together and the sex was fine. I thought it was the beginning of a real affair. I waited for him to call. He never did."

The country is full of women like these women—women waiting to hear from men they slept with once, or twice, or thrice. They are waiting in vain. They have met Hit-and-Run Lovers, a proliferating breed of men who score and soon after disappear. Some younger women are not devastated by their hit-and-run encounters. They accept them as part of the game, or even seek them out. But most females are left wondering, "What did I do wrong?"

The married woman is convinced the actor didn't like her breasts. They were too small.

The lawyer is sure the man who romanced her with such fervor and dumped her with such alacrity was too competitive—he was uncomfortable with the fact that she was a successful professional.

The woman who thought she had encountered her Prince Charming in the art gallery only to find that he galloped away as swiftly as he had appeared, is just plain puzzled, but she figures, "Maybe I slept with him too soon."

The truth is, no matter what physical attributes you have or don't have, whether you have sex on the first night or not, whether you are a successful professional or a secretary with no great career ambitions, has little to do with the fact that you will suddenly lose your charm after having sex with certain men.

Hit-and-Run Lovers act the way they do because they are driven by their *own* lacks and needs—and the needs are rarely sexual, although their behavior belies this, and the men themselves are convinced that lust is what keeps them needing so many woman so much.

Modus Operandi

Hit-and-Run Lovers pick up women in elevators, on the street, in buses and subways, getting out of cabs, at singles affairs, at parties, at museums, at discotheques, through friends, in restaurants—wherever they happen to find themselves or a woman who catches their ever-roving eyes. Since their life is centered on women, they have tunnel vision.

One not particularly good-looking man explained his thirty-year successful career as a Hit-and-Run Lover by saying: "There are an infinite number of lonely women in the world." He is obviously not averse to taking advantage of this sad and true fact.

Another better-looking and younger man told me about picking up women on the ten-block walk to his home from his office. Someone will catch his eye and he'll simply say, "You are a very pretty woman." He finds a lot of women who end up as his one-night stands this way.

Another divorced man is invited to a large number of press parties and openings in New York. He finds his sexual partners at these affairs and, occasionally, to his discomfort, he is found again by some of his previous victims.

"Sometimes a woman will come up to me at a party,"

he told me. "I don't recognize her, but something she says will tell me that I have slept with her. Then I'll say, 'Oh yes, of course I remember. It was wonderful, sweetie. I'm sorry I never called you again.' Sometimes I pass women on the street whom I've slept with, and I don't recognize them. Sometimes some of the women will telephone me. I don't see them again, but," he added proudly, "I'm always polite."

Hit-and-Run Lovers may be polite or even flattering, if that is what it takes to get you into bed or out of their lives, but there is little concern or empathy for a woman's feelings before, during, or after—except for the answer to the crucial question: Is she responding?

For Hit-and-Run Lovers, women are not real people.

Once the sexual act is over, they have served their purpose. Disposable and interchangeable, they are not thought of again; or, if they are, it is with a dimly felt sense of guilt which passes quickly—with one exception. The Vicious Hit-and-Run Lover not only thinks about his victims after he has bedded and dumped them—he actually gloats over the hurt he imagines he has inflicted, taking as much pleasure in fantasizing about a woman's pain as he did in his momentary sexual pleasure.

Luckily, the Vicious Hit-and-Run Lover who is out to deliberately hurt a woman is comparatively a rare type in the Hit-and-Run subculture. So, before we take a closer look at him, let us examine two other garden-variety Hit-and-Run Lovers. The Jock and the Perfection Seeker are men whom women are more likely to meet on the contemporary sex scene.

The Jock

Men referred to here as Jocks may not be interested in sports—although many of them are—but they share a kind of Jock mentality. Their vision of the world is purely macho. They feel a kinship with other men—an "us guys" feeling as opposed to "them." "Them" are women, who are regarded as alien, inferior, and as instruments to serve men. The Jock feels he is engaging in very "masculine" behavior by loving 'em and leaving 'em. After all, slam-bam-thank-you-ma'am is the way "real" men act.

Some Jock Hit-and-Runners boast to other men about their conquests, but often, after a certain age, the outright boasting stops. However, allusions to a lifestyle based on fast sexual encounters continue in more subtle forms.

One man told me about a group who continually ran into each other in a Los Angeles restaurant that stayed open all night. These men would arrive in the wee hours of the morning alone. Without it actually being said, it was understood between them that they had all come there after leaving a woman. The unstated code these men used was simple: "Where did you go tonight?" or "Did you have a good time tonight?" would be asked. The questions and ensuing answers were enough to establish an understanding that each had been with a woman.

Interestingly, for this group of men—all notorious womanizers—the most important part of the night was not the dates with women, and not the sex that had taken place, but this meeting with one another afterward.

"I remember," one of the group told me, "lying in bed with some broad right after having fucked her and thinking about going to the deli and wondering which of the guys was going to show up. What I wanted to do was get rid of the woman as fast as possible so I could go bullshit with the guys."

Although Jocks spend a lot of their time with women, they do not consider this time—except for its sexual finale—well spent. What is worthwhile for the Jock is time spent with other men, or in working (many of them are workaholics) or engaging in sports or other hobbies.

Indeed, many a Jock will admit to being bored most of the time by the women he finds himself with.

"The point of the evening," explained one man "is not to be stimulated intellectually, but to end up in the sack. So I start in on the woman immediately to figure out how I can get her there. I try to find out about her interests so I can either flatter her or make it appear we have a lot in common. The truth is I don't give a damn about her interests most of the time, or anything except whether I am going to fuck her."

Another man, an inveterate bridge player, who racked up fifty-three different conquests in 1977, which means a lot of time and energy spent on women, commented: "Frankly, I think more about cards than women."

When I asked him, since he so freely admitted he didn't care much for most of the women he slept with, why he then bothered with them, he said: "Well, it's like watching TV. It passes the time. Some shows turn you on, but you can't remember them. It's the same way with women. I can't remember most of them. It really doesn't mean anything to me. It's all over after the sex. Like a TV show, you stay with it until it's over."

"Do you ever feel you want to get the women out of there as soon as possible afterward?" I asked.

"Very often," he admitted.

Jocks—like this man—often join with other men (whom they value) to go on the prowl together for women (whom they don't value). It is then that scoring becomes doubly important. It is a game played for a spectator who counts, whose respect, acceptance, and admiration are important: a fellow male. A common scene in singles bars is two guys, both obviously on the hunt.

In some groups of men the phone numbers of women who are considered easy and desirable prey are passed around. A woman may be merely a commodity to the Jock Hit-and-Run Lover—devalued and dehumanized—but if he is able to provide desirable women to other men, then the female becomes valuable, still not as a human being, but as a marketable product. She is the means by which a man can gain status with other men and feel powerful and quite manly in the process.

A Los Angeles producer told me that passing along phone numbers of women they have slept with and don't want to see again is a common practice in his crowd and that some men eventually become known as "meat dealers" or "butchers." Meat dealers are famous in their circle for being able to provide, at a moment's notice, women for a friend or business acquaintance. The woman is not a call girl or hooker, because status would then be lost. She is someone whom the man knows, from personal experience, will have sex quickly. The term for handing down phone numbers in this group is "passing meat"—meat being the woman. The contempt these men have for women is evident.

Another successful Chicago executive told me that in his group of wealthy businessmen beautiful women get handed around from one to the other, much like the stock tips this group also exchanges.

"How do you think the woman feels when you don't call her after having sex with her?" I kept asking the acknowledged Hit-and-Run Lovers I interviewed. Generally, the men were surprised by the question and at a loss for an answer. Absorbed as they are in their own needs, they had never thought about women in this way before.

One answered: "The women are in it for the same thing I am. They don't give a damn about me either."

Sometimes this is true, the Hit-and-Run Lover will meet his female counterpart—a woman out just for a one-night stand herself. Female sexual adventurers are increasing with the sexual and social emancipation of women, but most women still go to bed with men in the hope that a relationship is beginning. They are hurt, puzzled, disappointed, and left questioning their own desirability when the Hit-and-Run Lover does not call again after sex.

Jocks know that the majority of women won't sleep with a man just for a night. They feel free to tell their male buddies that a "quickie" is all they're after, but with females they are devious. They cajole, flatter, or do whatever is necessary to get them into bed.

In contrast to the Jock, who is dishonest with women but candid with men about his limited interest in relationships, is another kind of Hit-and-Run Lover whose motives are more hidden from himself and others.

The Perfection Seeker

Perfection Seekers feel compelled to run from woman to woman just as much as Jocks do, but they think they bed-hop because they are searching for the perfect mate. Unlike the Jock, who never expects a woman to be perfect, the Perfection Seeker always hopes she will be.

The Jock prefers the company of men to women, but the Perfection Seeker, typically, is uncomfortable with other males, whom he regards as threats. He considers them more successful in business, or more adequate as men. His great insecurity vis-à-vis other men, makes the Perfection Seeker prefer women, and most of his friends are female. The women he gathers around him may be coworkers, the wives of friends, old school friends, and even ex-lovers, rescued from the ashes of his brief sexual fire.

Despite his bevy of female friends and lovers, the Perfection Seeker often considers himself a lonely man. This attitude contrasts sharply with the Jock, who has male cronies, is active and busy, and does not dwell on loneliness.

The Jock generally does not regret the absence of an enduring love relationship. The Perfection Seeker, however, feels genuinely sorry or guilty that his love life consists of a never-ending series of brief encounters. The Jock knows he is exploiting women and is open about it, but the Perfection Seeker is convinced that bedding and leaving women rapidly is part of his search for a more permanent relationship. The Perfection Seeker jumps from woman to woman, not because he devalues womankind like the Jock, but because he has an ever-alert and unrealistic eye for a female's fatal flaw.

There are two variations of the fatal-flaw principle. From the minute one kind of Perfection Seeker meets you, he starts to look for what is wrong. He knows the flaw is there—he just has to uncover it. Another kind of Perfection Seeker idealizes a woman initially. It isn't until after the sex act is consummated that the flaw appears.

One man who fits the second category remembered how this operated in his life.

"My career was in a mess then. I was very discontented with myself and I found women soothing. They were less judgmental than men. I needed the acceptance of women and I set out to get it. But right after sex I always found something wrong. I didn't like her legs, or her breasts, or something."

If it isn't legs or breasts it can be previously unnoticed wrinkles that now jump out at the Perfection Seeker and turn him off. Thighs will suddenly seem too fat, ankles too thick. Once he has spotted the fatal flaw, he is forced to set out again on his endless journey. He must find someone new. Somewhere out there must be someone, he feels, who will match his fantasy of perfection.

Sometimes the fantasy of a Perfection Seeker zeroes in on a specific.

One man recently insisted to his therapist that he had to have a woman with large breasts—not an uncommon fantasy of men, in general. The fact that during treatment he managed to get involved with a woman with small breasts was a source of amazement to him.

Another man has a scenario in his head: At a party or other public place he will see from afar a tall, blonde Nordic beauty with apple-red cheeks. She has arrived with another man but will meet him and find him more appealing and go off with him. Although this man keeps meeting short blondes or tall brunettes, he finds both lovely as people, and desirable sexually, he keeps his eyes roving and his body moving from bed to bed searching for his fantasy. Only then, he imagines, will he be able to form a permanent, monogamous relationship.

In addition to fixed visions of physical perfection, Perfection Seekers also often have more intellectualized fantasies. For example, they may think they are searching for the woman who turns them on so much they won't tire of her physically. Or they may feel they are looking for a bright, active, knowledgeable woman who will also look up to them as heroes. The fantasies of these men often have built-in contradictions, but they fail to recognize it. An intelligent, assertive woman would hardly engage in unquestioning hero worship, for example. Besides, she would undoubtedly evoke anxiety and insecurity.

The reason Perfection Seekers cling to their fantasies so tenaciously is because the fantasies are tools. They serve to keep Perfection Seekers from getting emotionally involved with the woman at hand. Around the corner may be someone more perfect, a woman who will match their dream. Of course they never find what they are looking for, which is precisely the point.

Sometimes before a fatal flaw is detected by the Perfection Seeker, a couple of meetings will have taken place.

More like the Jock than the Perfection Seeker is the next species of Hit-and-Run Lover. He has no idealistic fantasies about females either.

The Perpetual Kid

We have all seen young children with advanced cases of the "gimmes": "Gimme an ice cream cone," "Gimme a dime," "Gimme a ride on your truck"—whatever they see they want. If they can't get it instantly they cry, scream, or hit. They have not learned to wait for gratification, or indeed to value what they crave beyond the pleasure of the moment, which is quickly forgotten. Well, there are some men who look at women as if they are ice cream cones—with the gimme eyes of greedy children who demand instant gratification. These men see you, they like you, they want you right away, they get you—and then they couldn't care less about you.

Perpetual Kids have never grown out of an infantile narcissistic state. Their outlook on the world is self-centered. Everything is focused around their needs, and only their needs.

The world for Perpetual Kids is a most impersonal place. They don't relate to people. They just want something from them. Like the Jock, they chew women up and spit them out. But what differentiates the Perpetual Kid from the Jock is his orientation. Kids don't necessarily feel that women are inferior—they are just totally self-centered and unthinking in their approach to them.

Perpetual Kids, Jocks, and Perfection Seekers are devastating to tangle with, but the next two varieties of Hit-and-Run Lovers are even more deadly.

The Vicious Hit-and-Run Lover

There is an element of hostility to women present in all Hit-and-Run Lovers, which is expressed in the process of dehumanizing them. Even the Perfection Seeker is not looking at the real woman but is trying, instead, to match her to the picture in his head. Dehumanization results from some anger and loathing, but with the Vicious Hit-and-Run Lover the hostility runneth over and becomes sadism.

The Vicious Hit-and-Run Lover is not only out for sex, he is out for blood.

He is extremely hostile toward women. He takes joy in fooling and deceiving them, and he gloats at the thought of a woman suffering because of his actions.

When Jane, an attractive divorcee of thirty-two, met Tom, she had no idea what she was in for. Tom was a chauffeur for a large livery service catering to executives and celebrities. She met him when an executive from out of town who had used her services as a free-lance stenographer sent her home in the limousine he had hired for his stay in New York.

Tom romanced her by taking her driving in his limousine during off hours, dining out with her, stopping off for a drink at cute little bars. He was very romantic, often kissing her in the middle of a street and once in a grocery store during his courtship. Jane explained to Tom that she was seeing someone else but was not committed to him. Tom asked her to stop seeing the other person. She refused without knowing Tom better. This had all taken place before they slept together—Jane was somewhat reluctant because of her other involvement. Somewhere in the conversations they had, Jane remembers Tom bringing up the subject of one-night stands. Jane explained she had never slept with anyone just once. He had acted surprised, and now she realizes that he was also registering the fact in his mind.

Finally, after weeks of driving around in his limo, she consented to sleep with him and they went to his apartment. Jane did not hear from Tom again until about two months later when a limousine pulled up to the curb one day when she was walking her dog. It was Tom. He smiled and invited her into the car. She refused. He trailed her down the block cajoling. "Listen," he finally explained, "I didn't call you again because I was mad that you were seeing that other guy. Still seeing him?" he asked. She nodded her head. "Oh, what the hell difference does it make?" he said, smiling. "I've missed you. Hop in."

Explains Jane, "I must be really stupid or something, because I got into his car. We drove somewhere out in Queens and he was all over me again. He asked me to go down on him. I did. It was all lovey-dovey again, I thought. Then silence. It was a one-night stand for him—twice.

"When I ran into Tom once more about a year later, he wanted to have coffee with me. I refused and ran like hell. Three times would have made me a bigger fool than I already was."

Tom, a Vicious Hit-and-Run Lover, imagined each time how lousy Jane was going to feel. He got a thrill from knowing that she had—thanks to him—finally had a one-night stand with a man. He felt he was paying her back for not dumping the man she was going with for him. Like many Vicious Hit-and-Run Lovers, he got more satisfaction from the hurt he was inflicting than from the sexual pleasure he had received.

Some Vicious Hit-and-Run Lovers manifest their hostility to women by being sadistic during the sex act itself and hurting a partner physically. Jane remembers that Tom, on their first night together, was more anxious to have anal intercourse than anything else.

Anal sex need not be sadistic, but Jane feels that in Tom's case it was a desire to do something that he considered in his sick mind to be humiliating to her.

Other sadistic Hit-and-Run Lovers treat women roughly or even brutally, engaging in little foreplay, displaying no concern about a partner's readiness, digging nails into flesh during lovemaking, holding a woman so tight during embraces that they cause pain or leave bruises.

They also often deliberately put women into embarrassing situations in public, or denigrate them in front of others. Verbal abuse in private is common.

Erica, a thirty-four-year-old woman who now lives in Philadelphia, remembers having the bad luck to choose a Vicious Hit-and-Runner as her first lover in her hometown in the South:

"I was seventeen. He was a junior in college. He started taking me out one summer and tried to go to bed with me. I kept resisting, but finally gave in. When it was over, he called me a whore and walked out. Can you imagine how I felt?" she concluded.

The Vicious Hit-and-Run Lover is generally mercifully brief in his sadistic encounters. But another kind of Hit-and-Runner is out not for a sexual score but for an emotional hit. He'll hang around for as long as it takes to get it.

The Love-Me-Then-I'll-Leave-You Lover

Laura went out with Jim for six months. During that time he was attentive and loving. He would call her each day on the telephone and see her two or three times a week. He would tell her how crazy he was about her, and how much he loved her. Laura was a cautious person and she kept telling Jim it took her a while to fall in love. Finally, one romantic night after they had finished a couple of bottles of wine and spent the evening making love, she told Jim what she knew he had been yearning to hear. "I love you," she whispered into his ear. From that moment on, she remembers, it was downhill. "He seemed more distant, colder, he called me less often on the telephone, and all of a sudden he was gone. I really don't know what went wrong to this day."

What went wrong was inevitable with men like Jim,

who is not a One-Night Stander, but is a Hit-and-Run Lover nevertheless. Jim and his brother lovers have genuine feelings during the initial stages of a relationship and want the woman to love them in return. But as soon as they get what they want, as soon as the woman reciprocates the feeling and indicates some kind of warmth or love, it triggers a change. The man goes from desperately wanting and loving to not caring.

Men like this are often extensions of the Perfection Seeker. They, too, are actively seeking a fantasy, but they go one giant step further. The Perfection Seeker finds fatal flaws in women soon after sex takes place, but sex alone is not enough for the Love-Me-Then-I'll-Leave-You boys. They need not just a woman's body but her heart. It is only after they are sure they have gotten a woman involved emotionally that they begin to feel something is wrong. If they don't see a flaw, they may simply experience a sudden loss of feelings for the woman. Either way they have to go out and find someone new. Jocks, Perfection Seekers, and Vicious Hit-and-Runners exploit a woman sexually. The Love-Me-Then-I'll-Leave-You type exploits her emotionally, and the hurt can last much longer and be much more devastating. Women often feel rotten after one-night stands, but they get over it quickly. After all, the One-Night Standers don't hang around long enough for you to get attached to them. The Love-Me-Then-I'll-Leave-You type, however, makes sure he is around long enough to leave an emotional mark.

At the opposite end of the spectrum from the emotional hit man is the Hit-and-Run Lover who won't even court a woman for a night. He is the most hidden Hit-and-Run Lover of all. Unlike the Jock, he doesn't think that sexual exploitation of women is what the game is all about. Nor does he feel he is searching for a perfect woman. This kind of man operates within the context of the swinging scene, and what he thinks he is after is sexual kicks.

The Swinger

The orgy-goer—or -giver—is a man who believes he is sexually liberated, but what he has done, in the name of liberation or exploration, is institutionalize the one-night stand. At orgies the woman is a nameless and often faceless body, dehumanized even more than she is in the life of Jocks, where for at least a night she must be addressed personally.

The Swinger runs from woman to woman sexually, faster than any other Hit-and-Runner—sleeping with several women in one night at a Swinger's party. Liberation is not his game, although that may be his political cry. His game is anonymity and distance from women—there is no greater way to avoid intimacy than amidst the crush of bodies at an orgy. He is also often bored and depressed and uses sex rather desperately as a way of running from both of these emotional states.

The Swinger may choose to operate in private as well, taking delight in threesomes (generally two women and him), or exchanging partners with another couple.

No matter how he acts, the Swinger is no more liberated than any of the other Hit-and-Run Lovers. They are all driven men who must seek, compulsively, a never-ending stream of female conquests. Their actions are out of control whether they are consciously aware of it or not.

What Makes Them Tick

Speak to other men about these Don Juans, and they will generally assess them enviously as men with very high sex drives. Hit-and-Run Lovers often consider themselves lusty lads as well. Occasionally, though, you meet a man who realizes, however remotely, that lechery is not what keeps him looking, loving, and leaving.

One man in his fifties insisted that in his long life as a very active womanizer, he has never felt horny, never felt an intense sexual urge that made him go out and find a woman. Yet this man has a mountain of "little black books" and calendars in which all of his sexual encounters have been carefully recorded. In his closets are albums bulging with photographs of women who have come and gone in his life. Last year he slept with approximately fifty different women and had sexual encounters on an average of three or four times a week. There are days when he sleeps with more than one woman. In his youth his sexual activity was even greater. He claims that his many sexual adventures "just happen," but as therapists know, things that happen repeatedly and with such regularity don't "just happen." And one is forced to wonder that if, indeed, his encounters mean as little to him as he keeps insisting, why it is so necessary for him to keep such a careful record of each and every one of them.

What is the very active sexual lifestyle of this man, who claims he rarely feels sexy, really all about? Why do men become Hit-and-Run Lovers?

Lawrence Edwards, in his book *Lover: Confessions of a One-Night Stand* gives us a clue about the dynamics of Hit-and-Run Lovers. He explains what embarked him on the body-strewn path of the one-night stand: "The self-image for which I was burning was that of a sexual man." About women he says, "...I was drawn to them with an overwhelming urge to be accepted by them.... It is women who send me back to myself, even as I reach out to them, embrace them, enter them. I commune with myself through them. I create my self-image through them....

"The self-image of the sexual man is, in the end, his image of himself as a man."

Although he explains his need of women in the abstract so eloquently, he later in the book talks about his reactions to women specifically and a lot less poetically: "...the moment I'd climax, I'd turn away from whatever woman was with me and lie on my back staring at the ceiling and wonder what the hell I was doing there."

Wondering what the hell they are doing there is something one hears time and time again from Hit-and-Run Lovers of all kinds. One man who thought he had found his fantasy of the perfect woman—until he started living with her—told me how he felt compelled to run away from her. "One morning I woke up and she was still sleeping. I realized, looking at her lying there, that she had been merely a figment of my imagination. She was not the special person I thought she was, and I thought, 'What am I doing here?'"

Lawrence Edwards, when he said he was seeking "his image of himself as a man," supplied the answer to this man's question and his own.

If Hit-and-Run Lovers find themselves on strange mattresses, feeling boredom, disappointment, dissatisfaction, or even disgust, time and time again, it is because, in bedding women, they are really acting out personal tragedies. These men are alone in their many encounters, no matter who else is present. Rather than wrestling with lust, they are tangling with the question of how they feel about themselves. They harbor a great many doubts about themselves as men. Some are so obsessed with the whole process of womanizing that they don't actually experience any feeling of inadequacy, but on a subterranean level it is surely there. Their anxieties about acceptability apply not only to women but to other men to whom they feel inferior.

In another book, *A Letter from My Father*, W. Ward Smith recounts his endless sexual adventures, and admits: "All through my life I have always had a feeling of unreality—as if I was bluffing my way through. I have always felt that I was inefficient at whatever I was attempting—that even goes for sex. I have always had a notion that I was an inadequate lover—that my prick wasn't big enough or my tongue wasn't long enough—women have raved about my rod and in my youth my caresses, but I had the idea it was insincere flattery...."

What the Hit-and-Run Lover does with women is allay anxieties such as those described by Smith. Each time he conquers a woman he seeks reassurance he desperately needs—that he is a desirable, capable, lovable, strong, sexy fellow, after all.

Women are as necessary to Hit-and-Run Lovers as dope is to heroin addicts. The are a "fix," but the "fix" barely takes, surely doesn't last, and so the man, prodded by his poor self-image, sets out again and again to find assurance in the form of a new woman. The man is haunted. No matter how many conquests he racks up, like Ward Smith, he doesn't really believe the message that getting a woman into bed was designed to give him— that he is all right. In search of some ultimate proof of his manhood, the Hit-and-Run Lover continues his journey through the vaginas of the world. And an unsatisfying, often lonely journey it is, no matter how many orgasms occur along the way, because the ecstasy he is really seeking is self-respect and self-assurance.

Because they keep doing things that are supposed to provide them with proof of manhood, but never do, there is, indeed, often an air of unreality about the life of the Hit-and-Run Lover, which is why some of them need bulging address books, little black books, diaries, calendars, or photographs to record conquests. Convinced inwardly that they are imposters in the world, they need concrete proof to reassure themselves that these things really did happen to them, that they are, indeed, real.

Another thing that a man who hits and runs chronically is fleeing from is intimacy. If a woman gets close to him she will be able to see him as he sees himself, as a lousy, weak guy, so he keeps his unions brief.

One-night stands also serve to keep the woman from rejecting him. He is sure, because of his own poor self-image, that sooner or later he will be rebuffed—so he rejects first, either by telling himself in advance that the encounter will be brief, or by taking off fast.

But although the Hit-and-Run Lover in the deepest recesses of his soul feels rotten about himself, he rarely recognizes it consciously. If he senses that you are not responding to his advances, he will get rid of you quickly, finding reasons why you were not worth bothering about after all. He'll fasten on something wrong with your looks, your personality, or your lifestyle so that he doesn't have to examine his own behavior or look at his own faults. This way of handling possible rejection accounts for the behavior of many men who date you once and don't call again. Even if they haven't had sex with you, you have had a one-night stand.

How They Got That Way

What is there in the background of the Hit-and-Run Lovers that make them the way they are—slippery, elusive, sometimes devious, sometimes sadistic, sometimes immature, and, especially in the case of Perfection Seekers, obsessive?

Generally, their behavior with women in the present is colored by relationships in the past, either with parents or early experiences with females.

JOCKS: The Jock can have observed within his original family the way he now operates with women—that females were there essentially to serve men. This image from his home was fortified by the place of women in society. His mother was often a workhorse who catered to his father and doted on him, and the father accepted this as his due. Men in his family may have treated women outwardly with formal respect, but they nevertheless regarded them as inferiors or possessions that performed useful functions.

PERFECTION SEEKERS: The Perfection Seeker may have found conditions as a child in his home so anxiety provoking that he developed a set of character traits to reduce the anxiety. He became overinvolved with minutiae in order to avoid what was really bothering him.

A good example of this is one man who grew up with an alcoholic mother. His father had left home before he was nine and he blamed this on his mother, but he nevertheless felt guilty about his anger. To counteract the anxiety caused by guilt and rage, he became very meticulous. As a child he would spend hours cleaning the house, often staying up late scrubbing the bathtub. Rather than be inundated by his upsetting and scary feelings, he focused on getting spots out, making things tidy, neat, perfect.

When the boy matured and started dating women, he found himself expecting women to be as perfect as he expected everything else to be. Of course he never could find a woman who matched his ideal—they always did something wrong, causing him to want to leave.

One sign of a man who is a Perfection Seeker with women is that, like this man, he is obsessed about many things. He is apt to expect perfection in other areas of his life besides women. It is easier for the Perfection Seeker to dwell on the faults of things and people than to concentrate on his own imperfections.

Consciously, the Perfection Seeker is also an "if only" person. "If only this woman were better, I could get close to her," he thinks. But unconsciously he is terrified of the exposure of intimacy and finds fault in order to avoid closeness, which he feels would lead to rejection.

LOVE-ME-THEN-I'LL-LEAVE-YOU LOVERS: Men who make women love them before evaporating tend to have an obsessive-compulsive personality structure. They not only want a woman to match a dream of perfection, but they search for a kind of perfect love as well.

Such a man was Harry. Harry grew up with a mother who gave him love, but always with conditions attached. "I'd love you if you were not such a bad boy, or if you'll do this or that" was her constant message. Upon her son she heaped continual demands.

As an adult Harry harbored one dream of a perfect woman. Not only would she love him totally—unconditionally—in contrast to his mother; she would also have a baby round face, pale skin, and flowing blond hair. Finally Harry met a woman he felt matched the image he carried around in his head. At first the woman didn't appear to be very interested in Harry, but he pursued her, trying to attract her love.

Throughout the courtship Harry secretly felt as he always had—inadequate. He wasn't good-looking enough, he wasn't a good-enough lover.

Harry at last persuaded his dream woman to go away with him for a vacation. They spent a week at a beach resort and the woman started responding to Harry in the way he had always fantasized. She became very affectionate and tenderly took care of his every need. One evening, much to Harry's delight, the woman admitted that she loved him. Harry was euphoric and the couple spent a wonderful night together. In the morning Harry woke up first, with vague feelings of irritation, and went for a walk on the beach. Looking out at the sea, he suddenly felt as if he had left a stranger behind in the house. "What am I doing here?" Harry asked himself, feeling a sudden urge to return to the city and his job. Harry finally had obtained the love he wanted so desperately, and suddenly he found he had no use for it.

Harry dreamed about unconditional love, since he never received even a reasonable amount of it from his mother; but since he was used to its absence, it also made him feel uncomfortable. He was in an insoluble bind. The love he desired was also a threat.

Men who lose interest after you love them can also be understood as cases of arrested development.

Trying to obtain love is a common game during adolescence when both boys and girls are concerned about their adequacy and their acceptability to the opposite sex. During puberty it is important to find someone to love you, but it has little to do with how you feel about them. Love gratifies and supports the needy ego, but the minute you find you are loved, the other person has served his or her function.

Many men who have not resolved the question of their adequacy in adolescence still feel shaky about it as adults. They never know what they want from women or a relationship, since they are stuck in having to prove themselves above all.

PERPETUAL KIDS: The Perpetual Kid may have come from a background in which he felt deprived. Since his family didn't satisfy his needs, as an adult he feels he has to go after what he wants aggressively and snatch it instantly, or he will never get it.

It is also possible for the Perpetual Kid to have come from a home where his parents gave him everything he wanted. In this case he never learned to delay gratification or value what he received. As a grown-up he regards the acquisition of women as nothing more nor less than his due.

The Perfection Seeker and men who want women to love them before taking off, ultimately define women as "saviors." "If only she were perfect she would complete my life," "If only she loved me, I would feel O.K.," are common refrains in their lives.

Jocks define women as slaves—creatures to serve them.

Perpetual Kids look on women as goodies to be rapidly consumed. The Vicious Hit-and-Run Lover, however, defines women as helpless.

VICIOUS HIT-AND-RUN LOVERS: Sadists think they can pull their numbers on women because they aren't afraid of them. In contrast, men are to be feared. Feeling helpless inwardly themselves, Vicious Hit-and-Run Lovers won't choose men as victims for their hostile actions—after all, men could retaliate.

The Vicious Hit-and-Run Lover is an angry man. Either he is hostile to women because of injuries he feels he has received previously at the hands of women, or he is angry at the prototype of woman in his life—mother—and therefore takes out his anger on all women.

One young man in his twenties had a mother who constantly belittled him, comparing him to her husband, whom she said was "no good." When he grew up, this man found the only way he could enjoy himself was with strange women with whom he was brutal, digging fingernails into flesh, displaying no tenderness and no concern, entering his partner without caring whether she was ready sexually or not. His favorite form of intercourse was anal or oral—not uncommon among sadistic lovers—

and when a woman went down on him he would pull her hair hard, directing her.

Another man, also in his twenties, had a considerate mother, but he grew up thinking of himself as frail, because of a chronic childhood illness. He was shorter than most of his friends, and when they started dating as teenagers he felt that the girls he wanted were not attracted to him. He would watch enviously as they went out with other boys.

Because of repeated rejections, he became embittered toward women and felt inadequate around them. By his mid-twenties he had found that he liked hurting women and would bruise them in bear hugs. The frail child still hiding within him felt powerful while he was hurting women.

Sometimes the Vicious Hit-and-Run Lover is a man who is angry at males, not females. He feels less successful, less adequate than other men with whom he is competitive. His anger at men, however, is displaced onto women because he feels safer with them. With women he is in control—with men he is not.

This pattern of dumping his hostility on women started with his mother. As a child and adolescent he discovered he could be angry with his mother and she wouldn't reject him for it, while his father would punish him for the same kind of behavior.

Friends can also play a part in determining whether a man turns into a Hit-and-Run Lover or not. A Jock, for example, might have grown up in a house where the role of women was regarded as inferior, but if his teenage friends accepted women and respected them and he had early positive experiences with girls when he treated them well, he would not necessarily turn out to be a Hit-and-Run Lover.

On the other hand, a boy who came from a background where women were treated decently within his family, might have had a painful early experience with women. He may have been rejected by a girl he cared for deeply, or ridiculed by the girl or by his friends because of her—and this colored his future actions. He learned to reject first—and hurt before he got hurt. He turned into a one-night lover.

Situational Hit-and-Run Lovers

Not all men whom women meet fleetingly as one-night stands are specialists in sex on the run. For some it is only occasional or temporary behavior.

For example, there are men who will go out and find strangers to have sex with after a fight with a wife or girlfriend. "I'll show her," is what they are saying. If their self-esteem has been dealt a blow by a breakup or a fight, men may also use a new and fast conquest like a Band-Aid—to bind up the wounds to their ego.

Newly divorced and separated men are notorious Hit-and-Run Lovers, but most of them calm down after their bruises heal a bit (See Chapter 10). The ones who don't have had the makings of a Hit-and-Run Lover all along. There are a fair number of men who responded when they were young to the pressures of society toward marriage. Once sprung, however, they feel a joyous surge of liberation and end up wanting to sleep with the whole world—and they proceed to do so.

Another kind of situational Hit-and-Run Lover is the man who has a strong need to feel dominant during sex. He will run like hell from a woman he thinks is sexually assertive or demanding, even though what he considers to be demanding may sometimes be merely a request or suggestion. Men like this never see an assertive woman again, making her a one-night stand, but they are able to enjoy lengthy relationships with women who don't threaten their "on top" stance.

And, of course, when discussing one-night stands, one cannot discount chance. Occasionally a perfectly nice normal man will make a mistake. He will end up in bed with a woman he may have thought he liked, but who turns out to be hostile, uninteresting, or is herself uninterested and gives him the "get lost" message. Although the evening turns out to be a one-night stand, it is really just one big mistake.

Since men and women climb into bed with each other much faster these days than in the past, more genuine mistakes are probably being made—you don't always know with whom you are dealing.

But the availability of easy sex accounts also for an

increase in one-night stands that are not so benevolent in origin. Hit-and-Run Lovers have always been around (Who hasn't heard of the adventures of Don Juan?), but to wreak their havoc perpetual conquistadors used to have to go through a long courting routine. It wasn't easy to convince women who did not take sex lightly. Because seduction took longer, the number of sexual contacts racked up in the past by Hit-and-Run Lovers was reduced. Today opportunities are endless.

Sexual liberation has made it possible, as one Hit-and-Run Lover described it, "to leave one woman at home, go out to the supermarket, meet someone else at the checkout counter, and go to her apartment for a quickie before returning to the original lady waiting in bed."

Also adding to the increase of one-night stands in our society are the increasing number of women who are willing to assume what were formerly male prerogatives. For some this includes hitting and running, and for the same reasons—to be reassured about one's desirability and worth.

What the ease of achieving one-night stands has done for its devotees, however, is to take some of the flavor out of the whole game. If sex is being used as a compensation for feelings of inferiority, then you haven't gained much—or certainly what you wanted to, which is a feeling of power and achievement—when it's no trick to get a woman into bed.

Some Hit-and-Run Lovers have therefore upped their ante. They try to get a couple of women into bed with them at one time, or they turn to sex in its more esoteric forms—notably the swinging scene. But even at orgies the underlying need for reassurance and acceptance can raise its head. Recently a Hit-and-Run Lover turned Swinger was terribly impressed that in a tangle of bodies one female hand reached out to hold *his* hand. This note of personal acceptance did more for him than all the vaginas he entered that night.

How They End Up

What happens to Hit-and-Run Lovers? Do they go on forever indulging in one-night stands? or do they change?

Some Hit-and-Run Lovers begin to find their pattern of loving and leaving women unsatisfactory after a while.

Going through countless females without forming lasting liaisons may seem all right to a man in his twenties when responsibility is not very important, but by the time he hits his thirties or forties a Hit-and-Run Lover may begin to need something more. He may start to feel bored by sexual conquests, lonely, or even just plain tired of the pressure engendered by one-night stands. The repetitive business of meeting, planning, and making new conquests can be a drain.

He may also begin to feel out of step with his friends and business associates who have settled down. He may sense that his life with women does not match his career, which by then may have jelled and in which he is feeling more confident and comfortable. He can then decide to look around for a wife, or at least a woman with whom he can engage in a more enduring kind of relationship.

Significantly, since Hit-and-Run Lovers tend to be insecure men, when they finally settle down they generally do it with someone who will not threaten their shaky egos.

Their choice may be a very passive woman. It may also be someone much younger, toward whom they feel fatherly or superior, by virtue of their years. They may also choose someone they feel is socially inferior. An example of this would be a professional man who marries a clerk in a store.

Once married, the Hit-and-Run Lover tends to blame his wife when anything goes wrong. Matrimony has created a ready-made scapegoat for him.

The Hit-and-Run Lover demands strict monogamy from his wife—his shaky ego would be devastated by anything else. However, since he still needs the reassurance gained from conquering new women, the odds are that he will revert to character and start playing around again secretly.

In this way two needs are solved. The Hit-and-Run Lover has the respect and security that a primary alliance supplies, as well as the affirmation of desirability and worthiness he gets from new conquests.

Hit-and-Run Lovers who find themselves steady girlfriends instead of wives tend to indulge their habit on the side as well.

These men feel little guilt about cheating. Since most of them operate by a double standard, they feel, "What's

the big deal?" They are entitled to a little extra action
because, after all, that is what real men do.

Interestingly, when things go well in the life of the
married Hit-and-Run Lover, he treats his wife badly. He
bosses her around, blames her for the least little thing,
acts in general as undisputed king of the household. However, the minute a real crisis occurs, his behavior can
change abruptly.

Men who become Hit-and-Run Lovers are basically
insecure and, as a result, react very badly to stress. In a
real crunch they often crumple. A bad business reversal
can make them depressed; they will then display, at least
to a wife, the neediness and feeling of helplessness they
have been cloaking all along. They may start calling her
several times a day from the office, and once home, they
may never want to let her out of their sight. If things pick
up, however, you can count on the fact that the Hit-and-
Run Lover will go back to his old ways—acting superior
and being demanding and critical all the time.

The Perennial Bachelors

Some Hit-and-Run Lovers never marry, and for them
one-night stands become less and less fun.

An underlying depression haunts all womanizers,
and speeding from woman to woman is one way of avoiding it. But, no matter how much they run, depression
begins to catch up with them if they don't settle down.
Life becomes flat. In his middle years the Hit-and-Run
Lover feels discontented, unhappy, lonely. He has been
fucking his brains out, and what does it all mean? He has
placed a premium on sex, felt that it should lead to something, and when it doesn't he hasn't much left as a person.
The Hit-and-Run Lover suddenly doesn't look forward to
sex as much as he used to. He has become jaded.

Since getting women into bed takes up so much of
their life, Hit-and-Run Lovers fear aging and the loss of
sexual powers even more than does the average man.
Some try to stay young by adopting the latest fad in clothing. Many of them, in middle age, continue to judge themselves by the standards of young men. If they can't have
two orgasms in an hour, they fear they are on their way
out.

And, indeed, there is a real danger that their fears

will become a self-fulfilling prophecy. Many Hit-and-Run Lovers run into sexual problems. But what makes them less able to have sex is not so much the aging process but increasing depression, which dampens sexual function and depresses them still more.

Some Hit-and-Run Lovers start having bouts of impotence, and for many this will lead to avoidance of sex altogether. Eventually, they will repress erotic feelings altogether. The sexiest men in town will become asexual.

The luckier ones in this group will handle their problems by substituting the acquisition of wealth or status for women. They become totally career-oriented and workaholics.

Even more lucky are the group of men intelligent and motivated enough to evaluate their lives and realize something is wrong. There are some who, after figuring things out on their own, stop having one-night stands and start searching for a more intimate, enduring relationship. Others, realizing they are in trouble, go into therapy in search of a more fulfilling existence.

The unlucky ones among Hit-and-Run Lovers are those who don't change their ways. They end up as depressed human beings. These men go through the motions of living without greatly enjoying anything, including the women they needed so much, as they hopped from bed to bed.

Chapter 3

The Jugglers

Sandy met John at a Christmas party given by the conglomerate for which she worked. He seemed intelligent and witty. An attractive man, she thought. But he was there with another woman, so, after talking to him for a while, she drifted off.

"I'll come find you when the orchestra starts playing. I'd like to dance with you," he said. But Sandy found the party dull, the man she was seated next to at dinner impossible, so she left soon after the music began. She figured that was the end of John, since she had not given him her phone number. But two days later, early on a Sunday morning, the phone rang. It was John. He had been thinking about her since they met, he said. In fact, he remembered the neighborhood she said she lived in and had been there at a party the night before. He had looked for her, hoping, foolishly, that she had been invited too.

"What are you doing tonight?" he finally asked.

She was busy, she said. He tried to talk her into seeing him, but she couldn't and wouldn't. Finally, he got her to agree to a date the following Tuesday. Before he hung up, he said, "I'm glad I found you in the book. I was afraid I'd lost you."

Sandy was impressed by what seemed to be John's real interest in her. On Tuesday she was even more impressed by John himself. They talked and laughed a lot together and John told her she was "a special person." Finally, that night, although Sandy knew it was much too soon, they tumbled into bed together.

"When did you know you were going to sleep with me?" John whispered. "As soon as I saw you," said Sandy. It was all very romantic, and before they parted in the early morning John made another date with her for four days later. The next time they were together he told her wonderful things—that she had a very personal style about the way she dressed and that he loved it, that her hair was terrific, it swung in such a sexy way. Sometime that night he asked her: "Are you interested in a real relationship?"

Sandy was delighted by the question. She felt it showed serious interest. "Casual affairs are not for me. And you?" she asked. "Are you interested in a real relationship?"

He gave the answer she hoped for: "Yes."

Again, when they parted that night, they made a date for the following week. Sandy slept with John every week for the following two months, but she never quite knew when she would see him. After a while, he stopped making dates at the end of the evening and, instead, called a day or two ahead to ask her out. Sandy saw him sometimes in the middle of the week, sometimes on a Friday. She was very aware, however, that she never saw him on a Saturday. Sandy felt somewhat secure in the relationship because John phoned her every day, but the fact that he never saw her on a Saturday worried her. Was there another woman, she wondered?

What added to the worry that Sandy was beginning to feel were John's constant references to his friends—all female.

There was someone named Diane, someone else named Jane, and two others named Lauren and Barbara. His whole life seemed to be filled with females—friends, ex-lovers, one ex-wife, all of whom were part of his regular conversation.

Finally, one night at dinner, Sandy worked up the

courage to ask John: "Are you seeing someone else? Why don't you see me on Saturdays?"

John smiled and said: "Well, I am seeing someone else, but I'm not seeing her now, but if Saturday is worrying you, then we can see each other on Saturdays..."

And thereafter she saw John on Saturdays—sometimes. But his answer, "I'm seeing someone else, but I'm not seeing her now," haunted Sandy. What the hell did he mean by that?

On the one hand, it lulled her—it meant he wasn't seeing anybody else at the moment. On the other hand, it left the door open to another woman. A masterpiece of double-talk.

Adding to Sandy's worries was the fact that John had started to skip calling her for a day or two. By this time she also realized his pattern: if she saw John on a week night, she would not see him on the weekend; if she saw him on a weekend, that was it for the week.

Along about the fourth month of their affair, John would still keep in touch with Sandy quite regularly by telephone, but a week or two might go by without his asking her out. When they did see each other it was still wonderful. He was attentive and flattering and made her feel that she was indeed somebody special in his life. "God, do you know how wonderful it is just to talk with you? Do you know how many people don't understand what I am talking about?" he would say, or, "I feel so comfortable with you."

And sex with John continued to be very nice, except Sandy began to get the feeling that what he did with her in bed was a routine he had gotten down pat. He was not responding to her individually. John was too mechanical.

Sandy's malaise about John increased. There were too many references to other women. They were seeing each other with some regularity, but there was no increase in either time or interest on John's part. Sandy felt more and more confused about what was really going on.

Finally, she decided to confront John directly, after he hadn't seen her in three weeks at night, although he managed one quick drink date. When he called one morning to ask her out to lunch, she grabbed the chance.

Over their meal she asked him outright: "Are you seeing someone else? It's been three weeks since we've slept together."

John acted surprised. "Has it really been three weeks?" Sandy nodded.

"It isn't because of someone else. It's just that I've been so busy." He complained of a new client who was causing him all kinds of problems. He told her also of dinner parties and shows he had been invited to, all by women friends. But no threat was what he implied. They were just friends. She was his girlfriend.

His conversation and actions—he insisted on sleeping with her the very next night—were both reassuring and at the same time confusing to Sandy, but she let herself think only about the reassurance. She liked John too much to imperil the relationship further.

And so for a couple of more months she waited for his still fairly regular phone calls, but with increasing anxiety. She would see him every week for a while, which kept her reasonably happy; then, all of a sudden, he would skip a week or two. Sandy was sure now that she wasn't the only woman in John's life. Finally, when her anxiety was running high because two weeks had passed without John asking her out, she blurted out when he telephoned on a Friday morning, just to say "hello": "What are you doing this weekend?"

"I'm going away," he said.

Sandy hung up angry and distraught. She had been asking John to spend a weekend with her for months, and he always managed to find an excuse not to. The next day she decided to have it out with him. She called him and asked: "John, are you seeing other women?"

He answered, annoyed: "I'm seeing all kinds of people but I'm not *seeing* anyone."

"Does that mean you aren't really seeing me either?" she asked.

"Well, yes," answered John.

And that was the end of this contemporary love story. Sandy dumped John. Belatedly, she realized she had met a Juggler, the kind of man many women get involved with today—generally not out of choice, but because there are so many of them around.

Operating Procedures

Jugglers are woman junkies. They need a variety of women, just as men who engage in one-night stands do, but unlike Hit-and-Run Lovers, they are not hooked on brief sexual unions. Their addiction is to ongoing relationships—several at once—and in the course of their complicated love games many an atrocity may be committed.

For example, one well-known social scientist, while having an affair with a friend of mine, met and married another woman. He neglected to tell her about either the courtship or the marriage.

When my friend inadvertently found out about his new bride, her boyfriend seemed surprised at her agitation. He tried to reassure her by telling her she was more beautiful than his wife and that his marriage would not interfere with their affair. He seemed to think his explanation would soothe her. She, of course, left him instantly, and angrily.

The number of women that Jugglers rotate varies from man to man and from one time to another in their lives. Turnover is high, with women coming and going all the time. Three to four simultaneous affairs seems to be the norm, but a dedicated Juggler, especially if he has something going for him in the way of looks or personality, is limited these days only by lack of time and/or endurance.

A young lawyer, with a certain amount of style and a great deal of energy, described life during his busiest season: winter, when on a Saturday he can have breakfast with the woman he spent the previous night with, get rid of her, then invite someone else over to listen to opera in the afternoon. Before the day is over he can have a quick drink with a third woman and a date at night with a fourth. This man was careful to explain that he doesn't sleep with all his Saturday companions, although it is not uncommon for him to sleep with more than one woman in a day. The quick drink, for example, can be with someone he just wants to touch base with. He will meet her at a pub and complain about the amount of work he has to do that weekend—work that, of course, will take him away from her in a little over an hour.

This man is quite aware and somewhat delighted at how outrageous he can be, and confesses to all kinds of lies and deceits in dealing with women. He admits he often breaks dates "if something better comes along."

Unlike this man was a Juggler I talked to who never

lied to the women he became involved with and who made it a point of sleeping with each one at least once a week—two facts that made things a little hairy during a recent peak load period in his life when he had five affairs going simultaneously. Describing the time, planning, and energy it took to keep himself and his women happy, he complained, "It got a little frantic."

But despite occasional complaints and sporadic cutbacks on activities, "a little frantic" is the way a lot of Jugglers like to run their lives. They have a great deal of inner anxiety about being left alone, and to ward it off they fill up their days and nights. They want people around when they need them, which is why they rack up supplies of women—somewhere in the bunch will be one who is available when the need strikes, even if they call at the last moment.

It is anxiety about being left alone that differentiates the Juggler from the Hit-and-Run Lover in his basic attitude toward women. Hit-and-Run Lovers find it difficult to continue relationships, but Jugglers find it hard to end them, even if it is with someone they don't like very much. It is not uncommon for a Juggler to vow to break it off with a woman one week and to call her the next, despite his misgivings, because he "couldn't find anybody better" around that night. Jugglers must have back ups—women to fill up the empty spaces on their dance cards as they jig uneasily through life, haunted not only by trepidation about being alone but also by fear of rejection. A squadron of women is insurance against the sting of rebuff. If one woman leaves, there is always another for the Juggler to comfort himself with.

Devious Jugglers

A gut fear of rejection is also what makes large numbers of Jugglers so devious. The Juggler feels he can't take the chance of being honest, and he certainly can't risk putting all his eggs in one basket. What if you left? He would feel too awful. Self-centered and narcissistic, the dishonest Juggler sees only his own needs and, as a result, is unable to play fair with women.

He tries to keep each relationship secret from the others. He also tends to give false hope by sending out, to each of his women, messages like this: "I really love you, but I can't make up my mind. Don't leave me."

The dishonest Juggler wants all of his women to be exclusively his, but he considers himself to be completely free to engage in many relationships. Manipulative, dishonest Jugglers are motivated by the need for self-aggrandizement, which a multitude of women creates for them, and for protection against rejection.

Honest Jugglers

At the opposite end of the spectrum is the honest Juggler, who is able to be completely open with you about what he is up to. Very soon after a dating pattern is established, this kind of man lets you know that there are other women in his life and warns you that there is no hope for a committed relationship.

The honest Juggler may be juggling only temporarily—to get through a trying period in his life, for instance, when work takes priority over relationships, or while he is still licking his wounds after a divorce.

He may also juggle as a permanent way of life. He has genuine feelings and concerns for the women he sees, but he can't do anything but juggle because of his extreme anxiety about intimacy and rejection. In some respects the honest Juggler can be considered a relatively healthy person: He has come to terms with his peccadilloes. He understands the reasons why he doesn't do well in a committed relationship but is able to operate well within the limits of his capacity—in simultaneous relationships that stop just short of intimacy. A good example of this is a Chicago businessman who as a child was shifted from one foster home to another just as he became attached to each new set of parents. For him, attachments are too anxiety-provoking. He understands his problem but he can't change, so he is content to engage in long-term and caring, but uncommitted, relationships with more than one woman.

Cream-of-the-crop Jugglers are warm with the women in their lives, are truly interested in their welfare, and see them all regularly—generally once a week, and sometimes over entire weekends.

What sets the relatively "healthy" Juggler apart from the unhealthy ones is his complete honesty with women,

his feelings of guilt about his actions, and his accurate
self-knowledge.

A common problem that women have with honest
Jugglers is that they refuse to believe what they hear.
They are told not to count on a long-term commitment,
yet they cling to a belief that they will change the Juggler's mind. When neither love nor anything else develops
in the relationship, these women are often just as angry
or disappointed as those who have been lied to by a Juggler. But the fault is theirs.

Intermediate Jugglers

In between the honest Juggler and his completely
devious counterpart is an intermediate type—a man who
is almost honest, but not quite. He gives a woman the
feeling that she is special, but he also intimates that something else is going on in his life.

Often an intermediate Juggler is not candid at the
beginning of a relationship, but becomes increasingly
open about his juggling later on. This happens not
through any love of honesty but in response to pressure
from the woman who wants the relationship clarified. Intermediate types often deal in evasions and half-truths
throughout an affair, and create much confusion for the
women mixed up with them.

Clues and Tactics

Other emotions like frustration, resentment, and
anxiety about desirability, are also created in women by
Jugglers, but if you feel confusion, in particular, it is
often a good clue that you are up against a man who is
not dealing with a full deck. How can one not be confused
by the tactics of Jugglers? They often tell you one thing—
"Everything is wonderful between us," or "I adore you"—
and then act another way. They call at the last moment.
They disappear mysteriously. Most importantly, they
never intensify a relationship.

Another good sign that you are dealing with a Juggler is that the relationship continues but never progresses. No matter what is said, if a man sees you only
once a week or once every two weeks, something is wrong.

Men who don't play games want to see the woman they care for more often as time goes by.

Not only are Jugglers often inconsistent, with words not matching deeds, but they are also difficult to locate outside of business hours. They are busy making their rounds. Their routine consists of not only dining and bedding their stable of women, but also looking for fresh recruits. Jugglers, consciously or unconsciously, are always hunting for new women, and in their pursuit they get around—to parties, to various public events, to museums, to friends' houses for dinner parties where they can always be counted on as an extra, single, unattached male.

Jugglers are also prone to leave clues. They talk a lot about women friends. They tell you stories about a myriad of ex-girlfriends.

If you visit them at home, their phone may ring frequently. The voices at the other end of the line will almost always be female.

If they have an answering machine and they slip into the next room to play back messages, you will generally hear female voices as well. If the phone rings while you are there, your host may refuse to answer it, making some lame excuse like, "I don't want to be bothered while I'm with you."

Alexander Graham Bell made Jugglers possible. Phones are essential to their operation. Since a Juggler is always spreading himself out, a call can make up for his physical absence. Even if he only manages to see a woman once every week or two, by regular telephone calls he can keep her feeling needed and cherished.

One Juggler who uses the phone adeptly to maintain his habit, recently had a personal revelation that he found exciting. In the middle of the night he had a flash. He realized that he had never had a truly intimate relationship with anyone. He proceeded to announce his moment of illumination to the world by going down his telephone list of "regulars." He called four women and created, in at least two of them, the hope that they might be his first intimate relationship, since he had chosen to bare his soul to them. When last heard from, this man, despite his moment of truth, was as far from intimacy as ever.

Lunches and afterwork drinks are also ploys used by Jugglers. Not only are they not as time-consuming as evening dates, they require no sex—an advantage, since a man who is juggling several women may find it difficult to keep them all well bedded.

Generally, Jugglers are quite attentive and give you time at the beginning of the relationship. Apprehension about rejection runs high and they are anxious to nail down the affair. Once a Juggler feels sure of you, however, because you tell him you care, or through your obvious interest, he then feels free to get on with his act. He starts to substitute lunches, drinks, or phone calls for evening dates and sees other women more often. As one Juggler explained: "Two phone calls, a lunch, and a dinner date take care of four women in one day."

While the Juggler gives himself to a woman in only a limited way, he often expects her to be constantly available. The only thing that increases his own availability to her is his suspicion that she's becoming interested in someone else, or that she's fed up with him. Then his ardor is rekindled, and he tries to intensify the relationship again.

Who Their Women Are

Jugglers are often casual to the point of being downright careless in their treatment of women. They get away with such behavior because they tend to prey on insecure women—women who hang around no matter how unsatisfactory the relationship is or how unhappy it makes them, because they feel they will never be able to find another man. Generally, these women harbor, in spite of evidence to the contrary, a fantasy that eventually the Juggler will come around. He will learn to love them and change his ways.

A woman's helpless attitude also allows the Juggler to look down upon her. His contempt creates distance between himself and her—a distance he desires and needs, because he is afraid of intimacy.

Jugglers also are often attracted to women whom they feel are inferior to them socially, educationally, or intellectually, and for the same reason—to create an emotional distance they need because they fear intimacy.

One Juggler, during an interview, marveled at his own attraction to inferiors. "You know," he said, "I will sometimes break dates with first-rate women just to go out with some clerk from Brooklyn? I'll travel," he said with wonder, "to God knows where to take women I don't even like to bed."

Some Jugglers seek out women who will compensate for their own real or imagined lacks. One shy, introverted man, for example, is interested only in vivacious, outgoing women.

Others look for women who will look good to the world. Depending on the man, they may search for beauty, talent, wealth, or status. Jugglers may find someone who fits some of their requirements, but if a really healthy "together" woman comes along, they feel threatened and run away—one of the few times when Jugglers are able to break off relationships.

Another kind of Juggler goes with women he wants to hide. He picks women he is essentially ashamed of, but they are the only kind of women he feels comfortable with. Since he doesn't want his friends to meet them, he leads a very private social life.

Secure women usually make reasonable demands somewhere along the line in their relationships with Jugglers. They want increased intimacy or more consistent and sensitive behavior. The dishonest or intermediate Juggler often views these demands as a sign that the woman is becoming possessive. If he feels rejection in the wind, he may even turn nasty and attack a woman verbally, enumerating all her faults.

Since their own needs cannot be met, secure women generally leave the less-than-honest Juggler fairly soon.

Relationships can go on for a long time, however, with honest Jugglers who are interested in the welfare of the women in their lives. The women may not be entirely content, but they may be tired of the singles scene, or they may feel they are getting enough out of the relationship to continue until something better comes along. But even among healthy Jugglers the attrition rate is high. Most women eventually want something more than the Juggler has to offer. Because the healthy Juggler allows his women to see other men, many women drop out when they meet someone with whom they can have a more committed relationship.

Both healthy and unhealthy Jugglers may harbor fantasies about finding a perfect woman, but the healthy ones never fool themselves into thinking that the reason they juggle is because they can't find their dream girl. They realize their fantasies are just that—things that go on in the head that don't have much to do with real life. On the other hand, unhealthy Jugglers are often convinced that they are playing the field only until they find the perfect woman.

Such was the case with Peter. He started his career as a Juggler after a divorce in which he was rejected by his wife. At first he lied to women, using them for his own ends. As time went on, he decided that his actions were nothing to be proud of and he began to become more open and caring with women, although he always had to have a few affairs going at the same time. Many wonderful women have come into his life, and he has developed varying degrees of liking and respect for them, but he holds back from any single commitment. There is always something that doesn't match his dream of perfection, either physically or intellectually. Once he met a woman who matched his fantasy of a big blonde with a great body who was also sensitive and intelligent, but even with her there was one thing wrong. Explaining why he continued to go with her for two years but still had to see other women, he said: "I wondered what was wrong for a long time, and then I realized that with her there was no real passion."

For this man and many Jugglers like him, no one will ever be perfect enough.

The inner dynamics go something like this: "I don't want to commit myself because, as perfect as this relationship is, how do I know that tomorrow I am not going to meet someone better?"

When someone comes along who seems to match their ideal, these men will often change their idea of what constitutes perfection.

Fantasies of perfection, for Jugglers, are actually defenses against intimacy. They are afraid of intimacy for the same reasons they are so terrified of rejection. Inwardly they feel inadequate as people and as men. What Jugglers are really juggling are their grave doubts about being acceptable to others.

In a close, long-term, consistent relationship you may see through the Juggler's mask and perceive the insecure person lurking there. Once his real self is revealed, the Juggler is sure he will be rejected. Who else could love him when he doesn't love himself?

As long as the Juggler keeps rejection at bay by having many women, he avoids having to grapple with the thing that is really bothering him—his bad image of himself.

Women are important to the Juggler, as he will freely admit, but what he has never come to grips with is the fact that they are *too* important. He derives his feelings of acceptability and well-being from them instead of from within himself, as healthy men do. And because he is really a prisoner to women, needing them to feel good, there is an edge of hostility to his dealings with them. Since they have the power to crush him by rejection, better not to get too involved. Put them in their place. Make them interchangeable. Have lots of them so that what is crucial, a feeling of acceptability, will never be too threatened.

The women with whom Jugglers surround themselves are not just sex partners, but friends and acquaintances as well. Some of these women are ex-girlfriends who have defected from his ranks without acrimony, or with whom he juggles now only occasionally; others have always been platonic—wives of other men, or perhaps fellow workers.

One personable Juggler has a relationship with a woman that centers around his habit. She invites him to parties whenever she needs an escort, he invites her to parties he knows about. Each is free to find a new love interest at these affairs.

Jugglers often claim that they simply like females better than males, but the real reason they surround themselves with women is not only to ward off rejection—they are also uncomfortable with men. Something in their background makes them unable to compete with members of the same sex, so they turn away from men altogether. Most Jugglers have very few male friends.

Backgrounds

Their defection from male turf may have been caused by a poor male model as they grew up. Some Jugglers had aloof or otherwise unavailable fathers, which led to their present difficulty—they never learned how to relate to men properly.

If a Juggler had a dominating mother who was very close to him and whose forceful character made the presence of the father, by contrast, weak or unimportant, it may have made him feel in later life that men were not important or accessible to him.

Other Jugglers suffered from intense sibling rivalry as children. For example, one Detroit lawyer had an older brother who was favored by his mother. She made it clear that she considered the brother smarter, better-looking, and more capable. Her attitude made the lawyer feel, from an early age, that he was a loser among men, an image he carried over into his adult life, so that he is never at ease with males.

Peer-group differences preceded by problems with a father can also contribute to the formation of Jugglers. A shy, awkward boy who felt, as an adolescent, that he was out of step with the other boys around him, who were active in sports and busy dating girls, may never have been able to compare notes with males as a teenager, so that today he still can't deal with men in a friendly way.

Because the Juggler comes from a background that makes him feel uncomfortable or different from other men, he looks upon women as his savior in a lonely world. In times of trouble he went to his mother rather than his father and learned to be more comfortable talking to women. Women, therefore, have become understanding mothers to him. In contrast to men, they won't let you down or disown you, no matter what you do. This attitude, however, has a built-in ambivalence. It allows the Juggler to also feel superior to women, since they let you get away with murder.

Because the Juggler regards members of the opposite sex as understanding mothers—the only source of his comfort in the world—he can reject a woman by not accepting her fully, but he cannot stand to be rejected in any way by any woman. He would be desolate without his good mommy.

There is another kind of Juggler who, because of his problems in identifying with a male model in childhood, is left with hangups about his sexual identification. Inwardly he is in turmoil because of homosexual fantasies and desires. Silently, he fears he is either gay or bisexual.

This kind of man feels that a committed relationship is forever and that, once he is locked into one, it would be too embarrassing to both himself and his wife if suddenly his homosexuality emerged. He therefore hides his homosexual fears by going out with many women and not getting close to any one of them.

Some men become Jugglers only after the breakup of their marriage. The rejection they felt from a spouse coupled with a predisposition toward feeling insecure as a residue of childhood experiences, can make them terrified of rejection forever after, or at least for a while, and they juggle until they get over their hurt.

When Jugglers Marry

Generally, Jugglers bite the dust and get married after the life of juggling begins to pall, in their late thirties, forties, or even fifties.

The ones who have a chance at a decent marriage are the men who begin to see that juggling is not working out for them in the long run. They try to figure out what it is they are really doing. The truth begins to dawn that they are running from closeness and commitment and, either on their own or with the help of a therapist, they figure out why. An example of this is a forty-two-year-old executive whose mother began to rely on him at the age of twelve as the man in the house when her husband fell ill. From this experience he was left with the feeling that men let you down and women expect too much from you, so he conducted his life by avoiding men and preferring women but not letting anyone get too close. After realizing it was ghosts from his past rather than real women in his life whom he both needed and feared, he was able to resolve his ambivalent feelings and choose a suitable mate.

Men who work out their problems make a conscious choice. They balance the benefits to be derived from a single relationship—closeness, trust, security, and love—against the protection from rejection and shaky egos that multiple women provide, and they opt for monogamy.

Another kind of Juggler has a less healthy motivation for marriage. He makes a conscious decision to get married either because all his friends have done so, or because it might enhance his career, or because he may want the comfort and security of marriage. But he never really intends to give up juggling. He takes a bride but also keeps a stable on the side.

Others may begin by trying to be monogamous, but later find a single relationship too anxiety-provoking. So they revert to juggling.

One accountant, now in his late thirties and on his second wife, is currently having affairs not only with his secretary and several other women from his past, but also with his first wife.

"My files are never closed," he says. This man's insecurities make it necessary for him to gather up women and keep them in his life so that he can have them on call when he needs them. His current wife recently found out about his affair with the secretary and is threatening to leave him, but he wants to keep her—particularly after she rejected him—as well as his other women. Interestingly, he left many clues of his infidelity around the house, including the classic one of lipstick on his shirt.

Another husband managed to leave a diary of his appointments with other women in a place where his wife found it. Still another wandering spouse left nude photographs of his girlfriends in a drawer his wife had access to.

In the end it may lead to disaster for him, but leaving clues is part of the Juggler's neurosis—he must show the world he is desirable, lovable, and acceptable to many.

Of course, many women who are involved with Jugglers don't really want to know the truth, so they manage to ignore a myriad of subtle and obvious clues.

Often Jugglers find a wife who will accept a mutual agreement: it is all right to play around as long as our basic relationship is not threatened.

Most of these agreements are unspoken, but some are open. Wives who have their own fears about intimacy or sex may find some competition a relief. Some husbands tell their wives only half-truths. One famous author who does a lot of lecturing out of town, warned his wife before he married her that he would fool around with women he knew on the road. She was able to accept this as long as he remained faithful when he was home. What this wife does not know is that he does not confine his extramarital affairs to the lecture circuit. He juggles a couple of women on his home turf as well.

When a silent agreement exists and a wife can lead a fairly independent life, the juggling husband who is discreet is probably safe. But a wife who needs a man around fairly constantly may be greatly distressed when he is not available. Although he covers his dalliances with excuses about working late or traveling on business, the anxious wife often finds out about a woman or two. If discovered, the philandering Juggler may quit for a while, but it is hard to kick the habit. He is a junkie. He needs women in numbers to reduce his own anxieties, no matter how much stress he causes his wife in the process.

Some Jugglers manage their basic neurosis by withdrawing into themselves in a marriage. They spend most of their time in solitary activities—piles of work brought home, do-it-yourself projects, or sports like golf or tennis. It is a protective device. You can't get hurt by a woman if you are insulated from her by busyness.

The search for the perfect woman, used by certain Jugglers as a rationale for engaging in simultaneous relationships, can come into play in marriage too. As Jugglers grow older they tend to become disillusioned. Every woman they meet has faults. So, in a spirit of settling for second best, they decide to marry anyway. The idea that they have wives with major flaws serves two purposes: (1) If things don't work out, the Juggler has protected himself from getting hurt—his wife was inferior anyway. (2) Because his wife is not so terrific, the man feels perfectly justified in going out and finding other women to play with.

Jugglers tend to be chauvinistic in their marriages and often find the perfect vehicle for playing Big Daddy around the house. Since they generally marry later than other men, they often marry younger women with whom they can easily adopt a paternalistic attitude.

Within marriage the sexy Juggler becomes less sexy. A man who previously may have been bedding different women three or four or five times a week, settles down to the more normal sexual pattern within marriage—one or two times a week, or even much less. For the Juggler, a wife represents security more than sexuality.

If the Juggler is the kind of husband who withdraws into himself, sex may become an even scarcer item. He often becomes depressed in midlife, and depression is one of the most effective antiaphrodisiacs around. The wife of a Juggler who presented himself to her at the beginning of their relationship as a highly sexual man, finds herself puzzled and frustrated. Failing to recognize her husband's diminished sex drive as his problem, the wife may become concerned about her own desirability and adequacy. As a result of her insecurities and frustrations, she may be driven to divorce, to marriage counseling, or to affairs of her own.

Single Jugglers

Depression, sexual problems, and life in general, however, are worse for the Juggler who never marries. His fate is similar to the unregenerate Hit-and-Run Lover. Juggling is a way to escape the underlying depression that stalks those who engage in it; and as they age, chronic depression may overtake them. They have sought a sense of adequacy in sexual prowess, but they finally realize that sex alone does not make them feel adequate.

Not only does sex lose its meaning and its kick. Like Hit-and-Run Lovers, Jugglers often develop sexual problems such as impotence. They may also lose all interest in women and end up as loners, finicky old bachelors, solidifying a tendency toward pickiness that existed all along. Pickiness is a way of being in control of people and things so that your inadequacies don't show.

Occasionally, a solitary old bachelor will break out of the loneliness and unhappiness that has permeated his life. He may take a trip or make a brief attempt to find "someone," but generally the prognosis is not good for these men, unless they have developed other interests besides women along the way.

The only other Juggler whose fate may be worse is one who juggles in reaction to his fear of homosexuality or bisexuality. If he continues to have homosexual desires, but continues to play the game with women, he may eventually experience what therapists call "homosexual panic." It will make him avoid women altogether and suppress all sexual desires, even homosexual ones, resulting in an asexual pattern of behavior.

Others allow themselves to have an occasional homosexual experience, usually under the influence of alcohol or drugs. They blame the passing episode on the liquor or the drug, and, thus absolved—for the moment anyway—they revert to their heterosexual juggling.

The only chance this kind of man has to arrive at a satisfactory social adjustment is to finally acknowledge his sexual preferences and act on them. The Juggler then gives up on women and becomes a full-time homosexual. He generally doesn't give up altogether on juggling, however—he juggles now with men. When his attractions are divided between men and women, a man may choose to lead the life of a bisexual, maintaining an even more complex stable than before. He then collects, calls, and beds both men and women, adding yet another layer to the possibilities of life as a Juggler in the contemporary world.

Chapter 4

Sexually Stingy Lovers

Marvin is an advertising copywriter who lives in a suburb of New York. He is funny, bright, volatile—qualities that Ellen noticed from the moment she met him—in his house, with his wife.

Yes, Marvin is married and, of course, unhappily. He and his wife have been threatening to separate for years. Their sex life is erratic—because of their problems, Marvin insists. After all, he is a very sexy guy—or so he says.

And from the moment he met Ellen he certainly acted as if he was. Even with his wife in the same room, he came on strong. Moving close to Ellen, he screamed out—funny style, to everyone in the room—"Oh, I'm in love."

Walking Ellen to the front door by himself at the end of the evening, he whispered all kinds of indecent things in her ear.

Ellen was invited often after that to Marvin and Linda's house. She and Linda became fast friends. At the same time, Marvin kept trying to make out with Ellen. One night, when Linda asked Marvin to drop something off at Ellen's apartment, he got his first real chance and he seized it by seizing Ellen, despite her protests, and tried to make love to her.

It was against her principles to take a friend's husband as a lover, and Ellen told this to Marvin. Nevertheless, she was very amused by this lively man and was also intensely lonely—a newcomer to New York City without any male friends.

And so, when Marvin kept persisting with phone calls, and invitations to lunch and dinner, she finally succumbed one evening. Despite her qualms, she found herself in bed with Marvin, and it was great. Marvin was a nice, sexy guy—just like he said. And so Ellen figured she would have a nice affair with Marvin and try to keep it cool because of Linda and the complications.

Marvin called her the next day and told her how terrific it had been. He kept phoning her every day. He made a lunch date and they laughed together over omelettes at a restaurant near her office. He had his hand on her thigh under the table the whole time. He told her how turned on he was.

Ellen figured she would see him alone in her apartment soon. But although Marvin continued to phone her and to come to lunch and made tentative plans to come over on a weekend afternoon, he never quite made it.

His schedule with tennis kept interfering, or his meditation lesson, or he had to meet a male friend, or he had to do something with his daughter on one of the many nights his wife wasn't home. The latter was the only excuse that Ellen really understood.

But she wondered, should a sexy guy like Marvin prefer tennis or his male friends to her and the really nice sex they had had?

Ellen kept trying to get Marvin back to bed. She invited him to parties and to concerts she had tickets for, hoping they would end up in her apartment. It happened a couple of times, but that was all.

Finally Marvin began to complain about the pressure she was putting on him. All she wanted was sex, but he kept feeling the pressure as having to do with a more intense relationship, and so it ended with a screaming fight—not about the thing that was really wrong (why Marvin didn't want to have sex with her), but about the way she kept the apartment and why she couldn't get the bathroom faucet fixed.

Midway across the country, in Chicago, Helen was involved in the last throes of her marriage to Ned. It had been a marriage with a power failure ever since the wedding ceremony ten years before. Ned, who had been ardent before they lived together, ignored her sexually for a long time afterward.

At first Helen had tried to lure him to bed. But Ned always pleaded, "I'm tired." At the same time he put the blame on her by saying: "You like nice things? You like to go to nice places? You like to live well? Well, I'm working my ass off to make that happen for you."

Ned started, soon, getting up at five in the morning to arrive at his business early. At night, exhausted, he would climb into bed at nine o'clock to read or watch TV, and then would fall asleep. He also started being very critical of Helen, blaming her when anything went wrong, claiming she was inept or stupid. As Helen put it, "He created a very unloving atmosphere," and then, in response to questions about why there was not more sex, he would tell her she wasn't responsive enough to him as a person and that he was turned off.

Somewhere midway in the marriage, Ned, in his occasional attempts at lovemaking with Helen, became impotent, and he started an affair to prove there was nothing wrong with him. He operated better sexually with the other woman. He was interested and passionate. He stopped having sex with Helen altogether.

The only time the fires of passion burned for Ned since before their marriage was after Helen announced, "I want a divorce." Suddenly sex was a big thing for him again, but as far as Helen was concerned it was too late. She wanted out.

In Atlanta, Gloria met Bob at a friend's house. He went after her immediately and tried from the beginning to get her into bed. By the fourth date he succeeded. He and Gloria slept together, and as far as Gloria was concerned it was the beginning of a nice affair. After that, however, Bob would call her on the telephone regularly and have long chats, and he would see her once a week, but at the end of most of those evenings he would plead that he was tired from a rough day at work, or that he had an early-morning appointment, or that his ulcer was

bothering him—anything that would keep him from sex.
Gloria couldn't figure out what was going on.

For Sandy, in Los Angeles, sex had been great with
Robin, her husband, until Kevin, their first baby, was
born. Then, all of a sudden, Robin started avoiding her.
Sandy is sex-starved and angry. She has tried sexy clothing and has even made passes at her husband, who ignores the provocative clothing and rebuffs her advances.
Sandy doesn't know if there is something wrong with him
or her.

Marvin, Ned, Bob, and Robin are sexually Stingy
Lovers—men who are eager to maintain relationships but
who treat sex as something dangerous, to be avoided as
much as possible.

Stingy Lovers can be single, in which case they are
anxious to have sex with you soon after meeting you, but
once is almost enough for these men. Having had you a
couple of times, they no longer seem to want you sexually,
although they keep up the interest in other ways.

Sexually Stingy Lovers can also be married, but for
husbands the fires of passion burn bright until the ceremony, and only then are they magically snuffed out.
There are three other variations of this: (1) the husband,
like Robin, whose light goes out only after the first baby
is born; (2) the man who invites you to move in with him
and immediately goes into reverse, changing from a passionate lover to someone who cares less and less about
sex; and (3) a man whom psychiatrists see a lot of today—
the fellow who can operate very well sexually in a living-
together arrangement, but just let him decide to marry
his housemate and suddenly the same woman who used
to drive him crazy with excitement becomes a leper.

Ploys

A variety of excuses and ploys are used by Stingy
Lovers to avoid sex. Most commonly heard is the complaint, "I'm tired," often followed by, "I've had a rough
day at the office." But sexually Stingy Lovers also claim:
(1) they have to get to work early the next morning, or
(2) they have to work late that night, (3) they have to play
tennis or jog, or (4) they have to see their mothers or
children. They also kvetch about backaches and head-

aches. Their sinuses and hemorrhoids bother them, or they have headaches—and, anyway, it's too hot.

Some of them take you home and say goodbye so quickly in front of your door that they seem to evaporate before your eyes. Others sit and talk in your living room, and just when you start thinking about sex they stand up abruptly and plead late-night work or an early-morning appointment and take off like a sudden chill. They can also drink themselves into a stupor so that sex is no longer even a possibility. They are quite capable, too, of provoking an argument at the end of an evening when sex rears its threatening head.

Generally, the Stingy Lover, through adroit excuses, can avoid direct confrontations about sex. But, if you pin him down and want to know what is going on, he is apt to express regret over the fact that "sex doesn't really mean that much to me," or sadness because "the chemistry just isn't there between us."

Some Stingy Lovers will protest, however, that they don't know what you are talking about. They are as sexy as the next guy. They have just been tired or busy. If you pursue the theme you may be branded "demanding."

Others become angry and are liable to attack you in a variety of ways, often ending their diatribe with one inevitable conclusion: "If I'm not sexy, it's because you don't turn me on."

In marriage Stingy Lovers tend to either fall asleep in front of television sets, or stay up so late in front of them that all they are left staring at are test patterns. They also stay glued all weekend to televised sports events. It is common, too, for husbands to take tons of work home from the office or get involved in all kinds of projects that keep them occupied through dangerous parts of the night or weekends when sex might be expected.

A fine example of this is one handy husband who lives in a suburb of Detroit. He has built, in the past, everything from a home sauna to an organ. Currently he is holed up in his basement trying to construct a computer, a project that should take him safely through a couple of more years without much sex.

Of all the men discussed thus far, the sexually Stingy Lover does the most damage to a woman. You can be dumped unceremoniously by a Hit-and-Run Lover, or decide not to have anything more to do with a Juggler, and get over it after a certain period of mourning, but rare is the woman who leaves a relationship with a Stingy Lover without grave, lasting doubts about her own attractiveness and sex appeal.

The tendency is to blame the man's erotic indifference on whatever part of her body the woman feels worst about—a rear end that's too big, breasts that are too small, hips that are too wide, pores that are too big, a hidden scar.

Objectively, however, a woman could be a goddess, unflawed, and unmarked, and still the Stingy Lover would avoid sex with her as if she had a social disease. He is turned off not because of the woman herself but because of his own problems.

The Awares

Some of the Stingy Lovers who acknowledge the fact that they are turned off blame it on something in the personality or character of their wives or girlfriends. More often, however, they blame their sexual apathy on just what the woman fears—some physical flaw—small breasts, big hips, flabby thighs. In the process traumas are created:

One woman was told by her husband that her vagina had a bad odor and that was why he didn't want to sleep with her. She couldn't detect anything out of the ordinary herself, so she went to see her gynecologist. He told her there was nothing wrong with the odor from her vagina. Since her husband continued to complain, she went to another gynecologist, who also gave her genitals a clean bill of health. Since her husband hasn't let up, she still periodically takes herself in for checkups. She is unable to feel reassured that there is nothing wrong.

Other Stingy Lovers who are aware of their lack of desire are more gracious. They don't lay it on a woman. They know that something is wrong with them, but, as the cause of their problem, they point to something external. Typical scapegoats are businesses that aren't doing well, which cause Stingy Lovers to become depressed, a boss who makes life miserable, bills that can't be paid, parents who are sick, kids who are underfoot, a stock market that goes down, inflation that goes up.

No matter what these men point to as the culprit, they use it in the same way—to keep a panting woman at bay. They send out a message sure to stop a female dead in her tracks: "It would be unfair and cruel of you to add to my troubles by putting additional pressure on me about sex."

Unfortunately, Stingy Lovers always feel sex as pressure rather than pleasure.

Most of the men described genuinely feel the anxiety or depression they complain about, but among them there are also fakers who just pretend to be uptight about business, for example, in order to keep a woman from asking for sex.

The Unawares

The kinds of Stingy Lovers who are *not* consciously aware of their lack of desire generally feel, instead, just a vague sense of discomfort. The diffused anxiety disappears when they are doing something, so they tend to get obsessively involved in a wide variety of pursuits.

Many sexually Stingy Lovers become work addicts— going to their offices early and coming home late, going in on weekends, taking work home at night. Some drink or gamble.

Others lose themselves in a hobby or sport, as one young editor who became involved with a married man found out. She explained: "The only time he could see me was on weekend afternoons, lunch hours, or in the early evening. Well, after our first couple of times together, he would only meet me for lunch in restaurants. We had terrific lunches and terrific talks on the telephone, but if I invited him over to my place he always had to play tennis. He played tennis outdoors in the evening and on weekend afternoons in the summer. In the winter he switched his game to an indoor court. I began to think the only way I was ever going to get him into bed with me again was if I put on white shorts and sneakers."

The ex-wife of a Stingy Lover described her former husband's tactics: "He built model airplanes, he played cards with his cronies late into the night. He took up parachuting and he flew airplanes. But finally he found the perfect out—he became interested in ham radio. He could then stay up until all hours of the night because somewhere in the world, in a different time zone, there was someone awake he could talk to."

Another kind of semi-aware Stingy Lover is a very frightened man.

He feels extraordinarily vulnerable, and caution in all things is his motto. Most frightened men lead constricted lives and choose the safe, sure way of doing things, but there is a minority who act in a manner directly opposite to how they feel. They battle their terror by deliberately seeking out dangerous situations or occupations. They become, for example, test pilots. Whether the frightened man reacts to his dread by always looking death in the face, or whether he chooses to tiptoe through life—his reaction to sex is always the same. Sex makes the frightened man feel vulnerable, so he avoids it like the plague.

All sexually Stingy Lovers are men who feel to some degree inadequate, either consciously or unconsciously. Their sense of self-esteem is generally low, and often they use sex symbolically as proof that they are not up to snuff. Some fear that they are poor lovers, or that they will be unable to satisfy a woman. Others feel that their penises aren't large enough, so they avoid erotic situations in which their inadequacy would be revealed.

The Hidden Sex Life of the Stingy Lover

Except for a small number who repress their sexuality completely (burying it often in a heavy program of work or sports), Stingy Lovers don't give up sex *per se* at all. They just avoid it with women they are close to. They find their outlet in frequent masturbation, or, if they are married, they may carry on torrid affairs with other women while their wife is still on hold.

Single men who are sexually stingy with their girlfriends soon after the relationship starts, have a direct phobia about sex. But husbands who begin to avoid sex with their wives only after marriage, are reacting more to the commitment than to their sexual fears.

For the sexually stingy husband, intimacy creates anxiety. He often feels trapped in his marriage and apprehensive that his inadequacies will be revealed. His wife, by repeated contact, will realize that he is not as good a lover as other men, or that his body, particularly his penis, is not good enough. Adding to the stingy husband's woes is the fact that he becomes more dependent on his wife the closer he feels to her. And the more he relies on her, the more afraid he is that she will abandon him. Terrified and apprehensive, he begins to scrutinize the relationship as if through a microscope. In the process he loses all spontaneity—including the ability to have sex in response to desire.

The sexually stingy husband soon loses touch with his sexual feelings. If he consciously felt lust, he would have to act on it. And if he did, he wouldn't be good enough and his wife would leave him, or so he feels somewhere deep inside himself. In effect, withdrawal from sex is the Stingy Lover's way of running from commitment and its concomitant anxieties—the terror of being abandoned, the fear of being judged deficient by someone important.

Since intimacy is what causes Stingy Lovers to be inhibited, they often do better in more casual relationships—Hit-and-Run encounters, or longer affairs that are not taken too seriously.

One salesman told me about his first marriage to a woman with whom he had been having a wild affair. Before she became his wife, Rick remembers sleeping with her in all kinds of places in the heat of the moment—on the roof of her apartment house, on a pile of carpets in her father's store. "But right after the marriage, I don't know why, I just began avoiding her," he said. "I would go out and pick up waitresses with big tits, almost anybody. I would fuck all kinds of women who disgusted me. But Diane, at home, whom I really cared for, I couldn't stand the idea of going to bed with her. I blamed it on her getting fat, and her sloppy ways around the house. But that wasn't it. I finally had a long affair with a neighbor, and my marriage broke up."

Some husbands, however, turn out to be as turned off with their paramours as with their wives.

Although the sexually Stingy Lover is bad on follow-through, in marriage and affairs he can be great at the beginning of a relationship. The need to win a woman is so important to his ego that it allows him to forget his anxiety for the moment and to function sexually, sometimes in a very intense way. He may be constantly filled with desire. But the same thing that turns the Stingy Lover on so much one week may turn him off the next, causing bewilderment to the object of his passion when his ardor suddenly drops.

There are other Stingy Lovers, however, who never have strong desires, even at the beginning of affairs. Nevertheless, they know it is important to consummate a relationship, so they force themselves to take a woman to bed.

Often men with meager heterosexual yearnings have strong homosexual ones, but they deny their inclinations even to themselves. As a result, when they deal with women they are operating only on the smallest part of their sexual drive. On those rare occasions when they end up in a woman's bed—generally because they feel they should—these men often have homosexual fantasies while having heterosexual intercourse.

Hidden homosexuals make up only a small part of the population of Stingy Lovers, however, and since their brothers in stinginess come alive at the beginning of relationships, they are prone to have extramarital affairs. These liaisons, at least initially, not only help Stingy Lovers lose their anxiety and make them feel animated, they also provide reassurance that they are really O.K.

The Stingy Lover feels secure in his primary relationship, but it is not enough to make him feel adequate. He is a man who generally loses confidence in himself quickly, and marriage is no exception to this pattern.

Although affairs are very attractive to the married Stingy Lover, he has no desire to get rid of his wife. His low self-esteem and sense of inadequacy make him cling to her, but, paradoxically, the more secure he feels in his primary relationship, the more he feels free to play around.

Their Marriages

His ambivalences and affairs add tensions to marriages that are generally not smooth anyway.

Frequently, the Stingy Lover, who inwardly feels weak and dependent on his spouse, is outwardly concerned about being dominated by his wife. And, feeling unlovable in his inner depths, he also tends to worry about whether his wife really cares for him sufficiently. There is never enough that a wife can do to make up for the lacks felt by a man like this, and any differences that occur are interpreted by him as proof that his wife doesn't really love him.

The sexually Stingy Lover can be difficult to live with in many other ways as well. He may be gregarious and giving outside the home, but quiet, antagonistic, and miserly under his own roof.

Fearing that his underlying inadequacies will be revealed, or resentful that he has those feelings, he hides his true nature in public, showing himself to be an unhappy, anxious person only in the safety of his own home.

While some Stingy Lovers confine their miserliness only to sex and manage to be affectionate and generous otherwise, many others can be tight-fisted with money and emotions as well. They have to control things in order to feel safe. These men are often emotionally distant, do not show affection, and don't like to touch or be touched.

Arguments are common occurrences in the homes of Stingy Lovers. For one thing, they like to keep things in an uproar. There is always something they are angry about, something that annoys them, something that isn't right. Turmoil provides a cover for what is really going on—which isn't to say that genuine tensions don't exist. After all, the husband feels that his wife is after something he can't give her—sex; while the wife feels that her husband doesn't want to give her want she wants. As a result, he feels inadequate, she feels frustrated, and tempers fray easily. Fights break out over almost anything—she may pick on him for not giving her enough money, he may criticize her sloppy housekeeping—but in the background lurks the real reason for the fights; sex, and avoidance of intimacy, in general.

Adding to the tensions that adulterous Stingy Lovers create is their indiscreet behavior. Although they are afraid to be found out, they talk themselves into believing that their wife will never know, and, thus blinded, often take outrageous chances—having an affair with a wife's best friend, for example, or a close neighbor, or simply becoming blatant about their carryings-on. Carelessness in covering their tracks can also be caused by underlying guilt and a need to be caught and punished as expiation.

Lack of sexual interest, plus the possibility that her husband is having an affair, is enough to drive a wife up the wall. Many wives of Stingy Lovers spend endless hours alone or with friends trying to devise ways to be more alluring to their husbands. But they soon learn the futility of the Black Nightgown or Total Woman approach. None of the clichés work.

Since her husband wants the rest of the relationship, but not sex, the wife is in a constant dilemma. She is always trying to figure out whether the problem is his or hers.

Things are somewhat different for the wife of the Stingy Lover who admits the fault is his. If he confesses that something is wrong with him, then the woman is required to be very patient and nurse him through his work or health problem or whatever it is he thinks is the cause. But, after much nursing and unflagging patience, a point of exasperation is often reached when nothing changes.

Sometimes the wife of a Stingy Lover becomes fed up and walks out on him—but not without taking along some profound feelings of inadequacy about herself. She may find, to her surprise, that her husband suddenly ignites sexually when she begins to pack.

A successful career woman in New York who had a stormy marriage punctuated by many separations and reconciliations before her final divorce, was able to pinpoint her ex-husband's pattern in retrospect:

"Every time I left him he would come after me like a bull in heat. The minute he had me back, however, there I was horny again, and there he was doing everything else in the world but making love to me."

The Stingy Lover is able to suddenly spring into action when he is rejected, because then his fear of abandonment outweighs the fear of intimacy which blocked his sexuality. He becomes gung-ho about getting his woman back, and his anxiety dissipates. He is just as he was at the beginning of the relationship. But just let him win and, once again faced with intimacy, he is unable to function sexually.

Some rejected Stingy Lovers take another tack. When their wife decides to leave, they simply fall apart. Not only can't they operate sexually, they can't do anything else either. This behavior is either a conscious or unconscious attempt to win the women back by making her sorry for his condition. If the wife returns the outcome is always the same. He stays in the same old unsexy rut.

Sometimes it isn't the wife, but the Stingy Lover himself who decides to split when he becomes too guilty about not fulfilling what he considers to be her appropriate desires or when her sexual demands make him too uncomfortable. A wife's sexual demands may, indeed, have escalated, but often nothing has really changed; the tension at home has increased, so he feels the demands have, too.

To accommodate to the situation they find themselves in, some wives end up masturbating to get rid of their sexual frustration, but this generally leaves them feeling anything but satisfied. Others manage to suppress all of their sexual desires. Explained one woman: "After a couple of years of ignoring me, I became aware that my husband was having an affair. He practically threw the evidence in my lap. But I had two young children and I wasn't prepared to divorce him, so I kept quiet and turned myself off sexually and concentrated on raising my kids."

In the interest of preserving their marriage, some wives solve the dilemma another way. They have affairs of their own.

Since stingy husbands create a mounting sense of inadequacy in their wives, the temptation is strong for a wife to take a lover not only out of sexual need, but also to prove that she is attractive and still has sex appeal.

Thus, one often finds the marriage of a sexually Stingy Lover played out on an ironic note. Both husband and wife are having affairs at the same time and for the same reason: he, because of a basic feeling of inadequacy; she, because of the sense of inadequacy his neglect created. Both may find themselves better lovers with other partners.

Occasionally, in an affair, one or the other will find someone else and the marriage will end. If the husband remarries he is likely to repeat the pattern of stinginess with his new wife. Some marriages, however, go on forever. Despite the bickering, there may be some very good things between husband and wife. When they aren't fighting, and sex doesn't come up, they may like each other's company and enjoy many activities in common.

Stingy Lovers who manage to have smooth marriages are those who choose wives with low conscious sexual needs of their own. With them sex never becomes a problem. It simply never comes up.

Stingy Lovers can also operate better with much

younger women, or with those they regard as social inferiors. In both situations they feel superior and, therefore, less threatened. When not dealing with a peer, they
tend to be less anxious about their functioning. With a
younger wife they can rationalize by saying to themselves: "Well, naturally I don't have her energy—I'm
older." With social inferiors they think they have the right
to control the situation any way they want to, and, besides, how these women feel about them doesn't matter.
Their feelings aren't important.

Stingy Bachelors

The single sexually Stingy Lover can generally handle his problem better than a married man simply because
he can more easily manage to not date women frequently.
Also, girlfriends tend to believe his excuses—at least for
a while—either because they can't put two and two together, or because they want to believe him.

Nevertheless, most women eventually catch on or
become fed up by the lack of sex or lack of the man's actual
presence. Turnover in relationships is high among single
Stingy Lovers.

Things can end, too, when the Stingy Lover, responding to a woman's desire to see him more often as a
sign that she is "possessive," terminates the relationship
himself. He feels he is asserting masculine behavior by
refusing to be dominated.

If a relationship continues, how often the Stingy
Lover sees a woman pretty much depends on how much
pressure she does or does not exert.

Stingy Lovers want close liaisons and will have one
if they don't feel under the gun. They will see a woman
a lot if she isn't pushy about sex. If she is, or they think
she may be, they will space out their dates.

Liaisons that last are with women who, for reasons
of their own—lack of assertiveness, lack of sexual drive,
lack of a better alternative—don't put on the pressure.

This is true of a relationship that one sexually stingy
bachelor has had with a young woman for the past five
years. He doesn't sleep with her very much, and she never
complains.

Recently, as a result of therapy, he decided to end
his near-celibate existence and engage in sexual adven-

tures. The first woman he picked he pursued diligently, and when he finally got her into bed he found himself very turned on. But after enjoying himself a few times, he suddenly began to find work-related excuses to explain why he couldn't see her. He put her off, but she openly expressed her desire to see him more often. To him this was evidence that she wanted to bag him, that she was pushy, demanding, and not sufficiently understanding. He abruptly terminated their affair.

Undaunted by the failure of this relationship, he immediately tried to have sex with another woman. She was agreeable to necking with him on their first date but didn't want to have intercourse. In the middle of fooling around with her he suddenly stood up and announced, "I feel foolish," and walked out. After these two incidents he lamented to his therapist: "The only woman it seems to last with is Gloria." Gloria is the woman who is content to see him without sex.

Their Future

The chances of a Stingy Lover getting married are greatest while he is young. Later on, these men tend to become fussy, with ritualized habits and patterns that leave little room for others.

Masturbation is a big thing in the lives of Stingy Lovers at all times, and many of them in later life resort to it totally for sexual gratification, giving up on women altogether as they get older, or relegating them to the role of "buddies" with whom there is no expectation of sex.

Even if this happens, the Stingy Lover who doesn't marry generally does better in life than does the eternally single Hit-and-Run Lover or the unattached Juggler. He has displaced his anxieties about sex or sublimated his sexual energy into involvement in other activities. He has hobbies, sports, work, which tend to keep him busy, while the man who has focused his entire life on conquering women is left, ultimately, with nothing.

Stingy Lovers also tend to have better relationships with other men than do many of the Hit-and-Run Lovers and all of the Jugglers, although with their male buddies they often stay away from the subject of sex.

If the Stingy Lover were to express his ideas about

sex, he might sound like a square and a staunch guardian of the double standard. Many Stingy Lovers feel on some level that women who sleep with men are whores.

The Stingy Lover is anxious about sex, and frequently this anxiety is transposed into a punitive attitude toward women who are sexual. Some Stingy Lovers outwardly sound more liberal about sex, but don't let it fool you. Inwardly they also maintain puritanical standards about a woman's sexual conduct.

Causes

The madonna/prostitute syndrome, a common male attitude that associates sex with "bad" women and no sex with "good" women, plays into the sexual insecurities and problems about intimacy that plague the Stingy Lover.

No matter what went on before, with commitment comes the feeling that the wife is a good woman; and once defined as such, she also becomes untouchable.

One intelligent young wife who realized that this was her husband's problem, told how, in desperation, she tried to turn herself into a bad woman for a night.

Like Scheherazade, she decided to invent a tale—a naughty one—in order to excite her husband. She made up an elaborate fictitious account of a sexual adventure with two men that was supposed to have taken place before her marriage. Her husband, she explained, got very excited by her story, but he had to squelch his desire by reminding himself—and her—of her true role. He whispered: "Do you swear it's true? Do you swear it on the head of your son?" As a result, there was no sex that night either.

When a wife gives birth, things can get even worse for the man who unconsciously associates mother and motherhood with incest.

A woman in the role of parent can become a sexual no-no even if the kids she is taking care of are not his, as one man who married a divorced woman with two children found out:

"Everything was great until the whole family moved in after the wedding," he explained. "Then, all of a sudden, I saw her for the first time on a day-to-day basis with the kids. Her mother role suddenly became a big one in our life together, and the more I saw her as a mother, the less sexy she became to me. I guess you don't fuck Mommy," he lamented.

For some of the men who turn off after the birth of a child, the problem is not one of incest, however, but of hostility. This is true of men who don't want to be fathers—either consciously or unconsciously. They resent the additional responsibility and, blaming their wives for having the baby, they withdraw from sex as punishment.

Other men, who need to feel central in their relationship with a wife, feel usurped by a baby and retaliate by taking sex away from the woman who isn't paying enough attention to them.

Again, what is often blamed for the sexual turn-off is something that really has nothing to do with it. A young husband who entered therapy at the insistence of his wife claimed that he didn't want to sleep with her because of an odor from her skin that he found repugnant. Upon questioning, he admitted to his therapist that he had never noticed the odor before the baby was born. Eventually realizing what his real problem was (envy of the infant's place in his wife's life), he was able to resume the good sex life he had had with his wife before.

The idea that sex is a sin outside of marriage or when it is not for the purposes of procreation, is fostered by certain religions. Sexually stingy single men are not uncommon among men raised as Catholics, for example. As a bachelor, a young man reared in a religious home will sometimes give in to an urge and have sex, but he is so burdened by guilt afterward that he is reluctant to repeat the experience. In marriage the madonna/prostitute syndrome takes over—the wife becoming the "pure" woman with whom sex is out of the question.

Some Stingy Lovers identify sexuality with hostility and therefore withdraw from sex with a women they love because of fear and guilt about subjecting her to their aggression.

Others are afraid that their sex drive is too strong to be satisfied by just one woman. Therefore, in order not to jeopardize their marriage by affairs, they suppress sexual feelings altogether.

A small number of Stingy Lovers are men who suffer from a sexual dysfunction. They avoid sex as often as possible so as not to reveal their sexual problems—impotence or premature ejaculation, for example.

Backgrounds

What originally causes sexual stinginess in men varies greatly, but one study pointed to a common pattern in childhood. Many husbands who avoided sex with their wives reported close attachments to women as they grew up—mothers, sisters, aunts, and grandmothers. In many cases the men felt trapped and controlled, as children, by these adult women.

When they subsequently married, their childhood feelings came back to haunt them. In marriage they again felt trapped by a woman—this time their wife—and they revolted at the idea of again being controlled. They felt that sex was now something they *had* to indulge in as a marital duty.

Withdrawal from sex became a rebellion against the ghost of a controlling, overbearing, and demanding woman from the past.

In other cases, the Stingy Lover grew up in a home where his mother was constantly finding fault with his father. He felt under tremendous stress to perform better than his father. Since he found he couldn't live up to his mother's expectations, he later approached all women with an underlying expectation of failure.

Even when he isn't pressed by his wife to perform, a man may feel inadequate and become a Stingy Lover if his mother constantly denigrated his father. Seeing his male model regarded as inferior, he inferred from this that he, too, was inadequate.

Ironically, the mother who praised her son too much could also have turned him into a Stingy Lover. The boy whose mother thought everything he did was marvelous, knew better. Not everything was that terrific, he realized, so he stopped believing her at all. At the same time, he constantly tried to perform better to merit her praise, but since he didn't believe her compliments, no matter how good he was, he always felt as if he had failed. This sense of failure in the eyes of his mother he transferred into later dealings with all women.

Sidney, a twenty-nine-year-old lawyer, grew up with a mother who put down his father but never found fault with Sidney. Even as a youngster Sidney was expected to change light bulbs better than his father, to remember hopping lists better than his father, to do everything better. Sidney was a good student at school, but he never worked hard at what he did. When a school subject or a sport became too hard for him, he withdrew from it. He sought the easy way with women, too, as he got older. He went out only with those who seemed interested in him rather than seeking out women he desired on his own. His love affairs always ended up the same way. He would start out passionately involved with each woman, but soon he would start finding fault with her. He would withdraw not only sexually but emotionally. When a woman complained about his cool behavior, he always left saying they expected too much from him.

When Sidney was in his mid-twenties he met a younger woman whom he married after a short courtship. Although he liked her childlike and dependent ways at the beginning of the affair, he soon started to feel that she was too dependent. He began to criticize her for not being able to get her life together on her own. Her good looks, which originally attracted him, suddenly appeared drab and Sidney lost all sexual interest in her. When she began to show her unhappiness Sidney blamed himself for it and became resentful toward her because she made him feel guilty.

Sidney found himself in a marriage where, again, a woman depended on him too much, as his mother had, and he felt as resentful toward his wife as he did as a boy toward his mother.

Another kind of mother who can turn a son into a Stingy Lover is one who was sexually stimulating to her child. The anxiety thus provoked is repeated in all sexual encounters as an adult, causing him to avoid sex as much as possible. A single mother who parades a succession of lovers through the house can also create such resentment of female sexuality in a son that he expresses it later by withholding sex from all significant females.

Although smothering, overly protective, seductive, demanding, or overly critical mothers seem to play a part in the background of many Stingy Lovers, so do fathers who did not provide their sons with an adequate male model. A boy whose father is totally absent or away from home for long periods has no male figure to imitate as he grows into manhood. He also often feels responsible for taking his father's place in his mother's life. And since,

no matter what he does, he can never take the place of h
father and thus make up for his mother's unhappine
he often feels that he has failed. This feeling of failure
carried with him later into close relationships wi
women.

Occasionally, the cause of a lover's stinginess ma
be repressed incestuous wishes toward a female memb
of his family, as in the case of a man who shared a roo
with his younger sister until he was seventeen years ol
He describes his marriage as being "like between broth
and sister," and, since he avoids sex with his wife, he
not far wrong.

Current Increase

Today there seem to be more complaints about sex
ually stingy husbands in divorce courts, sex clinics, an
marriage counseling offices than there used to be. Som
people feel that the number of sexually stingy men ha
increased in our society. But it is hard to determin
whether men who withhold sex have multiplied or whethe
they have simply lost their cover.

Before the early 1960s a man could date a woma
for some time and get away without having sex becaus
women were supposed to be "saving themselves" for mar
riage.

And in marriage, in even earlier times, if a husband
didn't sleep with his wife very often it was either a relie
to her (because she didn't like sex anyway) or she felt she
had to put up with it to preserve her family unit. This
rationale, of course, was current before divorce became
a national pastime and, in the process, lost most of its
stigma, and before the sexual liberation of women made
wives feel that they were entitled to a good sex life.

The sexually Stingy Lover today stands more ex
posed than ever before in history. And the pressure is on
him from all sides.

For one thing, women of the seventies have increased
his basic fears. Females of the past may have been thought
passive and subservient, but it is hard to regard women
today as anything less than peers. Today's woman is often
as educated as the Stingy Lover and she may have just as
good a job. She can be outspoken as well. The aggressive
woman who is his equal is someone the Stingy Lover is

increasingly afraid to tangle with. Her potential for putting him down, in bed and out, is too great—or so he thinks.

Another thing that troubles the Stingy Lover about women today, is that they are more sexually experienced than in the past. He is worried now about how he compares to a woman's previous lovers, and he may withdraw in the face of competition.

Life was never much fun for the sexually Stingy Lover, but today he may find it impossible.

Chapter 5

Men Who Never Make Passes

Going one step further than the sexually Stingy Lover is the fellow who never ever makes passes. This man takes you to dinner, or the theater, or a movie, goes home with you, waits around your living room, and then after a while says something like, "It's late" and just packs up and goes home.

A middle-aged, prominent doctor in New York is famous for this kind of behavior. He dates sophisticated, attractive women, many of whom know one another. They have compared notes and they all say the same thing—he has never attempted sex with them, and they don't know anyone else with whom he has had an affair.

One New Year's Eve, he invited a thirty-eight-year-old dress designer to go out with him, stay over at his place, and bring a change of clothing. "Separate bedrooms," he assured her—and, to her amazement, he stuck to his word.

On the West Coast a twenty-five-year-old publicity woman recalled her frustration and bewilderment after going out with a movie director.

"He was so attractive and we got along fine, but although we went out several times, nothing happened even though I wanted it to. Twice he came over to watch television with me. Since the TV is in my bedroom, we both stretched out on the bed after the set was turned on. Wouldn't you think he would make a move then? I would have welcomed it. But no such luck. He never did and we never slept together."

On the East Coast a similar thing happened to a city planner. "I met Grant at a friend's birthday party. He asked me out to lunch and dinner a few times. We liked to talk to one another and we got into the habit of having long telephone conversations. A couple of times he came over and we sat together on the couch, and he told me the various things he liked about women and about his work.

"I thought he looked at me like he wanted to have sex, but he never made a pass. I certainly wasn't going to be the one to start anything, and so pretty soon I adjusted my thinking about him. I began to regard him as just a friend and started to look around for other men."

The dress designer, the publicist, and the city planner all admitted the same thing. As a result of their exposure to Men Who Never Make Passes, they alternated between wondering "What is wrong with him?" and "What is wrong with me?"—a common reaction to men who exhibit no sexual interest.

The dress designer thought the doctor was "crazy," but since he was her first date after being rejected in a love affair that had lasted five years, she found herself sinking into a depression. She was sure now that she was getting too old for men to find her attractive.

The young publicity woman said she thought her friend was "impotent"—but, at the same time, scrutinizing herself in the mirror, she decided that she was too fat and needed a different hairdo.

The city planner called Grant "a fag," but he made her feel so undesirable she went on a shopping spree and bought too many clothes that cost too much, in an attempt to make herself feel more appealing. Also, she slept with the first man who came along, in order to reassure herself of her desirability.

You don't have to tangle personally with asexual men to be aware of their presence in our society. They are sometimes called "neuters."

An East Coast politician is well known for his asexual

mage. He is in his fifties but he has never been married, has never been known to have an affair with a woman either, although he numbers women among his business associates and friends. The rumor of asexuality persists about a prominent politician in a large western state as well.

In less rarified circles the asexual can also be observed if one is astute. He can be found at large singles events. He is the man you spot standing all alone the entire evening. The room can be full of attractive, lonely, available women, but the asexual man does not talk to any of them. He may talk to no one at all, but if he does it is likely to be to another man. He never leaves with a woman, yet he is always back at the next singles event, where he again remains aloof. Or he may be the man who is friendly and affable with practically every woman in the room, but he never makes a choice. He goes home alone, also.

There are several kinds of Men Who Never Make Passes. Some are Complete Asexuals. They have suppressed almost all libidinous thoughts, fantasies, and desires. Sex seldom enters their heads, and they have no desires or erotic life with women, although they may occasionally have a sexy masturbatory fantasy.

Others are asexual in deed but not in thought. Functional Asexuals have desires that are alive and well, but they are unable to put them into action. Afraid to make a pass, they get rid of their sexual tension through frequent masturbation sparked by erotic fantasies, often of low-down lecherous females who come on very strong.

Some men will never make a pass themselves, but if a woman makes the first move, the Passive Male snaps into action.

Other men who seem to be asexual are actually Underground Sexuals. They would never think of making a pass at a woman they think is "respectable." They reserve their desire instead for streetwalkers or call girls.

One accountant who is an Underground Sexual turns his paid-for nights into imitations of normal dates. He uses only very attractive, high-priced call girls whom he wines and dines in style before having sex.

Another man whose sex life was hampered by his inability to have intercourse with anyone but prostitutes,

solved his problem in a very practical way. He married
his favorite "pro."

Other Men Who Never Make Passes are paralyzed
sexually only with women they think may be candidates
for a long or serious relationship. Selective Sexuals take
out women they like but leave fast at the end of an evening, saving sex for more anonymous encounters with
women they don't care about.

All Men Who Never Make Passes share a basic feeling
of inadequacy that usually started early in life. Doubts
about themselves crystallized as they grew older into specific fears about their capabilities as lovers or their ability
to sustain an intimate relationship.

Complete Asexuals

The Complete Asexual, oddly enough, has made the
most comfortable adjustment to his fears. He learned
early in life to transfer his desires from sex to other activities in which he felt more successful. One good example of this is Paul, a middle-aged lawyer who has never
had intercourse with a woman. Frail and thin as a child
he grew up feeling shy and awkward. He was not well co-
ordinated and was considered clumsy by everyone. But
Paul, who was aware of his problems and did not feel good
about himself initially, soon found a solution to his basic
lacks. His friends were active in sports, but he decided
since he wasn't a good player, to become the team manager instead. He found himself accepted and liked in this
role and began enjoying himself so much that he stopped
wanting to be a player.

When the time came, during adolescence, to date
girls, the same sort of adjustment took place. Paul originally wanted to take out the same lively, good-looking
girls his friends ended up dating, but after a few attempts
that failed, he turned himself into the girls' friend—someone they could talk to and come to with their problems.
Paul found himself so successful in his role of confidant
and buddy that he lost his original desire. He no longer
wanted to date girls. He was happy just to be their friend

When Paul grew up he carried his early adaptation
into adulthood. He was content to see a woman as a friend
but he had absolutely no desire to sleep with her.

Complete Asexuals, like Paul, often come from homes

where sex was either considered unimportant or looked down upon.

Paul's parents, for example, valued only things of the intellect or spirit and considered matters of the flesh "coarse." Classical music was what they approved of, and popular songs with sexual lyrics were considered inferior. Book with sex scenes were considered "trash."

Paul, in suppressing all his sexuality, not only removed himself from a part of life fraught with failure, he also incorporated his parents' values. His mother and father had conveyed the message that sex is not important—and he believed them, to the point of expunging it from his life. Also, since his parents showed no discernible interest in sex between themselves, Paul had no model for sexuality to pattern himself upon. This is often the case with Complete Asexuals.

Paul became an amiable bon vivant, successful in his career and active in the cultural events of the city he lived in. But the range of adjustment to life in general is wide among Complete Asexuals. Some become dry, remote scholars who, if they don't live in an ivory tower, cloister themselves behind mounds of books and papers. Work addiction is common to asexual men. They can spend long hours climbing corporate ladders, or fill up their days and nights tending to patients as doctors.

The Complete Asexual is remarkably free of tension and conflict. He suffers no psychic pain. He fully accepts his lack of sexual interest. It's part of his nature, he feels.

Functional Asexuals

On the other hand, the Functional Asexual is in a constant emotional dither. He is a mass of unfulfilled desires. He gets horny, he has sexual fantasies, but he freezes with a woman. Unlike the Complete Asexual man, who is at peace, the Functional Asexual is discontent, full of self-hatred and dread.

He cannot act on his desires because of two fears. He is in terror of a woman's rejection, but he is also in terror of *not* being rejected. "Suppose she *doesn't* reject me," he thinks, in panic. "Then I would fail!"

How this double emotional whammy can work is illustrated by the behavior of Rick, a thirty-two-year-old car salesman whose earliest sexual contacts were with prostitutes. Although he functioned fairly well with them, he found himself filled with doubts when he finally had intercourse with a girlfriend: Was he really a good lover? Was he really satisfying her?

His requests for reassurance from his girlfriend annoyed and irritated her, which, in turn, convinced Rick that he was an ineffectual bedmate. He became more and more timid about making advances to girls until, ultimately, he found it impossible to attempt intercourse at all.

For the past ten years he has dated women only until he felt they wanted intercourse. This system reduced his fears about rejection but increased his fear of not being able to perform well when the time was right. At this point of danger he always has to break off the relationship.

Functional Asexuals have often had an early experience with sex that was frightening or disconcerting. It could have been a girlfriend's anger, as in Rick's case, or it could have been a woman who made fun of his lovemaking.

Or a negative message about sex may have been conveyed by his parents. The man who has desires but can't act on them has often been taught to think of sex as dirty, bad, or sinful. The no-no messages in his mind conflict with the yes-yes urges in his groin, and he becomes paralyzed. He wants to, but feels he shouldn't, so he can't— at least with women.

Alone in his own bed his anxieties abate, since his concerns with women not only come from guilt about sex itself, but fear of rejection and doubts about his ability as a lover. In a heterosexual situation he feels at a woman's mercy. But alone he feels safe and in control. During masturbation the Functional Asexual does not have to worry about whether he will be accepted or not. There is no one to criticize his performance.

Interestingly, as he begins to date, the Functional Asexual is often filled with hope. In the back of his head is always the fantasy that somewhere in the world is a woman so warm, nurturing, and understanding that she will accept him no matter what happens. And occasionally—very occasionally—the asexual man will think he has met such a woman. If he feels warm and comfortable enough he may try the dreaded thing: sex. But, unfortunately, because he is filled with anxiety, he often climaxes too quickly. Premature ejaculation does nothing to rid him of his terror of failure and his fear of rebuff. The woman's reaction may be amazingly kind, understanding, and warm, just as in his fantasies, but it will not matter. The Functional Asexual will break off the sexual relationship and return to the deep freeze as far as females are concerned. His worse expectations have been realized. He has failed.

The Passive Male

The Passive Male, who wants a woman to make the first move, is waiting for sex to happen to him. If the opportunity arises he will not run. Not only will he respond to an overture, he may even turn out to be a good lover. He is simply playing it safe; he wants to be dead sure he won't be rejected. The only way to be absolutely certain, of course, is to leave the entire matter in the hands of the woman. He is playing the same role women have had to play for centuries.

The basic trouble with the sex life of the Passive Male is that women have not been trained to be sexual aggressors. A woman may even pick up the vibes that her date wants some action from her, but she may be afraid to do anything either. Like him, she fears rejection, but perhaps worse, something tells her, despite Women's Liberation, that it would not conform with her female role to take the lead. So they sit around—he waiting for her, she waiting for him—and chances are nothing will ever happen between them. Passive Males cannot make out with Passive Females. *Someone* has to begin.

Passive Males often lead pretty arid sex lives. One very attractive, well-spoken man who hadn't had sex for three years when I talked to him, told me about his lifelong pattern:

"I was twenty-one before I had intercourse. Before that, the closest I ever came was with a friend of my sister's who pursued me. She let me put my hand on her naked breast. Then I was in Italy one summer and I became friendly with a wealthy Italian man. He sent a girl to my room, and that's how it happened. I didn't have sex for years after that. I have always had great difficulty making overtures to girls. Once things get started, I am beautiful, but what I am not good at is initiating things.

I don't want to be thought a boor or a slob, so unless she comes on to me, rather than risk that, I'll withdraw."

This man is in his early forties, but Kenneth Keniston, Professor at M.I.T.'s School of Humanities and Social Science, in *The Uncommitted*, his classic study of alienated youth, reports that he found many young men of college age who could not initiate sex. Here are how four of them described their hangups:

—"If intercourse must result because of aggressive foreplay on the part of the boy, it is something I am incapable of doing."

—"My ideal partner would be an aggressive woman who would take the initiative in beginning preliminary activities."

—"When I go with a girl I am overly passive, and this is the usual reason for the break between us, which always seems to come."

—"My major sexual fantasy consists in girls just coming to me with no effort on my part and seducing me."

Kenneth Keniston found that passive men, like his subjects, often have very close relationships with strong mothers and weak relationships with absent or aloof fathers. These men tend to identify more with their mothers than their fathers, which results in great doubts about their own masculinity.

Many of these men are dependent personalities, wanting, even as adults, to be taken care of by women as they were by their mothers. By leaving it up to a female to initiate sex, they are, in effect, turning over the responsibility for their sex lives. The woman makes the first move and is the one in charge.

Some men who are passive sexually are passive in other areas of their life as well, preferring, for the most part to be followers rather than leaders, imitators rather than innovators in jobs, in public, in family life. Others confine their passivity to sex, the one area where they feel most vulnerable and feel worst if rebuffed. They are active and dynamic outside the bedroom.

Once involved in an affair, the Passive Male can be a wonderful companion to a woman, sensitive and understanding, capable of a long, caring relationship.

Some Passives, however, are secretly "macho." By waiting for a woman to make the first move, they are taking secret pride in making her do all the work. When she does what they want, they feel triumph. Unlike the other Passives, this type is really a hidden Aggressive. He needs to stay in control. The woman may make the first move, but he is convinced he made it happen and that he is, therefore, still in charge.

The Passive/Aggressive's macho thinking contains an edge of hostility toward women. There is some fear of women deep down in all Passive Males which potentially could give rise to antagonism, but most of them function benevolently. They think of women as motherly, nurturing creatures who will take care of them.

The Underground Sexual

In contrast, men who have sex only with prostitutes are woman haters—their malevolence sparked by a deep terror of women, whom they fear, on some level, will harm or control them.

Many of them have had parents who planted in them a deep-seated doubt about their basic worth. They may have had overly critical or overprotective mothers. The child felt that something was wrong with him if he was constantly criticized or not allowed to do things on his own.

A seductive mother may have left her son with the feeling that sex with "good" women is tinged with incest and, therefore, taboo.

An aloof mother who never showed much interest may have made her son feel unimportant.

A narcissistic, totally self-absorbed mother who made family life revolve around her, may have left her son feeling controlled by women and resentful because of it.

An embittered mother who always talked about how men are no good to women may have made her boy feel, since he was male, that he was that way, too.

Other mothers may have left the impression that sex is revolting and that a woman engages in it only as a duty. As a result, the man resorts to prostitutes. He doesn't want to inflict this terrible duty on ordinary women.

Generally the fathers in these situations either didn't or couldn't do anything to offset the mother's actions.

Certainly the madonna/prostitute syndrome plays

into the needs of the Underground Sexual. He neatly divides women into two categories—"bad" ones for sex, and "good" ones whom you dare not sully with your filthy lust.

He can only relate to women in a demeaned position. In effect, by dehumanizing the female whose favors he buys, he manages to reduce his anxieties about himself.

Since the prostitute is a "nothing," he doesn't worry about whether she will find him acceptable as a man. He knows she *has* to—that's what he has paid her for.

Some men who limit their love life to hookers have no social interaction of any kind with ordinary women. They go around with "the boys" and spend their time in activities that exclude females.

Many treat prostitutes like the dirt they think they are, sometimes releasing their hidden hatred of women by being sadistic, verbally abusing the "pro," or shoving her around.

Others, for whom prostitutes are their only contact with the opposite sex, try to be friendly. They may ask her about her life, or tell her their troubles, in an attempt to turn the transaction into a pseudo relationship. This kind of man is liable to take a call girl to dinner or go dancing with her before having sex.

Some Underground Sexuals may date ordinary women but reserve sex for prostitutes. They go out in the normal fashion because they feel they have to. They may move in circles where it is expected of them, or they may have to attend business functions, where men always escort women.

An Underground Sexual on a regular date will be visibly uncomfortable with the woman he is with, afraid of her expectations unless he feels it is absolutely clear to her that the relationship is to be platonic. The more that is spelled out in advance, the more relaxed and friendly he can be.

Generally Underground Sexuals have dealt with prostitutes all of their adult life, but occasionally the pattern starts only after a trauma. A New Jersey real estate man became so embittered toward women after a divorce in which he felt his wife stripped him financially, that he won't go near anyone but a call girl.

A small minority of the men who rely on hookers are antisocial. They live like hermits and resort to prostitutes in preference to going out and mingling with suitable women. Since this kind of man hides from people, you will probably never meet him.

The Selective Sexual

The man who ignores women he likes or looks up to, saving his sex for hit-and-run encounters or females he looks down upon, is similar in some ways to the Underground Sexual, the man hooked on hookers. Both have divided womankind into distinct camps. There are the women whose opinions you respect and who, therefore, scare you; and the others, with whom you are comfortable because you don't respect them and it doesn't matter to you what they think. The "bad" ones are for sex.

Such a man may have had a critical or demeaning mother who left him feeling that women you care about are to be feared. Or he may have experienced failure with girls that left him feeling unable to compete successfully with other men for a desirable woman. When, as an adolescent, he found he couldn't make out with the popular girls, he may have turned instead to girls who were unattractive, fat, handicapped, or stupid, or even the town's bad girl who would sleep with anybody. As an adult he continues his pattern of shunning competition by only going for undesirable women.

For him, sex has been defined as the great test in the sky. If you pass the test you are acceptable as a person and a man; if you fail, you are a weak, ineffectual, no-good son of a bitch. The godlike creature who hands out such a life-and-death grade is the woman you like—someone you could be serious about. To avoid the test is to arrange not to fail it.

Sometimes a man becomes paralyzed not by someone he likes but by someone he believes is his superior. This could be a woman who has a better education, someone much richer, or a woman from a higher social class.

Stanley came from a solid middle-class family and always felt in awe of people of money or high social standing. As a lover he had no problems in hit-and-run encounters, but he ran into trouble in relationships that seemed more important. When he met a woman whose parents were in the social register he found himself in her elegant Park Avenue apartment, unable to make a

move toward her sexually. Stanley was thunderstruck to
discover, after she had broken it off with him because he
wasn't interested in her physically, that she was known
to be promiscuous, with a reputation as a "nyphomaniac."

Men like Stanley don't pay much attention to what
women they look up to are really like. They worry too
much about possible rejection from a woman who counts,
or the part of society she symbolizes. A rebuff would be
so dire that they refuse to even take that great test in the
sky.

Some Selective Sexuals get tied into knots of anxiety
around women they are drawn to. As a defense against
the attraction, and possible rejection, they may be automatically hostile or sarcastic in initial interchanges.

Around attractive women they are also prone to irritability, outbursts of anger, or withdrawal into a "Mr.
Cool" stance.

If, despite their initial hostility and inner stress, a
relationship miraculously does start, it rarely lasts—because it cannot be consummated.

The Selective Sexual, throughout it all, continues
with his one-night stands, affairs with women he thinks
are "second class" or "dogs" or "pigs." There is not much
of a chance for anything more to grow from any one of
these encounters, because the minute this kind of man
sleeps with a woman he labels her, consciously or unconsciously, a "whore."

The Men in Hiding

Scattered among the Men Who Never Make Passes
are those who are hiding a sexual dysfunction like impotence or premature ejaculation. They are afraid to start
an affair because their failings will be revealed.

Also among them are men in flight from homosexuality. They are in such terror of their "gay" inclinations
that they cut off all sexual feelings rather than recognize
them.

Others keep their sex drives alive but avoid homosexual activity. They take women out but never make a
move toward them, saving sex for masturbation to homosexual fantasies. Some are "closet" homosexuals. A
social life with women is their camouflage.

Finally, there are Men Who Never Make Passes simply because they have a very low sex drive. Some men have less need for sex than others. Their physical make-up, not neurosis or a woman's lack of appeal, keeps them in neutral a good deal of the time. These men may be healthy from a psychological point of view, but because our society says that males are supposed to want a lot of sex, they are sometimes ashamed of their own lack of desire. Wanting to conform to what is considered "normal," they are apt to show up in sex clinics today asking for help.

Situational Asexuals

Some men become asexual only at a particular stress-ful or energy-consuming period in their life. Lack of sexual interest can occur as a result of prolonged illness, for example, or intense involvement with work. One Ph.D. candidate recalled being so caught up in research for his thesis that he woke up after four months had gone by and said, "Hey, I haven't had sex with anybody in a long time." He really hadn't missed it. Anything in a man's life that makes him feel anxious can cause a temporary bout of asexuality.

It is not uncommon, for instance, for a newly divorced man who has been rejected by his wife to stay away from sex for a while. There is a double purpose to his asexuality. He may fear any further rejection at a time when he is really hurting, or he may be extremely angry at women and express it indirectly by withholding sex.

The hate-all-women syndrome can be stimulated by women other than an ex-wife. A mother or—increasingly, these days—a boss or coworker can do it, too. What a man does is take the feeling of hatred he has for the boss, or business rival, and transfer it to the women he deals with in social situations.

Another increasingly large group of asexuals are the men (and women) who deliberately turn away from sex in reaction to the *sturm und drang* of contemporary life.

Voluntary celibates can range from the victims of several traumatic love affairs to those who are disgusted with casually sleeping around.

One recent convert to celibacy, who was quoted in the New York *Times*, attributed the breakup of his marriage to "Her low sex drive, not mine," which made his decision to take a vacation from sex ironic: "My ex-wife would never believe this, but I haven't slept with a woman for three, maybe four months. I lost count. I was always cheating on her. Since the separation I've had relationships with several women, none I gave a damn about. You might say I'm taking a sabbatical from sex, to sort out my feelings. I'm also going to a shrink twice a week."

Among the sexual runarounds who turn away from sex are those whose retirement may be permanent. They are the Hit-and-Run Lovers and Jugglers described earlier—the ones who in their later years lose all interest in women. Their exile from sex is not voluntary. It is a natural consequence of their psychological problems.

Another kind of man who may begin to shun sex is the guy who feels under the gun in our highly charged social climate.

He reacts to sexually or politically liberated women as threats. He may even be intimidated by women with good jobs. The man who considers the contemporary woman a menace may not want to tangle with her in bed. He turns, instead, to the prostitute, who is clearly a non-threatening woman.

The Selective Sexual who can only take "bad" women to bed may also turn to prostitutes these days. He finds it increasingly hard to separate good women from bad, since almost all the women he knows are having sex outside of marriage. He has no trouble labeling a hooker as "bad," however, so he shifts to paid-for sex.

Perhaps the largest group of men swelling the ranks of voluntary celibates are those who are weary of the tension in sex these days. They are the men who worry a lot about their sexual performance.

Since we live at a time when men don't consider the sex act a success unless the woman is satisfied, the majority of men suffer from performance anxiety to some degree. Those who feel the stress most acutely may settle for masturbation as less anxiety-producing than sweating it out with a woman. One man described the joy of masturbation this way: "Listen, there's no hassle in it. I take my sweet time. I have my own fantasy. I can do it as long or as quickly as I want, as often as I want, in whatever way I want, and with whomever I want. I don't have the feeling that somebody is saying to me, "So, schlemiel, do something. . . .""

This kind of man finds it a relief not to have someone monitoring his performance, but eventually he will get bored with masturbation, which is lonely. He will go back to women, as will most of the other voluntary celibates, who generally masturbate, too.

The Fate of Chronic Asexuals

What happens to men who have a lifelong history of not making passes?

Some of them change.

—If he's hot to get married, the man who relates to prostitutes may end up taking one of his girls as a bride. If he does, however, he will be very nervous if he doesn't know exactly where she is every minute of the day.

—The man who can't make it sexually with women he likes may tire of his seamy life of fly-by-night encounters or sex with women he despises. When this happens he may go to a therapist, or he may force himself to take some risks and initiate affairs with women he does like. The man who can't bring himself to try will never change, but the one who does may meet with one success and, thus encouraged, try again. One success can lead to others, so that eventually a self-cure is possible.

—The Passive Male who wants a woman to take the initiative may find someone he likes who makes a grab for him. The chances of this happening are greater today than in the past, with more women willing—even eager—to be the aggressor. If this kind of man marries, however, he will probably want his wife to take charge in other ways as well, and his bride had better be prepared. He may want her to arrange all their social activities and manage the family finances.

—The Complete Asexual feels hounded on all sides today by a culture that insists that he should have an active sex life. As a result he may show up in a sex clinic, where many of his kind are beginning to ask for help. The Complete Asexual is the most likely, of all the men we have discussed, to remain unchanged, however.

For him a world without women and sex is not the fate-worse-than-death that it would be for the Hit-and-Run Lover or the Juggler. The Complete Asexual is generally content with his life exactly as it is, and the worst thing anyone can do is try to convince him that he is wrong.

As Dr. Helen Singer Kaplan, head of the Human Sexuality Program at New York Hospital-Cornell Medical Center, recently put it: "For some people, sex is fraught with so much anxiety, anger, and negative emotion that it would be a better adaptation not to risk it."

Chapter 6

The Romantic Lovers

In contrast to most of the other men one meets today, the Romantic Lover would seem to be the answer to a woman's prayers. He comes on with love in his heart and commitment on his lips.

Love and commitment sounded mighty good to Phyllis, who had just been through two unsatisfactory affairs when she met Fred. One ex-lover had been a secret Hit-and-Run Lover when he wasn't with her. The other was a Juggler. So when Fred told her immediately how much he cared for her, and insisted that they see one another every night, she responded with delight. And when Fred started talking about marriage a week after knowing her, Phyllis was flattered and hopeful that at last she had met someone with whom she had a future.

The first signs of trouble in what looked like paradise started early, however. If she even talked to another man in Fred's presence it drove him wild with jealousy, and if Fred didn't know exactly where she was every minute she was away from him, he had fantasies of her being with another man.

But the real moment of truth came in their second

month together. Phyllis went on a trip to California with Fred and they lived together in a rented house.

Phyllis had many friends in San Francisco and she made plans to see them. Her appointments sent Fred up the wall. Every time she had lunch with someone it resulted in a scene. And every time she talked on the telephone he went crazy after she hung up. He wanted to go with her everywhere and be with her twenty-four hours a day. Phyllis realized she could have no life of her own. Feeling smothered and upset by Fred's demands, Phyllis packed up, caught a plane back home, and started to brood about yet another failed relationship.

If Phyllis, who is a bright woman, had not been starved for a caring and committed relationship, she would have realized something was wrong sooner.

Fred's love for her, announced just twenty-four hours after meeting her, couldn't have been real. He was infatuated with a fantasy. He didn't know what Phyllis was really like as a person.

All Romantic Lovers are like Fred. They fall in love almost instantly and want you to commit yourself to a relationship totally and quickly—much too quickly. One sign that you may be dealing with a Romantic Lover is the feeling that you are being rushed.

Other earmarks of the Romantic Lover are his dogged persistence while he is trying to capture you and his irrational jealousy.

One Romantic Lover saw a car parked in front of his girlfriend's house and was sure it belonged to a man. He waited outside the house all night trying to see who would emerge. In the early morning when no one appeared, he banged on her door, forced his way in, and ran up the stairs to her bedroom, which he found empty. It turned out that the car belonged to a visitor who was staying at the house next door.

After he has landed you and established a committed relationship, the Romantic's jealousy may seem to disappear. He tends to deny negative possibilities and convinces himself that everything is so wonderful that you couldn't possibly be interested in someone else. But the jealousy is merely dormant. It can emerge again if the Romantic Lover has to be separated from you even briefly.

During your absence he thinks about you obsessively, driving himself crazy by imagining all the men you are involved with.

When he speaks to you on the phone he will often try to ferret out who you have been with and when. He may call at odd hours—very late at night, for example—to make sure you are where you are supposed to be, and that you are there alone.

If you reject him, the tendency of the Romantic Lover is to cling to his lost love anyway. He continues to think about you obsessively long past the time when most men would have gotten over the affair. The Romantic Lover may even persist with bulldog determination in fruitless efforts to effect a reconciliation. There is magical thinking attached to his behavior. It goes something like this: "If I continue to think about you, it means you are thinking of me. If I stop, you will, too. If I persist in loving you, there's a chance you will love me. If I give up, you will, too."

The Romantic is obsessed with an idealized fantasy of love, and he goes through life looking for someone to fall in love with. When he finds a candidate for his affections he lavishes affection on her. His attentions are meant to overwhelm. At the same time that he surrounds her with his love, he puts a lot of pressure on her for closeness and commitment.

Often the woman doesn't like being pushed so hard. Her instincts are to resist being rushed into commitment, but her negative reactions are generally outweighed by positive delight at being so desired.

Because they learn after a while that women can resent pressure, some Romantic Lovers teach themselves to hold back at the beginning of an affair. They appear cool, but it is only part of their game plan. Inside they feel the same old urgency.

It is difficult for the average woman to resist the Romantic Lover—he makes her feel special, precious, that she is the most important person in the world.

In our culture women have been encouraged to look for that one man who will sweep them off their feet, make them hear bells ringing. The Romantic Lover seems to fit the bill.

Bedazzled and bemused, a woman doesn't recognize the strong pressure and overpowering attentiveness for what they are—strategies of control. The Romantic Lover must get the situation firmed up so he can relax.

The Romantic Lover is allergic to uncertainty. He needs immediate gratification and can't endure frustration. He is constitutionally afraid of failure, and if he doesn't get what he wants right away he is afflicted with tremendous anxiety—rejection and defeat loom.

The Romantic Lover, ingorant of his inner dynamics, recognizes the turmoil he's in, all right, but he confuses it with the fever of love. He translates tension as need: He absolutely *must* have this marvelous woman!

So he lays siege, determined to overcome. He surrounds his beloved with attentions. He hammers at her with declarations of passion. If she resists his efforts to get her to commit herself, he keeps at her with dogged persistence.

His front-line attack appears under the guise of love, but it is really an attempt to alleviate the crushing anxiety he is suffering from because the affair remains uncertain. This doesn't mean that the Romantic Lover is consciously manipulating. He does feel warmth and desire, but he is responding to his own needs rather than the qualities of the woman he is chasing.

The truth is, the Romantic Lover never recognizes the object of his desire as a person. Initially, he views you through the haze of his fantasy. He sees you only as an ideal. As the relationship progresses, he thinks of you in terms of what he wants from you rather than what you may require as an individual.

Basically, Romantic Lovers expect women to be extensions of themselves. Sometimes they will enrich their own incomplete lives by taking over your lifestyle, friends, and interests, but more often they insist that you conform to their patterns of life. They resist any attempt by a woman at independence or individuality.

If their beloved expresses a wish or opinion that differs from theirs, they may cajole, tease, change the subject, or distract her. They are subtle in their takeover tactics, and more often than not their love object is not aware that she is being controlled.

One Romantic Lover in Chicago, under the guise of "taking care of" his girlfriend, has begun to assume total responsibility for her. He won't let her do a thing. He says he is "protecting" her. What he is really doing is robbing her of all initiative and binding her to him by turning her into a complete dependent.

Making a woman believe she is being protected, as women should be, is a common tactic among Romantic Lovers, who often fall back on macho attitudes to rationalize their actions. If they find a woman who is looking for someone to take care of her and give her life meaning, they may seem to be a godsend.

Romantic Lovers hate competition of any kind, whether from a woman's job, from another man, or, increasingly these days, from a woman's career. They tend to ignore demands created by a woman's job—or, at best, treat her job as a nuisance, which it is to the Romantic Lover, since it gets in his way.

Said one secretary who was living with a Romantic Lover: "He wanted me to quit my job and just stay home with him. I refused to do this and it was always a source of contention between us."

"I could never make him understand that in order to write well I had to get a decent night's sleep," said a free-lance writer about her ex-boyfriend. "He loved to stay up half the night drinking, and no matter how many times I told him that it was important I get home early, he ignored it and tried to get me to go with him on his all-night rounds."

By binding you to him, by wanting you with him at all times, by trying, in effect, to own you, the Romantic Lover is expressing one of his most hidden needs. He often comes on strong and macho, but his take-charge attitude is really a camouflage for deep dependency. Underneath the bluster and positive manner of the Romantic Lover hides a narcissistic, self-centered child who wants "his woman" to take care of him.

This need may surface strongly during illness when the Romantic Lover expects you to wait on him hand and foot and be at his call continually. Demands upon a woman may increase markedly also when the Romantic Lover is having career problems and needs ego-boosting.

Despite his underlying insecurity, the Romantic Lover exhibits a sure, positive feeling about himself on the surface. His manner conveys the message: "I deserve to be loved."

The Urge-to-Merge Lover

One subspecies of Romantic Lover deviates in characteristics from the general class. This is the man who is not satisfied with merely possessing a woman. He wants to go one step further. He believes the romantic metaphor of love—that two become one flesh. He wants to fuse with his beloved.

The Urge-to-Merge Lover has a weak ego and a low sense of self-esteem. With little faith in his own identity, he requires someone else to give him strength, substance, identity.

He is a very frightened person. The Romantic Lover hides his insecurities behind a self-assured and brash manner, but the Urge-to-Merge Lover lets his underlying doubts show. He always seems shaky. Decision-making for him is difficult; he cannot take on responsibility. He is much less capable of dealing with the world around him than is the Romantic. He shares the Romantic's anxiety about failure, his ability to fall in love instantly, and the same desperate need to get a woman to commit herself to him, but he is afraid to express his feelings forcefully. He may not move into the relationship as quickly.

The Romantic Lover's protestations of love may seem to you, either consciously or unconsciously, phony, incredible. His love—too soon in full bloom—has an air of unreality to it, as do his threats that he will fall apart if his love isn't returned. Even if he appears hurt, desolate, and in despair, you sense that he will survive.

With the Urge-to-Merge Lover, however, you cannot be as sure. His vulnerabilities are real and apparent. He may, indeed, self-destruct, die from a broken heart.

If an Urge-to-Merge Lover establishes a relationship, it differs in certain respects from affairs with Romantics. The Romantic will be very demanding, want to be the prime mover, try to get you to conform your life to his. The Urge-to-Merge Lover will cede *all* responsibility to you. He will want you to make all decisions, and he will often build his life around yours completely.

Marriages

In marriage the Romantic is demanding and often unreasonable. The Urge-to-Merge Lover typically ends up henpecked, trying to do everything to please his wife. Both kinds of men tend to be monogamous. They are so wrapped up in the relationship they don't have time for anyone else.

Both Romantics and Urge-to-Merge Lovers, however, are doomed to disappointment in their relationships and marriages. They approach women as extensions of their fantasies, and no woman can live up to the pictures they have in their heads. When a woman doesn't, they feel cheated.

Neither Romantics nor Urge-to-Merge Lovers can ever perceive the role they play in creating their own disappointments. The Urge-to-Merge man usually ends up feeling very sorry for himself; the Romantic is more prone to get angry at his beloved. Both refuse to accept any responsibility for their fate.

Despite their disappointments, both Romantics and Urge-to-Merge Lovers tend to maintain their marriages because of their strong dependency needs. The man who feels merged with his wife will stay married forever. He is part of her. Occasionally, however, some Romantics who have bitched about their disappointments for years will deviate from the norm and, to everyone's shock, suddenly get out and look for a new, untarnished romance.

Work

The Romantic constantly dreads failure in work as well as in personal affairs. Sometimes his fear of failure makes him work doubly hard to prevent catastrophe, so he ends up being very successful instead.

The Urge-to-Merge Lover finds himself in complicated territory in business. He needs to identify himself with an authority figure in business as in love. He works well in harness, with someone telling him what to do and giving him reassuring pats on the back, but he will fail if promoted to a position where he has to operate independently.

Some of these men put all their emotional needs into the work basket. They merge with work, in a sense—becoming in the process workaholics. Their identity is shored up by their work activities; therefore, they don't have to gain their strength from a woman. Workaholics are often quite cool and distant at home with their wives.

Despite the Romantic's tendency to success, he and the Urge-to-Merge Lover are capable of making poor business and other decisions because of their tendency toward denial of anything negative.

A Romantic husband may be oblivious to the signs that a wife is having an affair. A Romantic executive may fail to see a dangerous situation brewing in his office as well. At home and in the office he behaves as if the fantasy he carries around with him is real. When life catches up with a Romantic—if he is fired, for example, or his wife announces her infidelity—he invariably blames the boss, the wife, the other man—anyone but himself.

Since the Romantic has a low tolerance for frustration, he tends to leave the field of combat when he encounters obstacles. It is not uncommon for Romantics to flit from one job to another.

Sex and Addictions

Alcoholism and drug abuse afflict a fairly high percentage of Romantics and Urge-to-Merge Lovers. Booze and grass reduce their sense of anxiety and sustain the illusions they live by. Cures are rare because they require confrontation with reality, which is hard for the Romantic.

Sex for Romantic Lovers can take two directions. Because they are such anxious personalities, their tension often manifests itself in a lowered sex drive or an inability to maintain erections.

The sex act itself is performance-oriented—Romantics are afraid of being evaluated by a woman and failing. Since sexual problems and fear of failure make intercourse less romantic than they would like it to be, they tend to avoid it, preferring often to merely hug or touch.

Others, however, channel their anxieties into an obsession with sex. For them the bed is an altar, and sex is the most romantic moment of all. They want to have sex around the clock.

Childhood Origins

Romantics often have had fathers who were either absent or withdrawn. Without close attachments to a male figure as children, they learned to project excessive love needs onto women.

Sometimes the father perpetually found fault with his son. The mother, on the other hand, never criticized her son's efforts. He therefore turned to his mother for praise—and later, to all women for confirmation of his adequacy.

Some Romantic Lovers had fathers with a strong and blustering demeanor that hid underlying feelings of weakness. Using such fathers as models, they too came on strong, denying negative aspects of their lives.

The families of Romantics were frequently not socially active; therefore, the child often found himself alone. Without much contact with the outside world, he learned to make up his own reality.

The Urge-to-Merge Lovers, however, often had fathers who were either fearful and dependent, like themselves, or overpowering authoritarians who required strict obedience. Rejecting the tyrannical father as a model, they became passive and dependent, wanting others to lead them.

Later Life

The Romantic Lover's life of fantasy usually catches up with him by the time he reaches forty. He often leaves behind him a series of failures in business and love.

Disillusioned, in midlife the Romantic Lover may decide to give up the attempt to realize his dream of perfect love. He doesn't give up the dream, however—merely the search for its fulfillment.

He may become glum, disenchanted, discontented, or depressed when he finally sees what the real world is like. But he never accepts it. He continues wishing that everything were closer to his fantasies.

At this point the Romantic Lover may increase his use of alcohol or drugs.

The Fantasy Lover

Romantic Lovers have always existed in our culture. Broken-promise laws were instituted to protect women against their impetuous ways. Nevertheless, until recently women have far outnumbered men as Romantic

Lovers, since for centuries they were taught to think of love as their only reason for being.

Today, women are abandoning fantasy and the dream of romantic love as their *raison d'être*. As men have difficulty coping with these realistic and independent contemporary women, the ratio of male Romantics may be increasing.

An increasingly large group of men, unable to find passive women willing to mold their lives around one man, are retreating from worldly love into a more perfect fantasy of love. They dream their dreams and leave women alone. In real life a Romantic can't control women the way he would like to, but in his imagination he can.

Women today are commenting about a new man on the scene—the Fantasy Lover, who won't go any further than the scenario in his head. Fantasy Lovers flirt with women, call them often on the telephone, give off all the signs that they are interested, but they never make a definitive move to turn the relationship into a real-life affair. Their love life is all foreplay.

One woman recently met such a fellow. He called her on the telephone constantly, talked suggestively to her, but never asked her out. After pondering how to explain his odd actions to her friends, she finally hit on the right description: "He's a breather who happens to know me."

Chapter 7

Unreliable Men

It happens to every woman. You meet a man. He asks you out. You have a wonderful time. At the end of the evening he says, "Call you in a couple of days," or, "I'll call you after the weekend," or "I'll call you next week."

So you sit by the telephone, afraid to leave the house because you'll miss his call. The only trouble is, he doesn't call you until long past the time he said he would. When, if he calls at all, you finally hear his voice on the other end of the wire, he appears oblivious to his original promise.

Or:

You go out with a man and he seems genuinely warm, interested, concerned. He seems to give out signals that he likes you but when he leaves he doesn't call you again for two or three or four weeks. Each time you see him it's great. But then he always disappears. You never do know when he is going to pop up again, and when he does he acts as if no significant time has elapsed since you last saw him.

Or:

You start seeing a man fairly regularly. Everything

is all right between you except for one thing. He is always late—sometimes very late—on each and every date.

Or:

A man you are seeing frequently breaks a date he's made with you.

Or:

You are married to a man who says he'll fix the toilet, mow the lawn, paint the front door. He agrees to almost everything, but carries through with very little.

If any of the above rings a bell, you have Unreliable Man.

The Unreliable Man drives women crazy. He says one thing and does another. Or he acts as though he loves being with you when he sees you, but then, by his neglect, implies that he doesn't care very much after all.

Understandably, the behavior of the Unreliable Man frustrates and confuses women, and sometimes makes them angry.

The problem of the man who says he'll call you in a couple of days and then doesn't, can be cleared up quickly. Generally, he doesn't mean to be unreliable, and he isn't really. The trouble is semantic. When he says, "I'll speak to you Wednesday or Thursday," he translates it in his head to mean, "You'll be hearing from me." It's his way of signing off. He is speaking metaphorically. What he doesn't realize is that women tend to be more literal in their dealings with men. If they hear Wednesday, they believe Wednesday, and they hang their hopes on it, gluing themselves to the telephone on that day.

These men may be more dependable in their dealings with male friends, and they are certainly more careful about promises to get in touch with someone about business, so a touch of unconscious sexism may come into play. You don't have to be that careful with women, is what their behavior implies. Nevertheless, for the most part, this type of man is not so much malevolent as he is a careless user of language, although sometimes he keeps things purposefully vague because he fears that more precision might lead to rejection. The solution to the problem is easy.

The next time a man says, "I'll call you next week," make him clarify. Without hostility. Does he really mean next week or sometime in the indefinite future? Or wait until after the fact, then tell him about the anxiety he causes.

Unfortunately, other kinds of Unreliable Men present more serious problems. With them it's not a question of semantics, but of their neurotic drives.

Let's look first at the man who plays hide and seek.

The Disappearing Lover

The tendency is to blame yourself. "What did I do wrong?" you wonder when he doesn't follow through. Such a question is not illogical, since the Disappearing Lover generally seems sincere and interested while he is with you, and he makes you feel that something real is going on.

But the fault is not with the woman.

For some men the disappearing act is a symptom of a total life pattern. They move in and out of jobs, they have on-again/off-again relationships with male friends, they see their relatives erratically.

Such men fear close contacts or affiliations of any kind. Subliminally, in terror of rejection, they forestall it by not allowing themselves to get involved with anything or anyone.

Other men, however, limit their hide-and-seek behavior to women. In affairs they can relate closely and warmly, but not on a sustained basis. They are threatened by continuous intimacy, fearing, on an unconscious level, that they will be either rejected or suffocated by the woman. In order to prevent the anxiety that intimacy provokes, they break the contact and dilute the intensity of the relationship by not seeing the woman for a while.

Once they regain a sense of distance, they are able to resume the affair and be warm and intimate for a day or two before anxiety creeps over them once more, causing them to withdraw.

Disappearing Lovers can maintain a relationship in which they draw close, then pull away for a long time, provided the woman is willing. But women tend to become discouraged in a relationship that never deepens or improves. For the woman who expects the relationship to intensify, no change may appear more like going downhill. Therefore, turnover is generally high in the love lives of these Unreliable Men.

Unlike the man whose phobia about sustained contact colors all his relationships, this Unreliable Man may be saved from loneliness by decent ongoing friendships with male friends.

The behavior of the Disappearing Lover is largely self-protective, but a close look at what goes on inside the man who is always late reveals some malevolence toward the woman.

The Chronic Latecomer

Men who are always late constantly worry, consciously or unconsciously, about whether they are being dominated, even if this feeling has no basis in reality. When they are late it is a deliberate, if unconscious, gesture to assert their autonomy. They feel a great inner need to control situations, and by being late they prove that they are running the show. Their lateness says, in effect: "I'm not going to be controlled by you or anyone else. I'll come when I damn well please!"

They may have set the time for the date themselves, but they come to feel you are in control because you are now expecting them to arrive at the appointed hour. They become angry and hostile and assert their independence by arriving late.

Men like this, either subtly or blatantly, often feel the need to control other aspects of the relationship as well. When they walk with you, for example, they may refuse to walk at your pace, and they decide where you will go, as a couple.

One woman who is involved with a Chronic Latecomer said: "All I have to do is say I feel like Chinese food, and Jim will see to it that we end up in a French restaurant."

There is a second, a rarer, kind of Chronic Latecomer, who dawdles not because he feels he must assert himself but because he is anxious about the impending contact.

He also doesn't understand what is making him drag his heels, and he is often quite apologetic about his behavior explaining, "I can never seem to get anywhere on time."

Once he gets where he is going, and the contact is

made, his anxiety dissipates—at least until the next time and the next date. He plays none of the dominating games with women that other latecomers do.

The Chronic Date-Breaker

The man who repeatedly breaks dates usually suffers from an overriding concern about his adequacy, and most of his behavior is an attempt to prove his masculinity. Overly sensitive about anyone's impinging on his independence or taking advantage of him, and thus proving him to be a wishy-washy character or a schmuck, he concentrates on proving that he is the guy in charge.

When he makes a date, even though he has done it of his own free will, like the Chronic Latecomer he feels controlled by the fact he has the appointment, and displaces this feeling onto you, seeing you as the one who is in command. Angry and resentful as a result, he breaks the date to prove that he's boss.

A much smaller number of men break dates because they are so overwhelmed by anxiety about intimacy that they must partially withdraw from the relationship by frequently breaking their rendezvous.

Some men who chronically break dates do it only with women. Others are unreliable with the whole world. They cancel engagements with friends as well as business appointments.

It is easier for a woman to understand the totally Unreliable Man. You often hear about his peccadilloes from his friends, and he himself may tell you about jobs he's lost in the past because of his problem.

You begin to realize that his date-breaking has nothing to do with you. His behavior is just one aspect of a lifelong pattern.

If the man restricts his date-breaking to women, however, you may not understand what's going on.

You may be inclined to blame yourself. Don't. It's his problem. He feels the threat of domination or engulfment solely from women, and he breaks dates as a somewhat hostile and aggressive assertion of independence. No woman is going to control him.

The Passive Resister

The unreliable husband who agrees to do something and then conveniently forgets about it is often a Passive Resister, with problems similar to those who are late and break dates. A husband who fails to do what he promises may be saying in effect: "You're not going to dominate me!"

Other men, however, break a promise simply because they are unable to say, "I don't want to do it." Underlying this is a fear that they will be rejected if they refuse. So, instead of saying, "No," or "I don't know how," or "I'm going to have a tough time doing it," or, "You're going to have to hold my hand while I do it," they acquiesce and then never get around to it.

There is a third group of Passive Resisters who are more hidden and subtle than the rest. They are the husbands who, when a wife asks them whether they want to do something or go somewhere, answer, "Do what you want. I don't care." They end up going to appointments that the wife has made, but under protest and with such grumbling and resistance that they might just as well have not gone. They, too, don't live up to their original implied promise, which was, "I'll go along with whatever you decide." Life with them is a constant tug of war.

Marriage itself can create unreliability in men where none existed before. Commitment makes many men feel under the gun. As husbands, they experience a sense of responsibility that creates pressure for them. The pressure is so intense that it makes them want to revolt to prove that they are still free. Almost defiantly, they act in an irresponsible way, to show they haven't lost their liberty.

Some husbands were discernibly unreliable even as suitors, but their wives, lost in romantic fantasies, refused to recognize it during courtship. Only after marriage, when romantic fantasies give way to reality, is the wife forced to confront her husband's character flaw.

The fate of marriages to Unreliable Men rests largely with the wife. If she is willing to adjust and assume responsibility for the two of them, things may work out reasonably well. If, on the other hand, she continually bridles at her husband's unreliable ways, or if she has a personal investment in playing a passive-dependent role in the relationship, she may turn out to be an unhappy person in a bad marriage.

Contributing to her unhappiness may be the irritating defense mechanisms of the unreliable husband, who often blames his wife for his inadequacies with statements like: "Why didn't you tell me before?" "Why didn't you remind me?" "If you were nicer to me I'd do it."

Psychological Causes

Unreliable Men, whether Passive Resisters, Date-Breakers, Latecomers, or Disappearing Lovers, have had three basic relationships with their parents.

Their mothers or fathers may have constantly criticized them for slipshod habits—not putting their toys away, not making their beds, dawdling. The parents looked on the child as unreliable and taught him to think about himself in the same way. As an adult he now acts in accordance with his underlying image of himself.

Other parents may have set unrealistic expectations. Such was the case with Joseph. His mother and father, both successful professionals, thought all their children had to achieve at the highest levels in whatever they did. Joseph's older brother and sister lived up to their parents' hopes. They were extraordinarily talented in art and were at the top of their classes in school. Joseph, on the other hand, could neither live up to his parents' expectations nor the achievements of his brother and sister. He started to dawdle over meals, was slow to get up in the morning, and was chronically late to classes. Sometimes he didn't show up in class at all. He could then blame his lack of good grades on missing the work rather than his own poor ability. With his friends he resisted going along with the plans of the group, and insisted on having his own way.

Later in life, as an adult, he never could get to his business appointments on time, and on dates with women he would always arrive late. Once he did arrive, however, he had to be the one to make all the plans for the evening as well.

Not until Joseph entered therapy, unhappy because of repeated failures in business and love, did he begin to see that his unreliable ways were a form of rebellion. Since he felt that he couldn't live up to his parents' extraordinarily high expectations, he deliberately refused to live up to any expectation from anybody else either.

Unreliability may also stem from unresolved battles for autonomy with parents. Most children go through a negative period of development when they do the opposite of what their mothers say in order to assert their individuality—even if it goes against their own best interests. For example, if a mother asks, "Why don't you have some chocolate ice cream?" they refuse, then burst into tears because chocolate ice cream is their favorite food. Some children never resolve their negative tendencies and as adults automatically react to all requests as if they were coming from parents—and they feel they have to resist.

Men who are unreliable only with women harbor early grudges against their mother specifically. Unreliability that is more diffused, however, stems from problems with fathers, or with both parents, or with some other significant adult.

No matter what their origins, the problems of the Unreliable Man multiply with age. When he is young his behavior is often excused on the grounds that he is an irresponsible youth, but once he's out of his twenties, the world becomes less tolerant. With the onset of middle age, the Unreliable Man may find it increasingly difficult to hang onto either jobs or relationships, or both.

Upward Trend

Unfortunately, there are indications that the number of Unreliables in our society is increasing.

One of the most noticeable signs is last-minute dating. Men who feel, "I can't plan my time ahead," have spread like a disease across the land. Many of them subscribe to the "hang-loose" or "laid-back" philosophy that is popular with young people.

Hanging loose is supposed to assert that you are an individual who won't be dictated to by stodgy conventions, but, in reality, not planning ahead is a device used by people who don't want to take responsibility for their own lives. By making hanging loose a virtue, a climate has been created in which more individuals can be unreliable and get away with it.

Also swelling the ranks of Unreliables in our society are the many males who feel that it is becoming harder and harder to be a man in our culture. Traditionally, men were automatically assumed to be the backbone of dependability in the family. Today, with the emergence of more and more women as breadwinners, men often feel that they have to prove themselves, and they are not sure they can. Linked to this dilemma is the pressure many young men feel to be successful and maintain at least a middle-class standard of living.

Many young men insulate themselves from what they fear will be defeat in the fierce competition they face from women and other men in life, by withdrawing from the battle. They reject all sense of obligation to others and the traditional male role of dependability, and deliberately adopt an attitude of irresponsibility. They become Unreliables.

Chapter 8

The Bastards

When Lois met Ben it seemed like love at first sight. He immediately liked the way she looked and the way she sounded, and he told her so. "There's no one like you," he kept saying during the first three weeks of their affair. He wanted to see her constantly and flattered her all the time, telling her how different she was from every other woman he had ever known.

The first hint Lois had about Ben's true character came in the fourth week she knew him. She had been invited to a Thanksgiving dinner at her sister's.

They decided that Ben would pick her up there afterward. He would catch up on some paperwork while she was gone.

Originally Ben was supposed to come for her at nine. "But by seven," explained Lois, "my sister's kids were getting cranky and my brother-in-law was logy from eating too much. I figured it would be better not to hang around, so I called Ben and asked him if he would come earlier.

"He immediately got angry. 'What do you think I'm doing here, playing with myself?' he yelled. 'I'm working. I can't run whenever you want me to. I was going to unpark my car and come and get you and then park it again. But now I'm not going to come at all.' He hung up."

Lois was dumbfounded and immediately started to blame herself. "Why," she lamented, "did I have to call him and ask him to come over early. I could have stuck it out."

Ben never apologized, but he kept on seeing Lois. Now, however, he started to criticize her. Lois had fallen into a routine of making dinner for him. He insisted that meals be ready exactly at seven. If dinner was even a few minutes late he made nasty comments.

Several times when Ben was going to pick her up in his car and she was less than ten minutes late, he had already driven away—to punish her.

The way she kept house was also subject to constant attack, and sometimes he would make denigrating cracks about her clothing. "He was totally inconsistent," complained Lois. "He would tell me one day that I was inappropriately dressed and that I should take off the dress I was wearing and burn it. Then, when I wore the same dress two weeks later, he would say, 'That's a nice dress. Where did you get it?'"

According to Lois, who has been seeing Ben for four years, life now has to run according to Ben's rules. "He gets hysterical if I even talk to somebody on the telephone and he can't get through. And if I'm not home from work by six-thirty he calls me a runaround. When I explain that I stopped off at the supermarket, he tells me there is something wrong with the way I run my life.

"As far as work is concerned, everything he does is important, but nothing that I do counts. If he has to change plans because of something that comes up in business, that's fine, and I should accept it without complaint. But nothing about my work is allowed to interfere with his plans.

"In general, Ben fancies himself a benevolent despot," says Lois. "He can be wonderfully generous sometimes, but it has to be out of his largesse. I must never make a request for or about anything."

Lois feels that Ben has a dream of a perfect woman, someone who will cook beautifully for him and have all meals ready exactly on time. Her house will always be spic and span, and she will never run out of toilet paper. "He even wants everything in the refrigerator to be in exactly the same place all the time. If anything is moved he gets mad.

"Anything is liable to cause trouble with Ben, and you never know when something will suddenly irritate him. Sometimes, when enough irritations build up, he walks out on me and disappears for a couple of weeks. He is walking out more and more. Once a month is about average now.

"I always have to call him to get back together again. He knows I'll call and he waits. When he comes back I always try to be extra careful not to anger him and I try to do whatever he wants."

Despite the constant torture she is subjected to, Lois is convinced that Ben cares for her deeply. "Maybe that's what is driving him crazy," she says.

For Jane it also started out as high romance. She met Jean-Pierre when they accidentally brushed against one another at a party at the U.N., where he worked. It was instant electricity. Jean-Pierre asked her out to lunch the next day, and when she arrived at the restaurant he was already seated, waiting. Opposite him at her place was a rose with a little card attached. It said, "I already love you."

Jean-Pierre saw Jane constantly for a month. He would grab her in darkened streets and kiss her with fervor, or he would run his hand up her back as they talked in candlelit coffeehouses.

When they slept together for the first time he looked deep into her eyes and said something afterward that touched her deeply: "From the moment I looked at you I knew you were a passionate woman."

The bloom on the romance between Jane and Jean-Pierre began to fade a bit in the fifth week. He started to be mysteriously absent from home when she called, and he did not call her on those nights either. Then she found a woman's necklace in his apartment. He laughed it off by saying it belonged to the girlfriend of a married man who had borrowed his apartment. She accepted this with some reservations until she found some condoms hidden under some magazines a couple of weeks later. Jean-Pierre laughed, called her jealous, and said it belonged to the same busy friend.

Soon Jean-Pierre said that he would like to meet some of Jane's friends, and the way he put it—"But you wouldn't do that for me, would you?"—she got the distinct impression he wanted to see if any of them might interest him.

Then one day he called to tell her that his mother was sick. He had to fly back to Europe. He was short of cash. Could she lend him some money? She did, and when he returned he did not mention paying it back. After that, he would borrow a five here, a ten there.

Once he asked her, with irritation, why she always wanted to make love as soon as he walked in? This made her stop being amorous the next few times she saw him. He then accused her of being cold and forced her to come to bed with him instantly, not allowing her even to insert her diaphragm.

At one point Jean-Pierre asked her if she wanted to go to a party some Africans from the U.N. were giving. It turned out that Jean-Pierre wasn't planning to attend. "They're short of women," he explained. Jane felt humiliated.

Jean-Pierre was becoming more and more open about his womanizing, telling Jane it was her fault because she often had to work evenings and couldn't see him.

By this time she was feeling sick about the relationship. She knew it was bad for her and she kept trying to leave. She would send him notes telling him it was all over, but then he would call and charm her into coming back. Besides, she was hooked on him sexually.

The final straw came one day while she was walking with Jean-Pierre in Soho. He spotted a good-looking black girl sitting in a parked car. "I've never had an American Black," he mused, staring at her.

Jane, angry and upset, asked, "Do you want to go over there?"

Jean-Pierre did not hesitate. "Yes," he said. The last thing that Jane saw through her tear-filled eyes as she walked away was Jean-Pierre making a beeline for the car. She refused to see him again. When she announced her irrevocable decision to him on the phone he kept repeating sadly, "Women always let me down." Years later, when she met him accidentally on the street, he said he could never figure out what went wrong between them.

Ben and Jean-Pierre are Bastards—a breed of men whose specialty is torturing and humiliating women.

There is no end to the kind of outrage Bastards are capable of committing. One young Bastard told me with pride about a choice caper. He was having an affair with a woman in her forties to whom he was attracted, it seemed, mostly because she was rich. One evening she introduced him to her daughter, who was home from college on vacation. He proceeded to seduce the daughter while still carrying on with the mother and then let Mom know, as if by accident, what had happened. He concluded his story with a laugh, saying: "But—do you know?—the mother was better in bed!"

Another Bastard is busy taunting his divorced girl-friend these days with goodies she can't have because she was bad. She dared to go out and get herself a job, against his wishes, so now he described the glamorous trips he had planned for the two of them, ending his taunting with, "But you can't go, you have to work."

A third man, when he comes back to his girlfriend after one of their many separations, always manages to let her know, as a finale to lovemaking, how many other women he has slept with in her absence.

A fourth admits that as a gambit to keep his wife in line, he compliments her only when she looks dowdy and demolishes her when she dresses up by saying, "You look better in your housecoat."

The girlfriend of a writer knows that when he leaves to have a manuscript typed he will probably end up sleeping with the typist in order to get the price reduced—or so he will claim. She never knows who has been at the apartment they share while she works, although she often finds blatant clues—hair in the sink, lipstick on cigarette butts.

Many women have had at least one Bastard in their lives. And they are left with strong memories of them—sometimes the strongest of all their love affairs. They remember the terrible times with Bastards—but also, alas, the powerful attraction that made them put up with the rest.

The Weak Bastard

There are two basic kinds of Bastards—one weak, the other charismatic. The Weak Bastard thinks of himself as unsuccessful in the world, whether or not it is true. Bastards are apt to set very high stakes for themselves. Even if they have achieved a modicum of success, they may feel like failures if they don't meet their own extraordinary expectations. Some Weak Bastards are correct in their assessment. They do, in fact, lead marginal lives and just scrape by.

The Weak Bastard's relationship to women is governed by his reaction to his real or fantasized inadequacies. When he feels particularly vulnerable he will compensate by making himself powerful at a woman's expense. He will yell at her, for example, when something has gone wrong at work. He feels guilty about being a rat, and in between bouts of hostility he will try to make amends. He can be sweet and solicitous, when he isn't being cruel.

The Charismatic Bastard

The Charismatic Bastard is a more fascinating creature. He is often a powerful figure with a compelling quality that draws people to him. Because he is basically a psychopath with a grandiose view of himself, he never feels guilty about his actions. Indeed, he feels comfortable, not only strong and sharp but on top of things, desirable, always right. He has a powerful persona, and when he isn't being a bastard he can exert overwhelming charm.

His charisma is often reinforced by wealth or status, for he is apt to be very successful in life.

It can be created by a dazzling brilliance. There are many extremely authoritarian, extraordinarily intelligent, cold superachievers who are Bastards. Many are found in the arts and professions. There are heads of departments at prestigious teaching hospitals who treat everyone around them with contempt. There are directors in Hollywood who behave like tyrants. And there are intellectuals who use biting, sarcastic wit to chew people up or cut them down to size.

The Bastard may even be an ordinary fellow, but one with catchy charm or contagious vitality. No matter what his station in life, the Bastard almost always sends out vibes that say: "I can add something wonderful to your life."

Bastards are consummate con men. When they are trying to snare you they will do whatever is necessary to attain their objective. They are masters of lies, flattery, exaggeration, wild promises.

What the Bastard is best at, however, is sniffing out

other people's vulnerabilities. He knows instinctively what they will respond to and plays upon their healthy or unhealthy needs, like a devilish virtuoso, to get what he wants.

He knows, for example, that most women want relationships with men, and he manipulates this desire. When he meets a woman he makes her feel that the possibility for a fantastic relationship has arrived and that she is a fortunate woman, indeed, to have caught the interest of such an unusual and wonderful person.

Tactics

Although he will change his tactics to suit the woman, the Bastard is particularly adept at catering to two needs that are commonly found in women because of their traditional role in our society—feelings of helplessness and dependency.

He presents himself as Mr. Strong, a "real man" upon whom a woman can lean. Although he is eager to offer his guidance and protection, she soon learns that the price is high. She must abandon all opinions and needs of her own that conflict in any way with his.

The Bastard is totally self-centered and self-serving. In his own special world he is at dead center, with everyone else merely circling around him catering to his needs. His satellites are never seen as people. They are simply objects who serve him. In the Bastard's universe there are no objective moral values. "Good" is what suits him. "Bad" is what doesn't.

Although he may come on like a rescuer or good samaritan, he has no real interest in helping a woman. He is interested only in getting a woman to fulfill *his* needs.

What the Bastard really wants is a servant, and not just a plain old drudge, either. His female slave must also love him and prove her devotion by doing whatever he wants, down to the smallest detail. He will bully, castigate, punish, shame, or withdraw into cold silences in order to turn her into a perfect serf.

The Bastard generally uses his woman to do all the menial tasks in life while he sits back like a king. He rarely helps on a regular basis with the housework, even when the woman has a job.

One married Bastard who is having an affair with his secretary makes her run errands for him on her lunch hour. He recently went so far as to have her choose a birthday present for his wife. Exploitation like this is common with Bastards who have affairs with their employees.

The Bastard, however, doesn't see the relationship as one of exploitation. From his point of view, he is the one who is put upon. He feels he is bending over backward most of the time to put up with the vagaries, the problems, the faults of the poor, incorrigible women he has had the bad luck to become involved with. His criticisms, threats, and punishments he sees as attempts to be helpful. He is trying to help you to master your shortcomings. Once he shapes you up you will be a better human being.

What a Bastard considers a fault in his woman may vary from one time to another. Ultimately, anything that gets in his way becomes a fault to which he responds with anger.

The Money Game

Although there is a lack of consistency about the things that irritate a Bastard, there are some areas in life that seem to be favorite targets for his sadistic games.

Money, for example, is one of his pet playgrounds. A Bastard generally hates to give a woman money, although he may beg, borrow, or steal from her without a qualm.

He needs to control other people, and in marriage money is one of his favorite devices to keep his wife in line.

The married Bastard may seem particularly crazy on the subject of money because he is really of two minds about it as far as women are concerned. He wants to retain power over his wife by keeping her economically dependent. At the same time he feels that she is a parasite for living off him.

Typically, he resolves the dilemma by giving his wife a minimal allowance, making her come to him for any "extras" and begrudging her every penny. In this way he can reward a wife for good behavior, punish her for bad, a system that constantly reminds a woman of her place—at his mercy. This *modus operandi* also alleviates one of the Bastard's greatest fears. He feels that everyone is out to take him in the same way that he is out to take them. By keeping watch over every cent, the Bastard reassures himself that he is not being taken advantage of.

Still, the same husband who is miserly with his wife will often spend freely on himself or pay dearly for things he shares—expensive apartments, for example, or high-priced meals in restaurants for the two of them, or luxurious vacations.

The seesawing back and forth between luxury and penuriousness is one of the things that helps keep wives of Bastards hanging in there.

"You get used to the good life very easily," explained one of these wives. The rich Bastard is liable to give his wife a mink coat as a present, if and when he feels like it, but if she dares ask for a cloth coat to replace one that is worn out, he is apt to think she is asking for too much.

It is characteristic of all Bastards to react to any kind of request as an infringement on their liberty and to feel imposed upon by everything and everyone. They impulsively attack when such feelings are invoked.

An example of this occurred recently at a ski resort where a Bastard and his wife were skiing together. She hit a rock, one ski came off, and she tumbled down the slope. While she was lying at the bottom, bruised and frightened, her husband, instead of expressing concern about her welfare, lashed out at her, screaming, "You stupid ass, now I have to go back up there and get your ski!"

A subject closely allied to money—and often, therefore, as much of a sore spot to the Bastard—is a woman's job.

Although he tends to think of a wife he supports as a leech, he often resists her getting a job, even if the extra income would come in handy, for three reasons:

1. The Bastard, who is always macho, genuinely feels that a woman's place is in the home catering to a man.

2. He wants to be a woman's whole life, and he fears a job would give her other interests.

3. He knows, too, that a salary would give his wife more financial independence and erode his absolute control of her.

One Bastard managed to retain his economic power in a tricky way when his wife returned to work against his wishes. He deducted just enough from her already meager household allowance to make her not much better off than she was before.

As far as work is concerned, a woman is damned if she does and damned if she doesn't. If she gets a job she has betrayed and deserted her husband, and he rarely lets her forget it. "Remember how nice it was before you went back to work?" is the constant refrain of one Bastard who claims that his relationship is miserable because his divorced girlfriend is too rushed to have sex with him now in the morning.

"Everything fell apart when you took a job," snorts another man continually, forgetting, of course, that he was terrible to his wife for the ten years before she resumed her career.

On the other hand, a wife who does not go to work is dismissed as a parasite, and treated accordingly. The Bastard then feels justified in not giving her much of his hard-earned money to spend.

The Bastard Pimp

Of course, there is another kind of Bastard who doesn't resent having a woman work. On the contrary, he loves it. He wants to sit back and live off her earnings. He is, in effect, a Pimp.

The ultimate example is the street Pimp, who makes his prostitutes go out and hustle, then takes all of their earnings, doling out sums for them to live on.

The street Pimp is able to get away with it because he is a clever student of human psychology. He chooses women with strong dependency needs and convinces them that he is really taking care of them and protecting them. He keeps his stable in line by setting up competition for his attentions. He punishes his girls by withholding his company and his sexual favors, and sometimes by beating them up. He rewards them by his presence and attentions. The Pimp sets it up so that his prostitutes are always vying with each other in order to please him, so he has several women catering to his needs at the same time, creating, in effect, the Bastard's version of heaven.

Extreme Bastards resemble street Pimps in some respects. They are capable of using their women to gain things from other men. They may want a girlfriend to sleep with someone, for example, to complete a business deal.

Pimps generally don't like their girls to have many friends outside of "the life," and Bastards, in general, are often unhappy about sharing their wives and girlfriends with others. They want to make a woman feel possessed, and many do so by complaining about anything and anyone that takes up her time. They are prone to criticize a woman's friends, for example, and they often get angry when they telephone and find the line busy or their quarry not at home.

It is common, too, for a Bastard to complain that his woman sees her relatives too much.

One husband is so possessive of his wife that he even became rankled by the amount of time she spent with their grown children, who would visit frequently. He wanted her to focus her attention on him, instead. His cure was to tell his wife of twenty-five years that he wanted a divorce. This made her frantic to please him so that he wouldn't leave. He ordered her to forbid their daughters to come over except on holidays. It broke this mother's heart to do so, but she obeyed him. His trick worked so well that this Bastard now refuses to tell his wife that the divorce is off. He will probably keep her dangling forever. He has found, after all these years, the perfect controlling device.

Sources of anger and irritation for the Bastard, however, are not limited to money, jobs, or other people intruding on a woman's life. Anything can cause trouble, and nothing can be predicted. In each relationship there are ongoing themes, but what sets a Bastard off can change from minute to minute and day to day, a fact that caused one woman, married to a Bastard for forty years, to complain: "I have tried, but I have never been able to learn to avoid the things that will make John mad. The same thing that drives him crazy one time won't bother him at another."

Inconsistency, an earmark of the Bastard, is one of his many manipulative devices. He likes to keep you off balance, and changeability is a good way to do it. The Bastard's selective memory also keeps you off keel. Typically, a Bastard remembers what he wants to and forgets what he doesn't, and twists things around to suit his convenience.

One example of this was given to me by an unhappy wife. Her husband told her, when she decided to resume her career as an actress, that he would pay for needed photographs and her union dues. Supposedly, he was trying to help her get started in her career, since he is one of those who regarded his wife as a leech. She landed one role on television and paid for her photographs out of her own salary, but when it came time to join the union she didn't have enough money and reminded her husband of his promise. His answer was, "I've done enough for you already." He had even made himself believe that he had paid for the photographs.

Public and Private Denigration

The rattiness of Bastards is not without a rationale, but the real reasons for their behavior are not the ones they use to justify themselves. The Bastard may think his abuse is an appropriate reaction to your provocations, but the truth is he likes your discomfort and enjoys, in particular, your humiliation. A Bastard takes pleasure in a woman's psychic pain for these reasons:

1. When a Bastard puts a woman down, he feels more important, by contrast. A Bastard always needs to feel above others, and he is continually proving his superiority at a woman's expense.

2. Because he has a basic macho orientation, he has to feel dominant in relationships with women, in particular. He assumes this as his rightful masculine role. By humiliating a woman and making her submit to him, he affirms his control of her and, in the process, his masculinity.

3. The Bastard is an angry man who harbors deep resentments about life in general. Hostility to a woman may have nothing to do with what he is really angry about. He is simply venting some of the rage he is always walking around with on a convenient scapegoat.

Unfortunately, a Bastard's torture is not limited to his private domain. This kind of man is quite capable of humiliating a woman in public as well. One nurse is always afraid to go to the ladies' room when she goes out with her Bastard and some friends. She knows that when she returns she will find him flirting openly with another woman.

Another Bastard always starts to eat if his girlfriend arrives late at a restaurant. When he is finished—naturally ahead of her—he simply gets up and goes home, leaving her to finish her meal alone or put down her knife and fork and trail after him.

An engineer recently left his girlfriend alone with his friends for an entire weekend they spent at a resort with three other couples. Angry at her for some infraction, he was punishing her in front of his friends by disappearing into another part of the hotel and neglecting her.

It is common, too, for a Bastard, in your presence, to complain to others about your many faults. Spontaneous cracks and snipes are staples in his repertoire. The Bastard, in the process of putting you down in company, generally puts outsiders in an equally embarrassing position. But, since he doesn't see his behavior as wrong, it is hard for the Bastard to realize how other people are reacting. Some Bastards wouldn't give a damn if they did.

Others, however, go out of their way in social situations to put on the charm and seem like nice, sweet guys who would give you the shirt off their backs. They show their true character only in private.

The Competitive Game

At business, it is not uncommon for the Bastard to be known as a Bastard to some of his fellow workers. He can relate to people only as inferiors or superiors. To people he thinks are inferiors he can be patronizing, but nice. With those in a superior position he may even fawn. But with people at his own level he must establish his superiority, and he is not above using cutting remarks, backbiting, and dirty corporate games to stamp down a rival.

Underneath it all, the Bastard is an extremely competitive person, but he has learned to express his feelings only indirectly. For example, the Bastard can be a murderous sportsman—playing deadly games of tennis, which he feels he *has* to win at all costs.

One prominent physician at a major West Coast teaching hospital, who is an accomplished jock, is always quick to find out what sport new staff members play so that he can challenge them to a game, win, and thereby establish his dominance.

One-upmanship is a common tactic. Bastards, in conversation, may casually let people know that they own the best car, go to the best restaurants, live in the best neighborhood, or that they were shrewd enough to make a million dollars in the stock market last year.

Friendships

Many Bastards are proud of the fact that they don't have many close friends. Their stance is that they are so strong they don't need anyone.

Others have friendships with men that center on traditional macho things—they talk about women in a demeaning way, and about business in a competitive way.

One Bastard, as a sign that he is a true buddy, makes it a practice to offer to share his women sexually with a friend—as a kind of after-dinner brandy for the boys.

It is rare for anything weighty to be discussed by a Bastard and his friends. Bastards are not profound thinkers, although they may be extremely intelligent. Their friendships are usually superficial.

Sometimes a Bastard will work at developing a small coterie of friends who regard him as a guru. He enjoys being the center of their attention.

With women, platonic relationships may exist if the Bastard sees them as inferior or nonthreatening, nurturing mother figures. The Bastard must feel in control, and a motherly type who comes on warm and understanding—an older woman, for instance—may be accepted as a friend, albeit a superficial one. The Bastard may also relate to a woman he can tutor—an underling at work, for example, to whom he is showing the ropes.

The women he gets mixed up with in affairs are in for it, however, unless they stop him right away.

Affairs

Behind his assured manner and brazenness, the Bastard is really a cautious fellow. He is always testing and will do only what he thinks he can get away with.

If he feels you will accept his behavior, he will be his own true self from the beginning of a relationship. If he is not sure how you'll react he will play it cool until you have in some way acknowledged that you are seriously involved. Once he feels he has captured you, he will begin to establish his dominance aggressively. The abuse begins but he is still testing. Each outrage a woman allows leads to further outrages.

Affairs with a Bastard are generally on again/off again. He is always walking out and coming back, or his girlfriend runs away but finds herself hooked and returns.

The single Bastard will usually play around with other women, feeling that this is his prerogative as a superior man. Although he rarely bothers to be subtle about it, he is generally not forthright either. He will neither confirm nor deny his other involvements, implying, "It's none of your business." This tactic, of course, throws a woman off balance, which makes him, in turn, feel powerful.

In general, after a relationship has gone on for a while and the Bastard feels clearly dominant in it, he will feel free to do whatever he wants. His attitude is: Either you go along with it or the hell with you. Never a paragon in this respect, the Bastard becomes, in time, even more uncaring, unfeeling, and insensitive to his girlfriend and her needs.

Affairs for single Bastards tend to be short-lived. Women with a modicum of health will escape, once they realize what the score is. Others leave when they realize that the Bastard, who is allergic to it, is not going to make a commitment to them. Unfortunately, their action is prompted more by lack of security in the relationship than abuse.

If a woman doesn't leave, the Bastard will generally become bored with her after a while, anyway. Bastards stick around, though, feeling bored, until something better comes along—and they always have an eye peeled for something better during their relationships.

When the Bastard is ready to split, he may become increasingly abusive, hoping he can force the woman to leave on her own. If, even then, she won't pack up, he may tell her he is bad for her and he has to leave for her sake. Endings to affairs with Bastards can be ugly and uncomfortable—but, then, so are the affairs themselves.

For the psychopathic Charismatic Bastard, any sense of loss at the end of a relationship is quite impersonal. He may regret losing a woman with a lot of money, for example, because some of the luxury he enjoyed is ended. He may feel sad, too, because his needs are no longer being met, but he doesn't mourn her. Bastards can only mourn themselves.

If a wife or girlfriend leaves before the Bastard is ready for her to go, particularly if she leaves for another man, he may suddenly become uncharacteristically frightened, lonely, plaintive, or apprehensive and want desperately to get her back. He will court her again, displaying generosity and sensitivity, but as solicitous as he may be while he is pursuing her, he reverts to type once she returns.

Why Women Put Up With It

In the face of the nightmare quality of affairs with Bastards, why do women stay?

There are seven basic reasons:

1. Women fall into the same trap with Bastards that they do in many of their relationships with men in our culture. They get stuck because they feel that any man—even a cruel one—is better than none at all. Being alone, to the majority of women in this country, implies failure, personal inadequacy, and unacceptability. In consequence, many women will put up with almost anything from a man.

"It's a couple society," one longtime wife of a Bastard sighed, explaining why she couldn't leave him.

"I can't stand being alone, and I'm afraid I won't find anybody else," said a woman who had just spent two hours telling me horror tales about her boyfriend.

2. When he isn't being cruel, the Charismatic Bastard can often be an exciting, dynamic person, and the Weak Bastard can be very sweet when he isn't being abusive. Both the charm and the sweetness are enough to keep women hanging in there.

3. The Bastard instinctively keeps a woman bound to him by playing cleverly on her ego needs. By constantly rejecting her, he creates a narcissistic wound—a crippling blow to her self-esteem. She reacts to rejection with an overwhelming need to undo his action so that she can feel good about herself again. She tries to get him to accept and love her, and since her whole sense of self-worth is

directed to accomplishing this aim, she feels she desperately needs him.

4. A woman may fall into a save-the-black-sheep syndrome, feeling that she will be the one to change the Bastard and make him into a better human being through her patience, understanding, and love.

5. A woman tends to rationalize the Bastard's behavior. He is a man with real difficulties, and once things get better for him he will act differently.

6. For certain women, Bastards are simply a bad habit—they are attracted to them. They mistake macho mannerisms and domineering qualities for the marks of a "real" man. These women consider men who don't come on like a Bastard to be weak, and a Bastard can always smell out this kind of woman.

7. A minority of women are genuine masochists. They seek punishment as expiation for an underlying sense of guilt and sin. Some women seem to be but really aren't masochists. They experience pain not as pleasure, and don't need it to reduce guilt. It is a means of keeping the man and maintaining the relationship. They are simply trying to change the Bastard's rejection into acceptance, and their pain into pleasure.

In sadomasochistic affairs the Bastard is always either annoyed or bored, his mate always on the defensive and hurt. They fight and disagree about a million things, but neither one can break away because each has strong dependency needs.

Partners in such affairs are actually addicted to one another and to the deadly games they play. The sadist needs a victim and knows he has found what he craves in his masochistic partner. He is hooked on torturing her. She, on the other hand, needs the pain to expiate her guilt and thereby feel worthy of being loved. Sadist and masochist both hate and desperately need one another and get locked into an existence that is a living hell.

Some marriages to Bastards fall into the sadomasochistic pattern, and many wives in these marriages feel abuse not as a threat but as love or attention.

The Bastard as Husband

Bastards, as a group, are slippery fellows and it is hard to get them to marry; but some take the plunge, usually when they are feeling vulnerable and depressed, and often as a reaction to a feeling of failure—in business, for example.

Some marry because, consciously or unconsciously, they know they will have trouble keeping a woman without a license. Spouses don't leave as quickly as girlfriends.

Many Bastards act like a gentleman until after the wedding. They first put a toe in the water, then start acting rotten and wait to see what happens. If their bride doesn't start packing, they escalate.

Other Bastards manage to be sweet for a decent amount of time, but become bastardly when they feel under pressure.

Unfortunately, a Bastard is good at creating tensions, often by misinterpreting things. He may, for example, react to his wife's wanting to hold hands in front of the TV set as a request for sex. Feeling this as pressure, he will blow his stack, seemingly about something else— for example, "Why did you change the station, I want to watch that game!"

Feeling under pressure, some Bastards resort to physical abuse. Wife beaters are one of the deadlier variety of Bastards.

Marriages to Bastards are always stormy. The Bastard may or may not be a Bastard with his children as a general rule, but he is easily irritated and can lose his temper with his children as well as with his wife. Cold, authoritarian, superachieving Bastards are apt to be demanding fathers who set extraordinarily high standards of accomplishment for their children. The atmosphere in the homes of all Bastards is always charged with fear and tension, and the whole family walks around on tiptoes trying not to upset the tyrant.

Unlike his single counterpart, who almost always plays around, the married Bastard may be monogamous, often because he is afraid to lose a wife through an affair. A fair number of husbands have problems with impotence and/or premature ejaculation. They are very concerned about their sexual inadequacy and compensate for it by making themselves feel powerful in other ways. They tear their wives down. Many is the Bastard who reacts to his impotence by becoming a wife beater.

It is not uncommon for single Bastards to suffer from sexual dysfunctions also. Even if he starts out sexually adequate, the Bastard may develop problems as an affair progresses.

Other Bastards are unsatisfactory lovers because they are so self-centered and self-absorbed that they are inconsiderate. Sometimes a sadistic Bastard will hurt a woman sexually, calling her foul names or entering her before she is ready.

Among the Bastards of the world, however, are a fair number of studs. Highly sexual men, very good at love-making, they often use their prowess as a hooker in the relationship, or as yet another weapon in their arsenal of controlling devices. They are capable of withholding sex when a woman does something to irritate them.

They can play even more vicious games. One Bastard only kisses and fondles his wife when she is doing the housework. When she doesn't respond in these circumstances, he berates her for not being spontaneous. When she is responsive and active in bed, he claims she is too demanding and is castrating him. If she lies still, he accuses her of being cold. He has admitted that these are calculated tactics to keep his wife in line.

Psychological Roots

Weak Bastards often come from overprotective homes. Having had everything done for them, they never developed a sense of achievement or adequacy. As adolescents their early feelings of inadequacy were reinforced when they felt less successful than their peers. Feeling rotten about themselves makes them angry and resentful toward the world. The hostility that burdens them slips out with women, who become the preferred victims for their rage because they are less powerful than men. Men can harm by retaliating; women cannot.

The psychopathic Charismatic Bastard had a much more traumatic background. His early home life had such a negative impact that, at a young age, he learned to cut himself off from feelings about other people. He disassociated himself from the world around him to save himself pain.

The Bastard may have witnessed a lot of verbal or physical abuse between his parents. Two Bastards told me about ugly divorces. In a violent home the Bastard learned to defend himself by paying lip service to other people's needs, but really only going after what he wanted. As an adult he still only goes after what he wants.

Very often the Bastard imitated a Bastard father who abused his mother. Figuring, if you can't beat 'em, join 'em, he too started to abuse his mother. She accepted this behavior from him, setting the pattern for his future relations with women. Other Bastards may not have abused their mothers but simply identified with their father and felt themselves as men in league against women.

A Bastard does only what he thinks he can get away with. This "testing" kind of behavior may have been provoked by parents who did not allow him to express himself as he grew up. To avoid punishment, he learned to see what his parents would tolerate before venturing anything.

Other Bastards came from permissive homes. Parents let them get away with murder, and they continue as grownups to expect to get whatever they want.

All Bastards share a feeling of hostility toward women. In some Bastards the anger is indirect. They hate the world, but take it out on women because they think of them as inferior objects who don't count.

In others, hatred of women is more direct, a reaction against critical and overdemanding mothers.

Bastards also tend to have a paranoid orientation. They are mistrustful about other people and their motives. They are antagonistic to women as both a defense and a reaction to distrust—they fear they will be abandoned in the relationship. The Bastard has problems with intimacy. He does want a relationship, but when he has one he begins, on an unconscious level, to feel anxious about the closeness and dependency it creates. He reacts by being a Bastard in order to create distance between himself and his partner. By his actions he is really protecting himself against the possibility of being hurt if his mate leaves him, but the Bastard doesn't realize this on a conscious level. He thinks of himself as a superior person who has the right to control others, and he considers his hostility an attempt to gain the upper hand he deserves.

Bastards who are wife beaters hate more intensely and are angrier than others of their species. They have frequently been beaten as children, or they may have witnessed their fathers brutalizing their mothers. Wife beaters are deeply disturbed, sick men. They get away with their behavior generally because their wives feel that, as women, they have no other choice but to stick it out with a husband—even one who is violent.

This acceptance, however, seems to be changing now. Shelters for battered women are springing up around the country, giving these wives not only a place to flee to but also the necessary counseling to permit them to end their dangerous liaisons.

Changing, too, are the prospects for the larger group of Bastards who don't resort to beatings, but rely instead on shame, sarcasm, verbal abuse, or an occasional slap or arm-twisting to keep their women in line, or force them into submission.

The Bastard generally abhors the social emancipation of women, and he has every reason to. The more liberated and self-respecting women become, the less helpless they feel about themselves. The more they realize they are not failures as human beings without a male companion, the harder it will be for the Bastard to play his obscene game.

Our social climate may be fostering Hit-and-Run Lovers, Jugglers, Asexual Men, and Stingy Lovers, but it is making life a little tougher for the Bastards of the world.

Chapter 9

Men with Sexual Dysfunctions

The Impotent Man

Marilyn is a sexy-looking young blonde with wild, curly hair and a curvaceous figure that she shows off by never wearing a bra. She keeps meeting eager young men who take one look at her and can't wait to take her to bed. Once they get her there, however, it is often a disaster. They are impotent. Marilyn is beginning to think something is wrong with her—something that turns men off.

Geraldine is the opposite in looks to Marilyn. She is a sedate and conservative-looking woman of forty-two. She has been married to the same man for seventeen years. She had a satisfactory sex life with her husband until two years ago, when he suddenly started having bouts of impotence. Now he not only is impotent when they make love, he tries to avoid sex altogether a good part of the time.

Rhoda is a divorcee who had a decent sex life with her ex-husband and had never met an impotent man in the three years she has been dating since her divorce—something that surprised her friends, who all had had plenty of experience with men who had sexual problems. Two months ago, however, she met a thrice-married and -divorced stockbroker who fell madly in love with her and wanted to be with her all the time. There was only one major flaw in their relationship. Although he kept trying to make love to her, he couldn't. He was impotent each and every time.

In this day of sexual liberation, impotence is something that most women will have experience with. It is estimated that more than 50 per cent of all men suffer from it, at least occasionally. For some it strikes every now and then. For others, impotence is a plague that threatens their entire sex life, coming and going with unpredictable regularity. Still other men "fail" for the first time after a period of normal functioning. For a very small number, impotence is all they know. They have never been able to get or maintain an erection.

Despite the fact that occasional impotence is so common that it can be considered a normal part of the male experience, when it strikes it can be one of life's most painful experiences.

A great deal of a man's self-esteem is wrapped up in his erections, and when one fails to materialize he is not only frustrated but also often humiliated and filled with a sense of powerlessness because he is unable to get his penis to perform.

Impotence almost invariably makes a man think less of himself as a man and as a human being. Therapists are used to hearing such self-damning descriptions as "a failure," "inadequate," and "less than a man" from the lips of suffering men.

Also hidden somewhere inside a man who experiences impotence is almost always the fear of ridicule and rejection by his partner. Sometimes this fear is transmuted into a diffuse, overall rotten feeling. Sometimes the man defends himself against his fears by attacking, blaming his impotence on you: "You're too fat," "too skinny," "too demanding," "too sarcastic," "too inactive," "too ugly," "too beautiful," "too smart," "too dumb."

Some men just plain lie. Many is the woman who has heard her would-be lover explain: "This is the first time this has ever happened to me," which, of course, is another way of making you feel that the impotence is somehow your fault.

Other men place the blame on outside forces: "I had

too much to drink," "I'm having too many problems at work," "I was too tired," "I shouldn't have eaten Mexican food—it always upsets my stomach!"

Rare is the man who will confess his impotence to another male. It is a standard part of male repartee to joke about occasionally not being able to "get it up," but men tend to maintain supermen facades with one another, and because of it they are careful to hide their troubles if they are plagued by chronic impotence.

First-Night Fright

One of the commonest kinds of impotence today takes place during initial sexual encounters. Many men on the singles scene suffer from opening-night jitters. They are anxious about their ability to perform or to please the new woman they are taking to bed for the first time. Unfortunately, their fear of failure turns into a self-fulfilling prophecy. They end up struggling with a limp penis.

Some of the more sensitive first-night failures are honest and open about it. They let you know ahead of time what is likely to happen, and that if it does you are not to worry.

By telegraphing the bad news they are, in effect, pleading for kindness and understanding, and if they are lucky enough to get it—if warmth, acceptance, and reassurance are forthcoming—they are able to achieve an erection the next time you get together, or even later that same night.

Other first-nighters, however, can be defensive and hostile. They, too, know all too well what's in the cards, but prefer to kiss without telling. Many are well aware that women tend to blame themselves when a man is impotent, but they figure: "If it's a toss-up between her feeling guilty and rotten about herself, or me feeling embarrassed and ashamed, let her be the one who suffers."

Most first-nighters are able, with familiarity or sympathy, to overcome their initial fears and go on to function normally, but for those who suffer from chronic impotence—the inability to have or maintain an erection most of the time—life is more complicated. These men tend to either hop from bed to bed, hoping their trouble will magically disappear with the right woman, or they avoid sex altogether. They are attracted to women, but then their mind leaps ahead to the next step—sex and the possibility of failure—and rather than risk disgrace, they don't even try.

Here's how one impotent man described a recent incident: "I met a woman who was with some friends on the beach. She looked great in her bikini and I found her very attractive. We all got to talking and the couple she was with invited us back to their house. I agreed to go. In the car she flirted with me the whole way and I flirted back, but as we approached their house I got to thinking that she would expect me to take her home and that probably I'd be expected to perform, so I suddenly told everyone I had to go and I took off. They must have thought I was crazy."

Sometimes a man suffering from chronic impotence, like the one who told me the following story, turns off his desire before he is required to act:

"I was having lunch at a counter restaurant, and there was a young, good-looking girl sitting next to me. We started a conversation. When we finished lunch I asked her if she wanted to go to the movies with me. She accepted. We went and I put my arms around her and then tried to feel her breasts. After the movie I asked her to come home with me. She said yes, but the minute she walked into my apartment I thought, What am I doing this for? I felt that she was too flat-chested and that sleeping with her would be like sleeping with a boy, so I gave her cab money and sent her home." Of course it wasn't the girl's body that turned this man off, but his own fear of failure. He had been finding one excuse after another not to get sexually involved with anyone for several months.

When a man thinks of himself as impotent, no matter what the cause, he often tries to develop compensations in other areas of his life. Some men make themselves feel more manly and powerful by becoming tyrants and bossing their wives around. Others insist on always being right about everything and anything. Still others turn to wife beating as a way of feeling powerful.

Other men prefer to escape. They turn to alcohol or drugs or become workaholics.

The Causes

What creates impotence, and what makes some men more vulnerable to it than others?

For a small number the cause is physical. Illnesses like diabetes, or medications such as those used to control high blood pressure, can interfere with normal sexual functioning. Liquor in large amounts and certain drugs can also be contributing factors in impotence, as can depression, which not only makes life go limp in general but causes the testosterone level to drop.

In the majority of cases, however, impotence is caused by psychological problems of one kind or another. Perfect proof of this is the fact that when men who are impotent with women masturbate (and most of them do) they have no trouble achieving or maintaining their erection and reaching orgasms.

1. Freud blamed impotence on Oedipal problems in early childhood that created feelings of fear and guilt associated with sex.

Between the ages of three and five it is normal for a boy to want to possess his mother and to harbor murderous wishes toward his father, whom he regards as a rival for his mother's affections. Besides secretly coveting his mother, he also dreads that his father will learn about his desires and punish him by castration.

In the normal course of development a boy resolves his sexual yearnings for his mother by substituting a more appropriate love object and solves his fear of his father by deciding to become like him. If, however, he does not resolve his early wish to possess his mother, he retains an underlying fear of castration as punishment. Whenever he experiences sexual excitement in later life, the old fear is invoked, unconsciously, and he feels enough anxiety and guilt to cause impotence in some cases.

2. Today, most mental health practitioners feel that a variety of other issues such as fear, shame, and anticipation of punishment for sexual excitement can be responsible for impotence. For example, if a boy was made to feel guilty about early attempts at masturbation, he

may respond to every sexual impulse thereafter with stress. If he was brought up in an intensely religious or puritanical house where sex was considered sinful or dirty, he may feel guilty about sexuality throughout his life.

Some men have had early traumas with sex. For example, one well-known author and wit of the twenties and thirties was having intercourse with his first girlfriend when her parents returned unexpectedly and caught them. He tried to jump out the window in his fright. He was restrained from doing away with himself, but he was impotent for the rest of his life. Current trauma can also do it. A man who discovers his wife has been unfaithful, for example, can become impotent.

3. Males who think of sex as an act of aggression often experience conflict that creates havoc during sex because they feel it is wrong to be aggressive with the woman they care about.

4. Others have specific phobias about female genitals, or vaginal secretions, or even sexual aromas. They manage not to have anything to do with the thing they are afraid of by becoming impotent.

5. Perhaps the single greatest cause of impotence today is the fear of failure that haunts insecure men. Not only do many men with poor self-images live in terror of not achieving an erection, they are also afraid of the consequences. They are sure that women will reject or abandon them for it, and their fears are enough to paralyze them sexually. They find they can't keep an erection, and once impotence strikes, they worry even more the next time around—and so, of course, it happens again. They get caught in a vicious circle—anxiety leading to impotence, impotence leading to anxiety, and so on.

6. Performance anxiety—a special form of fear of failure—is another prevalent cause of impotence today. When a man has an excessive need to please his partner, or even a competitive need to be better than other men in bed, he may end up becoming a spectator in his own event. Not being able to abandon himself to the passion of the moment, he becomes impotent. Here is how one man described a disturbing tendency to monitor himself. "Performing rather than enjoying is not natural. It's a drag, but I haven't been able to shake it. I'm too concerned about my partner's reaction rather than wallowing in my own

enjoyment. I'm always wondering, What's going on? Is she satisfied? Should I be doing more of this or that? You categorize. What do you think this one will go for? What do you think that one will go for? You start something and watch to see where it will go..."

7. Sexual demands of one kind or another may also create impotence. Such demands can come from outside forces—a wife who presses for sex as proof of her husband's love, or a casual or steady sex partner who wants more or different sex than the man is already providing. Even today some men feel that women who initiate sex are too demanding.

One attractive politician told me what happened to him on a recent first date: "After dinner we were driving home in my car. She reached over and grabbed my balls, just like that. I really didn't have sex on my mind, but I knew what she wanted from me, so I took her home. But no matter what she did, or I did, I couldn't get an erection. We were both demolished by the incident."

When a woman initiates sex or makes requests during the sex act itself, men sometimes feel they are being controlled. They resent a woman who calls the shots, and they express their resentment by not delivering the goods. Impotence is their way of showing who's "boss."

Sexual demands that lead to impotence don't always come from a woman, however. They can be self-created. Many men have high and unrealistic expectations of themselves based on distorted and exaggerated beliefs as to how other men function. From an early age they have heard other men brag about their conquests and prowess, not realizing how many of the tales were lies. They also see superstuds in action in porno films and they feel they can't perform as tirelessly or as well. They may realize, too, that their penises are not as large as those of porno film stars and therefore feel that their organs are inferior.

It's common for men to wonder, "Why can't I be more like the other guys?" And the notion that they must be inferior is enough to create real failure—impotence.

Also contributing to impotence caused by feelings of inadequacy vis-à-vis other men, is the fact that women are sexually more experienced today. The insecure man fears he will be compared to other lovers and found wanting.

A young songwriter told me about some men in her life whose fear of competition did them in:

Her blue eyes opened wide as she said, "Honestly, I don't know what's happening. I've come across impotence three times lately. Each time it was with someone I had known for a while beforehand, but it was the first time we were in bed together. All three finally confessed the same thing. They think I am beautiful [she is], but because I hang out with rock stars, they think that people like Mick Jagger are in my bed all the time. They think I must be a sexual connoisseur and that they can't come close to what the other guys have done. So they can't do anything. It's not true of course. It's all in their heads. I haven't been to bed with that many people. In fact, my current boyfriend thinks I'm sexually naive."

8. Rejection and career or financial failures are also common causes of impotence. Divorced men, especially if their wives have walked out on them, sometimes suffer from sexual troubles for a while. So do men who have been fired or unemployed for a long time, and epidemics of impotence have been reported each time the stock market takes a steep plunge.

Men's sexuality is more fragile than popular mythology and the macho stance would have us believe, and anything that makes a man feel powerless can affect it. On the other hand, something that makes a male feel more powerful can turn the tables as well.

One woman reported going out with a publicity man whose career was in a decline. He was impotent with her each and every time until one day he took her into a room in his house that was plastered with pictures of himself and powerful figures in the movie industry. She appeared impressed, and that, together with the heady ambience, was enough for him to be potent for the first—and only—time in their relationship.

Another woman reported that a wealthy dentist was unable to perform sexually with her until she picked him up at his office one evening. There, in an environment where he felt successful and powerful, he was able to get an erection for the first time.

9. The guilt created by infidelity can also make a man impotent with his wife, his mistress, or both.

One straying mate reported taking his secretary to bed right after visiting his wife in the hospital, where she was recuperating from an operation. He had been sexually successful with his employee many times in the past, but this particular occasion was so guilt-provoking that he couldn't do anything.

10. Impotence can be a signal or a weapon in interpersonal relationships. When a husband begins to dislike his wife or develops an aversion to her because she has gained weight, aged, or become sloppy, he may in effect reject her by becoming impotent.

A man who feels his wife is dominating and resents it can express his anger and also reassert his control over her by present her with a limp penis.

The cuckold who has discovered that his wife is having an affair can wreak his revenge by not functioning in their defiled marital bed.

11. Also implicated in many cases of impotence is that greatest sexual saboteur of all in men's lives: intimacy.

Just as the fear of closeness can help turn a man into a Hit-and-Run Lover, a Juggler, or a sexually Stingy Lover, so can intimacy stop the show altogether for certain men.

Large numbers of men have trouble integrating sex with intimacy. Long-term or committed relationships invoke complex psychological reactions that interfere in one way or another with sexual functioning. Some of the things that can cause sexual failure are a man's fear of rejection, abandonment, domination, or suffocation by a woman who is important to him. A man may also unconsciously identify the woman he cares for with his mother.

These conflicts do not come into play as strongly or as often in casual sexual encounters.

A man's impotence in a close relationship may also be caused by a lack of intimacy with his parents in his early life.

A man whose parents abused or neglected him, or who were not present because of death or abandonment, may have failed to develop a fundamental capacity to trust and love. As a result, the intimacy of sexual relations is too threatening. He becomes trapped in a crippling conflict. He desires sexual gratification, but the anxiety that comes from being close to a woman immobilizes him and prevents its fulfillment.

A thirty-eight-year-old corporate executive told me

about his problem. He had been placed in foster homes at an early age by his mother. Over his third scotch he confessed: "Sexually I have always been best with rejecting women. The minute a woman is accepting or loving, then goodbye Charlie. Frequency falls off, and I can't get it up. I can be with a rejecting woman every night and still be turned on. There is one woman I have strong feelings for, but I can't get it up with her. I introduced her to pot. I turned her on and me off." He laughed bitterly.

12. An important cause of impotence is sexual ignorance and/or the failure to communicate one's sexual needs to a partner.

Many men in this country have received little or no sex education. According to one study, boys are told even less than girls. As a result, they bumble through their first experiences and stumble along for the rest of their lives filled with insecurity and anxiety, never sure they are doing the right thing or how they compare to other men.

Sexual ignorance can extend even to the middle-aged man who fails to recognize his changing sexual needs due to age. He may expect to function just as he did when he was young. He worries when it takes him longer to respond, and he may push himself into frequent sex even though he has no real desire. The result is that he fails.

It is not uncommon for a husband in his fifties to expect to achieve a rapid erection at the mere touch of a woman, just as he did in his youth. He doesn't understand that he may have to be stimulated more intensely now in order to achieve a firm erection, and since he is unable to communicate this to his wife, he becomes impotent merely because of insufficient foreplay.

13. Finally, another cause of impotence is the kind of women some men sleep with. One kind who can cause sexual troubles is the woman who gives off an aura of vulnerability. "Don't hurt me physically or emotionally. If you're not serious, don't make love to me," she seems to be saying. For the male who needs to release anger and aggression during sex—and some men do—this kind of woman can be a turn-on, he loves hurting her despite, or because of, her implied plea. A tyrant who needs someone to tyrannize over will also turn into a sexual dynamo with a woman who appears fragile. But some men are afraid of hurting women—either physically or emotionally—and

for them a vulnerable woman can be the cause of impotence.

Another group of women are deliberate sexual saboteurs. They create pressure and tension just before sex, for example, or they make themselves physically repulsive, or they actually frustrate a partner's desires during the sex act itself. Generally such malicious reactions occur in the context of a troubled relationship.

Some women who don't create impotence may nevertheless welcome it. They have concerns about their own sexuality, or they need to make themselves feel worthwhile by doing something for a man. They either nurse him along, or play the stoic martyr to his impotence.

As for "castrating" women, some women, of course, are so controlling and bossy they would turn any man off. But an efficient, aggressive, or assertive woman is not a ball-breaker *per se*. A self-assured and forthright woman may, indeed, threaten an insecure man enough to make him impotent, but she will not inhibit or frighten a man who thinks well of himself.

When women encounter impotency, their reaction is a reflection of their feelings about themselves. If a woman feels secure about herself, she will understand that it's the man's problem and not blame herself. If she is insecure, she will feel varying degrees of responsibility. She may blame her ineptness as a lover or some part of her body that she feels badly about. A woman with a poor self-image will feel that she has caused the impotence even when a man takes pains to explain that it happens all the time.

Occasionally a woman will react with overt anger and hostility. Reported one man who slept with a well-known television personality: "When I couldn't get it up she clenched her fist, pounded it on the mattress, and screamed. 'Goddam you!'" But most women, according to men I have spoken to, are amazingly kind and sympathetic to a bed partner who is impotent.

The Premature Ejaculator

The most common of all male sexual dysfunctions is premature ejaculation. The man who suffers from it is unable to exert voluntary control over his ejaculatory reflex. Once aroused, he reaches orgasm almost instantly.

Most premature ejaculators climax just before or immediately upon entering the vagina. Some are capable of several thrusts before they come, others ejaculate after just a few minutes of foreplay, and some lose control merely at the sight of a woman disrobing.

There is a story about a famous Hollywood comedian who was a great womanizer and notorious for precipitous orgasms during sex. He had been seeking a cure for his condition his whole life. A friend once gave him a new medication to apply to his penis to numb it and slow down his responses. The next time the comedian was with his girlfriend he eagerly pulled out the tube and rubbed it on as instructed. The slight stimulation of the massaging motion, together with her watching him, was all he needed. He came before he had finished applying the ointment.

Premature ejaculation not only short-circuits a woman's sexual pleasure but the man's as well. Once the premature ejaculator is aroused, there is often a lessening or absence of erotic sensation, and as he reaches orgasm he may have very little sensation.

Premature ejaculators are not generally aware of their sexual anesthesia. If they undergo sex therapy it is only after they achieve control that they suddenly enjoy sex more and realize what they have been missing.

Some men think that fast orgasm is normal and desirable. No less a figure than Kinsey considered it to be a mark of male superiority.

Young men, in particular, may have such an urgent need for release that their quick orgasms may not bother them. But after the first flush of youth, men who suffer from chronic premature ejaculation generally feel extremely unhappy about their condition. Not only do they think that their own sexual pleasure is incomplete and too brief, they also feel guilty because they have deprived their partner of pleasure. Inevitably, they consider themselves sexually inadequate.

The level of psychological discomfort of the premature ejaculator may be even higher than that of the man who suffers from impotence. It is harder for a man to blame his rapid ejaculation on either the woman or outside problems when he has become excited, achieved erection, and reached orgasm.

Nevertheless, certain men attempt to dump the problem on you even though it is ridiculous to do so.

The commonest face-saving technique is a masterful tactic. It is a reproach that sounds like a compliment: "You are too sexy," or, "You excite me too much."

Another common defensive reaction is to get angry or sullen and refuse to talk about it. "Let me alone," the premature ejaculator growls, conveying the feeling that somehow it is all your fault.

Very often a man will simply exude "Woe is me" vibes. Some apologize: "God, how awful. I'm very sorry."

Some attempt to stonewall it by ignoring what has just taken place, or taking the "You're crazy" attitude, implying "What's the matter? That's the way guys fuck."

Others react to their anxiety and shame by avoiding sexual contacts as much as possible.

No matter how the premature ejaculator handles himself, women aren't bothered as much by this type of sexual failure as they are by impotence. When a man can't maintain an erection you feel completely undesirable, but a man's hasty orgasm—while it may leave you just as unfulfilled—at least doesn't tamper with your view of yourself as a viable object of desire.

Eventually, however, if the relationship lasts for any length of time, in marriage or out, resentment begins to set in. Sex therapists report that it is often the angry and frustrated wife who insists on treatment.

What Causes It

There are actually two kinds of premature ejaculation. The first spans a man's entire sex life.

The second is situationally induced. It is a man's reaction to a particular woman or a specific set of circumstances, and it is generally part of a power struggle between a couple.

For example, one middle-aged husband in Minneapolis has a wife who recently became liberated enough to initiate sex occasionally. This man feels so threatened by her actions that he ejaculates prematurely only when she has made the first move.

For many men, premature ejaculation is an expression of resentment or fear of being dominated by a woman. According to one theory, a husband may think that if the wife wants him to hold back his orgasms, she is attempting to control him. He fights her control by coming too quickly.

Masters and Johnson feel that the chronic premature ejaculator may simply be the victim of a bad habit that is hard to shake. The pattern may have been set by stressful conditions in initial sexual encounters that made a man want to "finish off" quickly—for example, sex in the back seat of a car with the fear of discovery, or in the living room of a girl's home when her parents are expected back.

Sometimes a man who seems to be a premature ejaculator is really just sexually ignorant. One forty-four-year-old salesman I interviewed told me: "It wasn't until ten years ago that I learned that sex isn't something you do as fast as possible."

Another man explained: "I was in my late twenties when a woman told me that I shouldn't come so quickly. Until then I had no idea. No one ever told me."

Thus enlightened, these men set about learning to hold back, which is what all men have to do. The natural thing is to ejaculate when you feel like it, which, for most men, is pretty quickly.

One of the men quoted above said: "I started asking other guys how they did it, and most of them said the same thing: 'Think about something else.'"

Some men do mathematical problems when they feel they are getting too excited, others dig nails into palms, still others flex their sphincter muscles and claim this works.

Some men who are troubled by premature ejaculation are desperate enough to masturbate alone before they have sex with a woman. "The second time is much less of a problem," said one. Others use creams and ointments that anesthetize the penis.

The masters of sex—men with perfect control—that I spoke to say they have merely learned to recognize the moment just before orgasm. When they feel its approach they cut down or stop stimulation altogether for a little while, and resume activity only when they have cooled down a bit.

According to sex therapists, one of the things that chronic premature ejaculators have never learned to do is recognize that important signal of impending orgasm. Once orgasm begins, there is no stopping it. Premature

ejaculators reach the point of no return without awareness. It is their anxiety about adequacy and performance
that distracts them and prevents them from recognizing
body signals.

Sex therapists during treatment concentrate on getting a man to pay more attention to his own sensations
so that he can catch himself in time.

Many men who suffer from premature ejaculation
eventually become impotent. Others switch from premature ejaculation to retarded ejaculation. These transitions
from bad to worse generally take place over a number of
years and frequently within the context of marriage. A
typical case is that of an art director who married a woman
who was a virgin. In the early part of the marriage, since
she didn't know what to expect, she put up with the premature ejaculation of her husband. As the years passed,
however, she started to recognize his trouble as the source
of her frustration and began accusing him of being selfish
and not doing a good job. The shift of her attitude from
tolerant and accepting to critical and blaming wounded
the man deeply. He symbolically tried to avoid her criti-
cism by becoming impotent.

Not all premature ejaculators become impotent, however, and the thing that may preserve the sexual act—
impaired as it may be—for certain men, is the double standard.

If a man firmly believes that women primarily serve
men during sex, he will not be unduly affected by negative
feedback because of his performance. For the man who
is disturbed, however, effective help is available.

By using new techniques developed over the past few
years, sex clinics are now achieving an 80 to 100 per cent
cure rate.

The Retarded Ejaculator

We all hear a lot about impotence and premature
ejaculation, and chances are good that if you are active
on the singles scene you will eventually encounter both.
But one hears little about the retarded ejaculator—probably because he is a much rarer creature and because, at
first, he seems to be quite normal. He has desires, he
responds to sexual stimuli, and he achieves a firm erection. However, no matter how much stimulation he re-

ceives and no matter how long intercourse goes on, he can't reach an orgasm, although he urgently desires one.

Retarded ejaculation, which is also referred to as ejaculatory incompetence, comes in six different flavors:

1. At its mildest it occurs only in specific circumstances that provoke anxiety. A man may find himself unable to climax with only one specific woman, or he may have a problem only in situations where guilt or conflict are present. One man who was angry at his wife for betraying a secret to a friend, was unable to "let go" and ejaculate the night he found out about it. Another old bachelor, who prided himself on his womanizing over the years, found himself suddenly confronted with a new breed of woman in his fifty-fifth year—women whom he felt were using him only for sex. With these women he was unable to ejaculate. When the situation was reversed, however, and he was with a woman he was using only for sex, he was able to function normally.

2. In one of its commonest forms, it takes place only when a man is trying to ejaculate in a woman's vagina. The man fails no matter what he tries, and he may try everything—fantasies, dirty talk, provocative records, alcohol. Men who can't climax in a vagina are able to finally "let go" if they withdraw and allow a woman to bring them to orgasm through oral or manual stimulation.

3. For some men the mere touch of a women is enough to paralyze them; they can't climax even when she uses every trick in the book: mouth, fingers, rubbing the penis between her breasts. They can reach orgasm only by masturbating themselves in the woman's presence, and even then there is a great deal of anxiety. They may have to distract themselves by fantasies while masturbating.

4. Others have to banish a woman before they can have an orgasm. They themselves may have to leave the room, and sometimes they may have to wait several hours until the heterosexual contact has worn off before they can masturbate successfully. Men like this often eventually give up on sex with women altogether and rely solely on masturbation for release.

5. The rarest form is also the severest. Men who suffer from it are the equivalent of completely "frigid" women. They can't ejaculate under any circumstances.

6. A man may be able to achieve only half an orgasm.

In the first stages of lovemaking he responds normally. He feels desire and experiences pleasure, achieves a strong erection, and senses impending orgasm, but instead of ejaculating in a spurt with several thrusting movements, which is the norm, his semen merely seeps out. There are no thrusts and he feels no pleasure in orgasm.

The male orgasm consists of two separate phases—ejaculation and emission. The man who has only half an orgasm suffers from inhibition of the ejaculation phase. The others I've discussed experience problems with both ejaculation and emission.

Half orgasms never become a chronic problem. They are quite common, however, as a transient phenomenon, occurring most frequently when a man is tired or in conflict. For example, if a man is uptight about feeling too close to a partner during sex, he may freeze himself out of the situation symbolically by anesthetizing his climax.

As with other sexual dysfunctions, retarded ejaculation in its many forms may be either a primary condition (one that has plagued a man from the beginning of his sex life) or secondary (the onset occurring only after a period of normal functioning).

Men who have never experienced retarded ejaculation often make the mistake of envying the man who suffers from it. They admire him as a superstud who can have intercourse interminably and maintain an erection forever. They are unaware of the pain these men feel as a result of their dysfunction.

Sometimes a man who suffers from retarded ejaculation will pose as a sexual athlete. One man who did just that was encountered recently by a sex therapist from the East at a bar in Las Vegas. He was capitalizing on his affliction by operating as a male prostitute. He specialized in picking up lonely, angry wives, ready for revenge, waiting with a drink while their husbands gambled in the casinos. Since he never climaxed, he could take on one after the other. It is possible that some of the famous great lovers of the world attained their reputation by fraud. They may have been men who couldn't ejaculate, posing as lovers who didn't want to climax in order to prolong the act.

Men who suffer from retarded ejaculation are not above faking an orgasm in order to hide their problem.

If they do, they generally masturbate later when they are alone. Just as many premature ejaculators become impotent eventually because they anticipate failure, so do a fair number of retarded ejaculators.

Psychological Origins

This sexual problem is a withholding action, and some men may not want to "let go" because of unresolved Oedipal problems from early childhood. They fear unconsciously that they will be castrated or injured by ejaculating into a woman's vagina, which symbolically is associated with their mother's genitals.

Some men relive another infantile trauma. They feared, as children, that their mother would abandon them, and now, as adults, they think their wife will leave them if they should soil her by "letting go."

Retarded ejaculation often has its roots in hostility. Men who feel angry, consciously or unconsciously, and are afraid to express it, may hold back in sex by not being able to ejaculate.

Destructive elements in a marriage can create sexual problems too. For example, a lawyer who felt he was constantly giving in to his wife in other ways chose to rebel in just one way—by withholding his semen from her. Another man who had great conflicts about commitment felt he had been trapped into marrying his wife. He discovered in therapy that he was unable to ejaculate in his wife's vagina because, on an unconscious level, he felt the marriage was not consummated if he failed to climax.

Some men are troubled by retarded ejaculation only after an emotional trauma. For example, two men who had left their wives and children for another woman told me that their problems began only after their new loves walked out on them.

The madonna/prostitute complex, wherein a man feels that sex is only for "bad" women, may come into play in retarded ejaculation, as it does in so many other male sexual patterns. A husband may have an underlying fear that his "good" wife will leave him if he defiles her with his sperm.

Women's Reactions

If a woman has trouble reaching orgasm, she may find the lengthy intercourse possible with a retarded ejaculator helpful—at first. But eventually, when a partner is repeatedly unable to climax, the woman questions her own desirability.

This concern is painfully real if the retarded ejaculator is unfair and directly or indirectly blames her by saying something like, "This has never happened before," or by indicating that if she moved differently, was more provocative, or had done something differently, he would have had no trouble. Some men try to ignore the whole thing and let a woman draw her own conclusions. Since most women don't know about retarded ejaculation as a sexual dysfunction, silence on the man's part almost invariably makes the woman blame herself.

Even when a man is honest and tells her that the problem is his, it is hard for an insecure woman to feel that she isn't to blame.

Because retarded ejaculation is embarrassing and humiliating to a man, many sufferers either run from woman to woman or avoid sex altogether. They take whatever pleasure and solace they can in lonely, solitary masturbation.

The Man Who Lacks Desire

A new classification has recently been added to the sexual dysfunctions that men suffer from. It is inhibited sexual desire—the impairment of the desire phase of sexual response. More and more men are turning up in sex clinics and in therapists' offices complaining that they have no interest in sex.

Without being officially recognized as a dysfunction, wives have certainly known about it—the lack of sex in large numbers of marriages may be one of the best-kept secrets of the ages. Its presence is finally being hinted at by therapists and marriage counselors, who report that while it used to be men who claimed that they weren't getting enough sex from their wives, it is now wives who are complaining that they need more sex.

The average couple copulates once or twice every week, yet an astounding number of husbands and wives go for three, four, five weeks, months, or, in some cases, years, without sex. According to a recent survey reported in the *American Journal of Psychiatry*, one third of the couples studied had ceased having intercourse for long periods of time.

One would think this would be true of only older couples, but young and healthy obviously does not always mean sexy. Seventy-six percent of the abstaining couples were less than thirty-nine years old. One of the reasons given for the most lengthy periods—three months or longer—was lack of desire.

Women, of course, suffer from lack of desire as well as men. But until recently it was assumed to be almost normal—that women were simply not as interested in sex as men. Just as that theory is now open to question, so is the assumption that has previously operated about men—that they are always ready, willing, and able to have sex.

As this book has already pointed out, many men are neither ready, nor willing, nor able always to have sex; and, as those who suffer from lack of desire will tell you, there are males who for long periods of time don't give a damn about having intercourse. But against the prevailing myths of male sexuality, awareness of this class of men comes as a surprise to the general public.

Some of the men who suffer from lack of desire— Asexuals and Stingy Lovers—have already been discussed. But men who suffer from lack of desire need not be Asexuals (men who have never felt a sexual urge in their adult lives) or Stingy Lovers (men who actively withhold sex from a partner). They may simply be unable to give because they have no inner erotic spark to ignite the fire.

The largest group of men who suffer from lack of desire are husbands who turn off to their wives at various stages in their marriage.

They complain of boredom, of sex with the same person all the time, or in the same old way, and sometimes set routines make this complaint legitimate, but often such bitching masks more profound psychological reasons.

Very often, as I noted before, husbands turn off to wives soon after marriage, or when babies are born. These husbands, many of whom were quite interested and passionate before, are reacting either to intimacy, which frightens them because it will reveal their inadequacies, or to commitment, which makes them feel trapped, or to a new sense of responsibility, which may make them feel overwhelmed, overburdened, and resentful. These men, in essence, uninvolve themselves and withdraw by snuffing out erotic feelings for their wives.

Lack of desire as a reaction to intimacy, commitment, or responsibility occurs in the early part of a marriage, and it seems to happen overnight. The young husband engages in sex with great frequency until he feels committed, and then—boom—it's all over. He couldn't care less. Or he is an ardent and interested husband until the first or second baby is born, and then suddenly he is apathetic.

When ardor dims in middle age, however, the reasons are different. Men between thirty and fifty go through an identity crisis. The man in a midlife crisis reviews his emotional and professional life and often feels that he has made the wrong choices in life and love.

He feels unhappy with his marriage but he stays in it. He generally rationalizes this behavior by claiming lack of money or responsibility to the children. But the real reason he doesn't split is his own strong dependency needs. He doesn't know he has them; all he feels is that he is stuck in the marriage and that he resents it. He acts out his annoyance and anger by cutting off his sexual feelings.

Other husbands who turn off in midlife are responding to a new and frightening awareness of death. Suddenly acutely conscious of their mortality, they set about preserving themselves. They take up tennis and jogging with a vengeance. They go religiously to the gym. They lose weight. There is one activity they suddenly shun, however—sex with their wives. Somewhere in their psyches they remember the common male myth that sex is depleting, the same myth that keeps prizefighters in training from having sex and that makes coaches admonish players to abstain before a game.

If they don't embrace a spartan physical-fitness routine, they may become workaholics or addicted to spectator sports, spending long hours in front of television sets watching any and every contest in football, baseball, hockey, and basketball. Sometimes they react to the sports they are viewing with the passion they are not spending elsewhere. The first shooting of a television set occurred a couple of years ago when the team a man was rooting for lost.

Generally, wives faced with husbands who lose interest in sex have predictable reactions. If a husband turns off early in marriage, it may come as a shock, particularly if he has previously been active and ardent in bed. If he turns off in midlife, he may do so quite abruptly, and the older wife may also be jolted. Some men, however, gradually peter out over the years until they are down to zero. The wife has by then become accustomed to the law of diminishing returns, but she is puzzled. She wonders if she is unattractive, if she is getting old or fat. She may also be frustrated and angry if her sexuality has bloomed in her mid-years and now, with stronger desires, she is stuck with a man with none at all. Ultimately she may wonder if her husband is having an affair.

She may be right. Some husbands who have lost all desire for their wives play around with other women. Particularly prone to adultery is the husband facing his midlife crisis. A new love is looked upon as the magic wand that will make things good for him again—he will feel young, exciting, and virile once more, or for the first time.

Some husbands manage to cut off sexual feelings for their wives as an excuse to start the affair they have been fantasizing about. "She doesn't turn me on, so I have a right to find someone who does," is how they think. And what they find is often a younger, supposedly sexier woman to play extramarital games with. With others it is the reverse—they start affairs, and it is their guilt that dampens their desire for their wives.

Not all husbands have affairs, however. Some don't because they are turned off to everyone. Others fear the repercussion on their marriage. They know, since they aren't functioning well sexually, that their wives might be crushed if they learned that their husbands were functioning better with someone else. Others truly believe in monogamy. Ironically, it is in monogamous marriages that lack of desire surfaces most frequently.

Occasionally, a husband's lack of desire is the outcome of a long period of unsatisfying sex. As I have pointed out before, some men who suffer from premature ejaculation, retarded ejaculation, and impotence eventually turn off from women altogether. Even if sexual dysfunction is not present, lack of desire may be the byproduct of a man's ignorance or failure or unwillingness to request the kind of stimulation he needs.

There are husbands, however, who use their wife's sexual unresponsiveness or ineptness to cloak their own low sex drives. They bitch and moan about their "frigid" spouses, but they also never manage to find other outlets for their dammed-up desires.

There is one husband in Philadelphia, for example, who is constantly complaining about his wife's lack of interest in sex and how this frustrates him. He hangs out in bars and is always picking up women. But when he does he always gets so drunk that he never quite gets to bed with them.

A husband with a similar story about his wife finally, after many years of complaining, found himself a girlfriend, a woman who was visiting Los Angeles, where he resided. He used the fact that she lived across the country as an excuse for not seeing her very often. She finally took a job in his city. But when she did so, he managed to be so busy in his own career that he could only see her twice a year.

For the most part, single men who suffer from lack of desire have an easier time evading their problem. The pattern is there all along, but they are able to keep the truth from themselves for years if they hop from woman to woman. It is only when they allow the dust to settle that their inherent trouble with desire catches up with them.

This dynamic haunts the love life of a notorious womanizer who operates on New York's chic Upper East Side bar scene. Most of his affairs are one-night stands and brief affairs in which he comes on like a sexual dynamo. He has had three longer relationships in his life, however, and in each one the same thing has happened. He started out very sexually demanding, but his ardor soon began slipping to the point where he ended up sleeping side by side with the woman he cared about without sex taking place for weeks on end. Each of his long affairs finally ended because of lack of sex.

Like many men who are forced to face the truth about their condition, this man manages to rationalize his problem by downgrading the importance of sex. "What has sex got to do with our relationship?" he exclaimed to his most recent long-term love when she started to complain about the lack of action. "Sex isn't important. It's companionship that counts!" he insisted. So far he has not found a woman who feels that love without sex is any better than sex without love (which is his other speciality). But he may.

If a man who suffers from lack of desire marries a woman with as little appetite as his own, they may live happily ever after. More of these celibate or near-celibate marriages exist than we are aware of.

Lack of desire is not always chronic or long-lasting. As I pointed out in the chapter on Men Who Never Make Passes, for some men lack of desire can be a transient thing, caused by physical illness, extreme fatigue, overwork, loss of a loved one, loss of a job, or loss of status. Mental depression is also a notorious desire killer.

But whether lack of desire is transient or chronic, the one thing that can get some men going again—if even only for a brief while—is the fear of loss. If a woman threatens to leave because she is too frustrated, a man may suddenly go into action. Terror of being abandoned usually surmounts any anxieties about intimacy, commitment, or aging that may have inhibited him. Once the situation is stabilized again, however, desire will fade once more.

Today's Woman and Sexual Problems

Are sexual dysfunctions—impotence, in particular, and lack of desire most recently—increasing?

There are good reasons to assume that they are.

Tensions in sex and between the sexes have increased in recent times. Many men worry a great deal more about satisfying a woman than about satisfying themselves. They feel that getting into a woman's bed is like taking a final exam. The exam is harder if you know you are also going to be compared to other men and graded accordingly.

Other men react to today's assertive woman, who may openly want sex, with the same terror they used to feel toward their critical or demanding mothers. When you think you are taking a very important test—one on which your masculinity depends—or when alarm bells about women go off in your head, you are apt to fail sexually.

For young men, in particular, initial sexual experiences may be more stressful than in the past. At one time a boy could make a pass at a girl and be reasonably sure he would be refused. This behavior was part of getting to know the game. You could neck and pet, which is a good way to learn about sex gradually, before you have to take the plunge and "go all the way."

Today, a boy's advances may be accepted quite soon—too soon for some young males. Like his older counterpart, a boy may be aware that he has to satisfy his sex mate, but since he is young and inexperienced, he may not be sure how to do it. Feeling under the gun, he too may fail.

Older husbands today may face wives who, waking up in midlife to what they have been missing, may suddenly insist on more sex or different sex. The middle-aged man who is grappling with the feeling that his sexual powers are waning may become unsettled and even resentful, and he, too, may fail as a result.

Men who can't say "no" are also swelling the ranks of impotent men. Many women now overtly indicate that they want to sleep with a man, and if he does not reciprocate the feeling, but responds only because he thinks he should, he may be left with a body that rebels. He really doesn't want to have sex, so his penis refuses to become erect, even if he goes through all the appropriate actions of a lover.

Men now have to learn to say "no" just as women do.

Chapter 10

Divorced Men

They are the walking wounded—the Divorced Men of America—a legion that makes up a considerable part of the male population of our country.

Divorced Men rarely emerge from marriage—whether they were the ones who took the initiative or not—without immediate emotional repercussions that generally last between one and two years.

Sometimes they feel tremendous ambivalence and guilt. "I suffered terrible pangs about my wife and kids," one man said. "I thought about all the things I hadn't done for them. At the same time I dreamed of screwing eighteen girls a week in my new pad. Only my new pad was terrible. It was in the middle of a slum. I could have afforded better, but I wanted it to leak back to my wife, through my kids, that I was living in a slum and doing penance. And, instead of going out and screwing eighteen girls a week, all I could do for the first three months was lie there, looking out the window, and cry. At night I dreamed of how sweet my wife was and the good times we had.

"When I finally stopped crying, I discovered how

lonely I was. It came as a surprise, and it was humiliating because I had prided myself on being a man with many intellectual resources.

"I couldn't even read, and I couldn't stand one week of loneliness, so I started going out again, but instead of screwing the millions of girls I wanted to, I ended up going steadily with one woman. She was totally unsuitable, I realized after the first two weeks, and I knew it wouldn't last, but I couldn't stand being alone."

Screwing as many women as possible is on many a Divorced Man's agenda, and one told me how he tried to do it: "It got so that I didn't get home for days at a time. I would end up going from one woman's apartment to another. I carried extra pairs of socks and clean underwear around with me in my briefcase. I would wake up in the morning never sure who I was with. Finally, I got sick of that and settled down with the woman I'm still living with."

Another tried to have the best of both worlds. He combined an ongoing relationship with scores of women on the side: "I would spend every weekend with Jennifer and her kid and have lunch with her once a week, and the rest of the time I was balling everything in sight. I was completely out of control and without a conscience. While I was still seeing Jennifer I met a woman I thought I was in love with. She was living with another man at the time. I spent a lot of effort trying to get her to move out and come live with me. She did, and within two weeks I had lost all interest in her. I lost Jennifer when the second woman moved in, and then I tried getting Jennifer to come back to me. She finally did, but that didn't keep me from picking up girls and screwing them whenever I could, even though I was seeing her."

Initially, Divorced Men may feel anger more than anything else: "All I kept thinking about was that cunt sneaking out and having an affair with my friend. She said it started after we decided to separate, but I bet it was going on for years—all those years I was breaking my back to support her. Well, I made sure she didn't get much of my money. Let *him* support her!"

Some feel hostile to all women: "I was resentful about women my whole life because I was afraid they would turn me down if I asked them to put out. After I was divorced, this fear suddenly grew so large that I walked around with a chip on my shoulder toward every woman I met."

Sometimes Divorced Men feel helpless: "The simplest thing suddenly became a big deal after Dinah left. I didn't know how to make a cup of coffee or run a washing machine. I suddenly felt like a baby."

Occasionally, men regard divorce as liberation: "It was such a relief," explained one. "The marriage had been bad for years, and at the end the tension was so tight that anything was liable to cause a big fight. I couldn't even concentrate on driving when I was with her, and once I ran into another car. So after the separation there was a sense of exhilaration. I had left everything behind and I was starting a fresh life."

Sometimes the liberation a man feels is from fidelity: "I never cheated on my wife in the five years we lived together, and since she was a model, she had some beautiful friends. Some of them used to come on to me when she wasn't around, but I was faithful to her, tempting as they were. But within a month after we split, I had screwed every one of them."

The Stages of Reaction

No matter what the Divorced Man feels at first—whether liberation, remorse, pain, unfocused lust, a sense of dislocation, or fear of the future—before he is able to relate well to a woman again, he must go through a series of predictable stages of reaction.

Not everyone passes through in the same order, or with the same intensity. Everything is worse for the man who has been rejected by his wife—but the point is that each man journeys through the following predictable post-divorce phases, no matter what his age or basic orientation toward life:

1. *State of shock:* In this phase a man feels as if life has become unreal. Like a robot, he attends to his everyday tasks automatically and without feeling. He gets up and goes to work lifelessly; he eats without tasting the food. Everything seems alien and at a distance. He tends to be immune to women until this period has passed.

Shock, for certain men, can lead into a period of denial and uncharacteristic behavior. A moderate drinker or nondrinker may suddenly imbibe heavily, a formerly decorous, quiet, well-behaved man may raise hell when he goes out. A stay-at-home may run around. Men in this period of denial feel that their uncharacteristic actions are in response to a new sense of freedom, but what they are doing, in fact, is trying to cut themselves off from the past.

2. *Grief and mourning:* A certain amount of grief at the end of a marriage is healthy. Healthy Mourners feel some sadness or a sense of loss or waste about all those years together. The man who grieves in a healthy way generally tends to assess what caused his marriage to break up, and he uses the knowledge to live more wisely in the future.

Unhealthy Mourners, on the other hand, become obsessed about what has occurred and sink into bottomless wells of self-pity. They ruminate continually and are visibly preoccupied. By keeping their thoughts on wife and marriage, they, in effect, hold onto the relationship. They feel, subliminally, that if they stopped thinking about it, the marriage would die. Their magical thought process goes like this: "If I continue to think about my wife, she will keep on thinking about me." They are apt to talk about their wives or the divorce all the time, as well.

Since the Unhealthy Mourner keeps his wife with him in this way, even though he is divorced, he can't respond to other women appropriately. He feels, for one thing, that she is still there and is watching him, or that if he responds to a woman, she will respond to another man.

Some Unhealthy Mourners go out with women in response to behests from friends, but they do so automatically and without much interest. Others date as a provocative act toward their wives. They think their wives will somehow know, and become jealous. Men in the mourning stage, whether handling their grief in a healthy or unhealthy way, are bad bets for women who want a good relationship. They are still too absorbed in themselves and in their past.

3. *Anger and protest:* A man may go into this stage first, and only after he simmers down will he begin to feel a sense of shock or grief. He gets angry at his spouse, at fate, at the world, at the divorce settlement. Rage, as an initial reaction to divorce, is often a defense mechanism for the man who feels guilty about the breakup of his

marriage. He doesn't have to feel the discomfort of remorse if he can be mad at his wife and at the dirty blow
life has dealt him.

Anger is sometimes a protection against a sense of
vulnerability as well. A man who feels helpless because
of his fate may compensate by rage. Fury is a good an-
tidote to helplessness. It makes a man feel strong.

Men are particularly dangerous in this post-divorce
phase. They may take out on other women the fury they
feel toward their wives. Unhealthy Mourners and Angry
Men are prone to want to do women in. They can use
women only for sex; they can act rudely or with lack of
consideration.

Some Angry Men go to the opposite extreme. They
are enraged, but also so guilty about their emotions that
they bend over backward to be nice about everything all
the time. Their goody-goody behavior is just as extreme
as that of the man who acts out his ire.

The Angry Divorced Man, whether enraged or ov-
ernice, confuses women, since he tends to overreact to
things that don't warrant it. For example, a man whose
wife cheated on him may become furious if his new woman
makes a date to see a friend from out of town without
him. He reacts to her as if she were his lying wife. The
feeling is appropriate, but it is directed at the wrong object.

4. *Reorganization:* Having gone through shock, anger, and mourning, in any order, a man should be able
to pick up the pieces and start life anew. He begins to see
women and relate to them, not as symbols or reminders
of the past, but as human beings in their own right. This
stage, if all goes well, will lead to the final resolution of
divorce—the choice of another partner.

Survival Tactics

During the separation blues men employ diverse survival tactics.

Some become recluses. They don't go near man,
woman, or dog for a while. Others keep up with their
male friends and shun only women. They cut off their
erotic feelings and become asexual. Some of these are discussed in Chapter 5. Men who shun women are ambivalent—they retain a residual attachment to their former

spouse. The pain of the divorce is too much for them. They can't take the chance of being rejected or hurt any more.

Other men fasten onto another woman quickly. Intensely lonely after divorce, they react badly to their radically changed lifestyle and yearn for stability. These men tend to get involved with sympathetic, accepting women who nurse them along the bumpy path to recovery and help them regain faith in themselves as men and lovers once more.

An unusually dependent man may make his first affair after divorce his last. He feels a great need to replace what he has lost, so he rushes into remarriage. In reality, he may be a desperate man. Not only is he unable to stand being alone, but all that laundry and meal-making is too much for him.

More often, however, after the woman in the first affair has fulfilled her function—after she has bound up a man's wounds, that is, applied a Band-Aid to his self-esteem, and made him somewhat whole again—he leaves her. "I'll always remember you with gratitude," he says. He may even have a tear in his eye as they part. He is not lying when he says he will remember her warmly, but as nice as the relationship was while he needed her, he surely isn't ready to settle down again yet, so he moves on. Being the first woman in a divorced man's new life is generally a thankless task if you want to be more than a Florence Nightingale.

For a lot of men, divorce is not the end of the marriage. They continue to play games with their wives and children. They may adopt the hairshirt approach to life after divorce, choosing to live in the most deprived and squalid way possible for a while. Their purpose is to make an ex-wife feel guilty and/or to expiate their own sense of guilt.

Others never quite take their feet out of the door. They may choose, for example, to set up their tent in an apartment down the block from the old family homestead. They may forget to change their mailing address so that they have to come by regularly to see what the postman has dropped off—and perhaps to see who has dropped in. One man who always managed to come by unexpectedly on the weekends when the kids were visiting *him*, to pick up baseball bats or gloves, finally found what he was really looking for—his wife enjoying herself with a new lover while the children were away.

A certain number take a what-the-hell approach to the marital disaster. Divorce has made their life into a shambles anyway. They may throw over all their responsibilities, quit their job and live on unemployment for a while, or take a series of fly-by-night jobs. One newly divorced man I met had recently given up his own business and taken a job as a clerk in a health food store. Another man did his cast-responsibility-to-the-winds act in a more dramatic way. He went on a year-long gambling spree in Europe and Las Vegas and managed to lose $150,000—his entire life's savings, which left him with zero, since he had given everything else to his ex-wife.

Some who act in this way are surfacing a long-felt resentment about women and marriage—a commitment that is too burdensome. Many of them were married too early in life and, once divorced, they revert to an irresponsible adolescent state.

Others become vindictive in abandoning responsibility. "Let her take care of the kids, she's making a good salary," said one man who is currently drifting from one low-paying job to another in order to avoid keeping up his child-support payments. Particularly if they are angry at the divorce settlement, some men will change legal residence to other states, or manage to withdraw their assets from accounts in their own names in order to avoid further support payments.

It is very common for a Divorced Man to try to recapture his youth after divorce, particularly if he is middle-aged. He may dye his hair, lose weight, or, these days, resort to a face lift. He imitates, in effect, what a discarded woman traditionally did—and often still does. Even if he doesn't try to alter his appearance, there is one thing he is sure to do—chase after as many women as he can to affirm his attractiveness and desirability. A large, and growing, number of Divorced Men want only young girls. One man in his late forties admitted that his cutoff year for women was twenty-five. "After that, they want to marry you," he said. Frequently this rationalization masks an underlying need to retain youth, or a fear of entering a peer relationship.

A space salesman sobered up after a protracted young-girl period, but only after a shock. He looked down at the latest in his series of practically anonymous young girls and broke out into a sweat. "Christ! She looked just like my daughter!"

Prognosis

For a while the frenzied sexual activity of the newly sprung husband may make him feel more vibrant than he ever has before, affirming the wisdom of the separation in case he had doubted it. Sooner or later, though, the novelty wears off and may be replaced by depression. Then the wiser men take off their running shoes and start to look for a more meaningful relationship. Others, less wise, try to outsprint their depression by a frantic—though progressively disappointing—sexual pace.

The modes of behavior I've described are usually transient. Recluses come out of hiding after they stop mourning. Men who have rejected responsibility resume their roles as solid citizens once anger has abated. Middle-aged men get tired of young chicks and start to warm their feet by the fire with someone closer to their own age. Men who have hopped from bed to bed in search of re-assurance come to a halt once they feel better about themselves.

Except for the men who get stuck. Never resolving their anger or mourning, they become permanent emotional cripples as far as women are concerned. They are basically narcissistic, self-centered men. Once burned, they see smoke ever after when they get close to a woman. They go on, after divorce, to become the equivalent of old bachelors, indulging in one-night stands or juggling several women at once, or going from one affair to another. It is increasingly common in our society to encounter a man five, ten, fifteen, or twenty years after his divorce still sowing his wild oats.

Some Newly Divorced Men suffer from sexual problems for a while. Particularly if they have been rejected by a wife, they may feel inadequate as men and respond with impotence. Impotence may result from depression. Also, anxiety about pleasing new women for a man who hasn't been near anyone but his wife for many years, can cause dysfunction.

When you go out with Divorced Men you may be heir not only to his emotional and sexual problems, but to troubles connected with his children. Some men manage to see you only sporadically, pleading weekends with children and other parental responsibilities. Their daddy duties are real, but men like this also use their children as rationalizations for their true motivation—they don't want to get too close to anyone.

Others are cavalier about having casual sleepover dates on weekends when their children visit. They may justify this behavior as being good for the kids—"They have to know what life is all about"—but the children may, quite naturally, resent the intruder in their mother's place, and treat you coldly or even hostilely or raise hell to direct their father's attention back to themselves.

Some fathers want to make their dates into surrogate mothers on weekends. You schlep with the kids to bowling alleys and zoos, and end up preparing snacks and meals for the whole family. Often men who turn dates into housewives are comfortable only with women in domestic or maternal roles, but they cast you in the role too soon, without the prelude of courtship or the benefit of marriage.

Ex-husbands often spend an inordinate amount of time talking about their ex-wives. If they do, you can be sure they are not really relating to you, but using their previous relationship to avoid the present one. Or they use their reduced financial circumstances to escape another close entanglement. They plead they can't afford it. Money is an easy excuse. What is more important to the man, a previous lifestyle or a relationship? If he offers a diminished bank account as a defense against possible remarriage, he isn't ready for love.

Unless he exhibits signs of being stuck in one of the post-divorce stages, a Divorced Man will be ready for a long-term relationship and/or marriage a year or two after his separation. *Before* then, he will not be ready even if you are. *After* that, he will be prepared to accept an identity other than that of Divorced Man and move toward becoming a Steady Lover or even a Husband.

Chapter 11

Kinky Lovers

Some men want women to engage in the kinkier forms of sex, and their number seems to be growing. A thirty-six-year-old department store buyer told me about her recent initiation into one of the contemporary world's more popular bed sports: "I had been going with Leonard for six months. During that time, while he made love to me he would fantasize verbally about another woman being in bed with us. I am fairly liberal in my attitudes and, because I knew it stimulated him, I played along with his fantasy. I would tell him what we would all do together. I thought it would be confined to fantasy. I was shocked one night when I arrived at his apartment to find another woman there. He introduced her to me as an old friend who had come by for a drink. It didn't take me long to figure out what was really going on.

"We all had dinner together, and then, on the pretext of building a fire, he maneuvered us into his den, where there was a big studio bed. Suddenly he was kissing me, with her watching, and then he began undressing me. I protested, but he kept telling me that it was me he loved and that she would just add to our fun as a couple.

"I felt ambivalent about what was happening. I was

resentful because he had set me up for this. At the same time, all that fantasizing had some effect on me. I was curious. I went along with it and it was O.K., but I would never do it again with him or anyone else. It really isn't my cup of tea. I prefer one-to-one sex."

Another woman met a Kinky Lover soon after her divorce. "He lived in the building I had just moved into," she told me. "We went out together for a couple of weeks, and then he started asking me if I had ever been to bed with another woman. I could see that the idea turned him on. I told him I hadn't, but that didn't stop him from asking me to invite one of my friends over so that we could all go to bed together. He called me prudish and old-fashioned when I wouldn't do it."

A woman I know recalled a telephone conversation with one of her husband's friends: "We had done a lot of talking about sex in the past. But it was just talk in general rather than anything personal. One night he called and totally shocked me. He was going to an orgy the following evening and wanted to know if I would go. When I told him I would just watch but not participate, he told me to forget it."

Two women told me about men who kept pressuring them to take part in a "threesome," which is the current term for what is also referred to as a *ménage à trois*. Whatever you call it, it adds up to the same—three in a bed. Most of the trios consist of two women and a man, the combination men favor. Less often, the threesome involves two men and a woman, which some women prefer.

One of the women who was being pressured was rather desperate when she recounted her story. Her boyfriend of six years was seeing another woman, and she was trying everything to get him back. The bait he was holding out was specific: She had to find another woman so he could watch the two females make love. She was willing to do even this. Anything to get him back, but she couldn't find a woman who was willing to go along with their "scene."

She called me later to tell me she had finally hired a call girl, but even though she had done what he wanted, he didn't come back to her. It seems all he really wanted to do was demean her. And he succeeded.

Orgies and threesomes have always been common in male fantasy, as the ancient art of India, Persia, and Japan testify, but more men daydream about multiple sex partners today because of the proliferation of kinky sex in men's magazines and pornographic films. Our culture not only advertises the outer limits of sex, but encourages the acting out of every pornographic dream in order to reach new peaks of fulfillment. Unfortunately, the experience never matches the dream. Fantasy is always better than reality, as one television producer found out:

"I was visiting the Coast and was invited by a business acquaintance to come to his home one night. He said he was having a party. I had no idea what kind of party he meant. When I arrived I found wall-to-wall nude bodies. I had always wondered about orgies, but seeing that crush of bodies was like looking at merchandise on a sales counter at Macy's. In a flash I decided this wasn't for me. I wouldn't even take off my coat. I waved hello and goodbye to my host, who was coming toward me stark naked with an erection. I got out of there fast."

Another man I spoke to had no such qualms. In his fifty-five years he had tried everything—threesomes a couple of times a year, orgies whenever available. He slept with a woman once on the behest of her husband, who wanted to watch, and he picked up a beautiful woman at a costume ball only to discover when he took her home that she was a he. "I slept with 'her' anyway," he laughed, "and pretended her anus was a vagina."

Why Men Get Into Kink

There are a a number of reasons why men become swingers. Here are thirteen of them:

1. A good proportion of the men who indulge in exotic forms of sex suffer from a symptom of depression—ahedonia—the inability to take pleasure in anything. These men try new kinds of sex, hoping to find a lasting source of pleasure. They never do. One jaded thirty-two-year-old bachelor who complained that sex had lost its kick because "nobody holds out any more," said, "I finally tried sex with a group that met every Friday night. I thought it was going to be great. The atmosphere was terrific. They even had a swimming pool. The first two times I found it exciting. Then it became the same old thing again."

2. A man may be dissatisfied with normal sex not because of depression and ahedonia but because of unrealistic expectations. He feels that sex always has to be

an earth-moving, bell-ringing experience, a common myth in our society, fostered by movies and books. When regular sex fails to live up to its advance notices, he begins to search for something to give him that missing extra kick. One accountant who wanders from woman to woman in search of the ultimate turn-on said, "I always hope the next girl I meet will have something sensational or different to offer erotically. But after three times the sex always wears off and then the relationship goes." He is currently seeking the ever-elusive thrill at orgies held at a private club in Manhattan.

3. A number of swingers seek in sex the answer to all of life's problems. They may be alienated or lonely, feel helpless and overwhelmed by life, but they think, "If I can get fulfillment in sex, the rest of my existence will become better." The number of men who expect sex to accomplish what nature never intended it to is growing. These misguided seekers are looking for happiness and spiritual fulfillment where it isn't.

4. A man may be simply bored with the mundane quality of his life and searching for thrills. He feels he should be having a wonderful, rich, full life and can't handle it when it turns out to be a normal existence with repetitive tasks and continual obligations. He turns to exotic sex to add color to his drab life and make himself feel "special."

5. Insecure men with fears about their adequacy who, although they feel inferior, have to show the world they are superior, often try to be in the vanguard. Some acquire the newest gadget, are the first to try a new restaurant or read the latest book. Others restrict their quest for novelty to sex. They dabble in orgies and threesomes like comparative shoppers. They are following the newest style and testing the latest product.

6. Swinging may be associated with youth. Middle-aged men sometimes seek rejuvenation in kinky sex, generally with younger partners, who add to the feeling that they are dipping into the fountain of youth. Other middle-aged men take to any and all forms of sex with a vengeance after a divorce. They are determined to make up for what they missed while they were restricted to one partner in marriage.

7. Some men use exotic sex as an escape from reality and responsibility, as a flight from business tensions or

pressures associated with relationships. Men like this want to get lost in the sensation of the moment with no strings attached. If group sex becomes a long-term habit, it is an indication of an underlying problem with intimacy. If it is just done as a passing phase—during a time of business troubles, for example, or right after a divorce—it may not be pathological, but a respite from burdensome cares or memories.

8. A husband who finds it difficult to be monogamous but wants to keep a committed relationship, sometimes finds a comfortable solution to his two warring needs. He invites his wife to take part in group sex with other couples. It's a way of having your cake and eating it too.

9. A husband whose marriage is in trouble may use swinging with a wife as a way to spice up a sex life that has gone sour. Sex is symbolic for him—if sex is working, the marriage is. Extramarital coupling may add a little extra thrill for a while, but marriage problems don't stay solved for long with a fillip of exotic sex.

10. Men who try to mold themselves into a *Playboy* image of manhood may take part in group sex and threesomes to add to their view of themselves as swinging bachelors.

11. A man who wants to aggrandize himself will turn to threesomes specifically. He feels, for the moment, powerful because he is able to satisfy two women at once. He is also like a potentate, with two female slaves catering to him simultaneously.

12. A fair number of men who experiment with orgies suffer from sexual difficulties like impotence or premature ejaculation. They hope the extra stimulation will enable them to function better. Whether this works or not, they don't need to fear recriminations or feel guilty. Sex at an orgy is impersonal and anonymous.

13. A man may try group sex once or twice simply because he is curious. His interest has been piqued by pornography. Once his curiosity is satisfied, he will let well enough alone. If kinky sex is merely a matter of experimentation, it isn't necessarily a sign of neurosis. Only if a man makes it a regular habit does he have problems.

Some of the men I've described suffer from a poor self-image. Sex for them, and all the men who take part in orgies, is a shallow experience, a device to reassure themselves about their own adequacy. Interestingly, many of these men downgrade the experience. They go to an orgy, say afterward that it was boring, then go on to plan the next orgy.

Some kinky sex afficionados are immature individuals, stuck in an infantile stage. The sexuality of babies is polymorphous—infants do anything they feel like, when they feel like it. Men who engage in kinky sex often need to gratify their every urge, no matter what form it takes, just like babies.

Other Kinky Lovers are fixated in adolescence, when sex, in fact as well as fantasy, is used to make one feel more adequate and powerful. These are men who feel aggrandized by multiple sex partners.

For still others, group sex satisfies a voyeuristic need. The act of watching is almost as good as doing.

A Kinky Lover who tries to pressure you to join him in group sex is saying: "Sex with you is not enough, I need more pleasure." Generally the sex is not good enough only because of a recurrent fantasy. When a man dreams about more than one body, one person cannot be fulfilling.

The Kinky Lover may also be revealing that he is bothered by shared intimacy. He is admitting, in effect, "I have to dilute it," or, "I can't stand it."

For some, kinky sex is a way of asserting control in a relationship. They like to force you to comply with their wish for kink, and even try to get you to supply the extra woman for a threesome. In this way they receive double pleasure: (1) you give in to their demands, and (2) you yield in a way humiliating to you. You are, in effect, procuring for them.

Asking a woman to engage in kinky sex is often a way to show hostility. The woman who was trying to get her lover back and finally hired a call girl to join them in bed told me that her boyfriend only wanted to see her perform cunnilingus on another woman. For him, this was a shameful act and he was proving his contempt for her by making her do it.

Cunnilingus or not, many men feel inwardly that they are demeaning a woman by making her sleep with another man or woman. Nor are they necessarily consistent. The same fellow who may ask one woman to take part in an orgy or threesome may not do it with another.

One husband who was no longer in love with his wife kept pressing her to swing with other couples, or at least to take part in sex with another woman. Ostensibly, it was to improve their sex life, but he was also angry with her.

He divorced his wife finally and soon after met another woman. He confessed to his therapist that he wouldn't dream of asking his new woman to do anything except make love to him. A suggestion for kink would be disrespectful to her and he would be jealous.

Men who genuinely care for a woman rarely want to share her. He had contempt for his wife but loved his new companion.

Basically, Kinky Lovers have a negative attitude toward women. For them, women are objects to be used, means to an end, instruments for their own gratification—not human beings with needs of their own. It is rare, however, that Kinky Lovers have any inkling of their underlying feelings.

The dehumanization of women in group sex is often an outlet for anger and resentment by men who feel threatened by women. Kinky sex may be increasing today precisely because more men feel intimidated by contemporary women. By making them into anonymous objects these men transform women into less powerful beings, bring them down to size, put them in their place.

How Women Respond

Some women are curious about sex experimentation themselves. They want to try it and they do. Others have a need to feel subjugated by a man. They give in to the request not because they desire the act itself but because they need to be submissive. They translate a man's desire for their participation as a sign of love. Or a woman may react by feeling like a man's partner in crime. A sense of camaraderie makes them feel closer to their bedmate; they may even enjoy going out with him to seduce other women or other couples for sex games.

Other women may take part in the experience but feel demeaned by the episode. Once they are in bed, some feel competitive and are jealous of the man's attentions to the other woman. Or they may find themselves in a strange new alliance, teaming up with the other woman against the man. Said one attractive divorcee: "He started ordering her around so much when we were all in bed together that I began to feel for her and dislike him. He was always a bully and chauvinist, and I knew it, but on that night I saw it more clearly than ever. It ended up with both of us putting on our clothes and walking out on him."

Occasionally, a woman may discover that she enjoys the woman sexually more than the man. One for whom this was true told me: "We couldn't wait for him to leave. We sent him out for the newspaper in the morning just so that we could be alone."

Most women, however, are turned off by proposals for threesomes and orgies, and they decline either graciously or angrily. They feel humiliated by the request and interpret it as a sign that the man does not really care for them. They are usually right. The man who makes such a request is rarely in love.

On the other hand, some kinky-sounding proposals or acts by men may not really be kinky at all. One generation's perversion is another one's fad. For example, oral sex was considered perverted by our grandmothers and great-grandmothers. Today it is a common practice.

Considerable sexual experimentation is going on in our world. Many men and women like to fool around with sex toys like vibrators, or to exchange fantasies while making love, or to use mirrors to watch. Some men enjoy using obscenities during sex, and some want you to talk dirty to them. Still others want to try anal sex.

None of these things are cause for outrage or alarm if done in the spirit of experimentation rather than exploitation. Nothing in these practices need make you feel demeaned or harmed. If you feel like experimenting, go ahead, and don't worry.

A woman should not allow herself to get involved in anything she has genuine qualms about, no matter how much pressure is applied. If something turns you off or frightens you, you shouldn't do it because you are afraid of losing the man, or because you want to please him.

A famous story about Lenny Bruce should serve as a warning. He kept pressuring his wife to have sex with another woman and him, and when she finally did he called her a lesbian.

If a man has empathy and respect for you, he will drop his request if you turn him down. If he doesn't, then think twice about him. If he isn't considerate about this, he won't be in other ways either.

The Sadomasochistic Man

Sadomasochism has become much more evident in our culture in the past few years. Its influence can be felt in some high-fashion photography and in men's magazines, from the slickest to the raunchiest. One of the hottest photographers today, Hemut Newton, who, in certain chic circles is almost a cult, pictures women in dog collars. Women appear in other submissive roles as well.

In case you haven't guessed, sadomasochism is a perversion. In relationships where it occurs, one partner forcefully dominates, and the other submits excessively. The inflicting and receiving of pain are integral to the interaction.

The pain may be psychic. Acts meant to humiliate, embarrass, or degrade are heaped upon the masochist by the sadist. It can also be physical, ranging from heavy beatings at one extreme, to the more common spankings. Bondage, in which the masochist is tied up by the sadist, is a traditional sadomasochistic practice.

Love bites, small pinches, and slight scratching can occur in normal lovemaking, and, although these may resemble sadomasochistic acts, they cannot be considered pathological if they occur as a response to passion.

During sex, for the true masochist and sadist, some kind of script is generally acted out in which pain is consciously inflicted in a controlled way. The sadist must hurt the masochist enough to satisfy but not enough to damage, and a certain amount of trust is implied between the two partners. There is a tendency to rely on ritual. The use of costumes is not unusual in sadomasochistic sex. Masochistic men who go to prostitutes to be abused often want to dress up as dogs or babies or even French maids. Leather is often worn by sadists, and on the gay scene there are "leather bars," where sadists and masochists meet one another. A whip is a common tool of sadists.

If you get around much, you may meet a man who may hint about his perverted sexual tastes after a while.

A young woman writer who was suffering from writer's block told me about meeting an executive of a large corporation who, after taking her out to dinner a couple of times and listening to her work problems, sug-

gested a solution. She needed a strong man to tell her
what to do, he said. He would spend some time with her
and would lock her in a room and tie her to her chair in
front of the typewriter. He would only let her out after
she had produced some work. If she didn't do any work
she would be spanked. As he unfolded his scheme for
helping her, he revealed that he was a veteran of sadistic
affairs and enjoyed hitting women on the buttocks,
punching them lightly on the breasts and vagina, and
making them dress up in costumes. The writer wisely
decided that he was not the answer to her block.

One woman who flirted with her own masochism
with a lover described how he would rip clothes off her
with his bare hands or take a razor blade and cut them
off her. "He always bought me new dresses afterward,"
she said. A television production assistant told me about
two men who wanted her to tie them up during sex. And
one man, who is physically big but has a gentle soul, was
dismayed recently when a woman he had started to make
love to suddenly asked him to slap her. He couldn't do it,
although it frustrated and upset her.

A masochist needs a sadist, and vice versa, and a
joke in SM circles starts by asking, "What's the definition
of a tragedy?" The answer: "When a masochist meets another masochist."

What Turns People Into Sadists and Masochists

Karen Horney called sadism a neurotic need for superiority. Sadists frequently are fearful people who frustrate, exploit, humiliate, or enslave as a way of demon-
strating their strength and the weakness of others. The
unknowns of life frighten sadists, and they armor themselves against their dreads by a distorted show of power.
Sadists also frequently feel they are treated as unimportant in the world, and they act out their resentment
through brutality.

Masochists are fearful about life and its unknown
terrors, too, but they solve their dread in an opposite way.
They flaunt their helplessness. They accept exploitation
and humiliation to prove they are unthreatening, uncom-
petitive, and loving, no matter what. In this way they seek

to enlist others, notably sadists, to protect them against the terrors of the world.

Sadism and masochism are two sides of the same coin. The person who is sadistic punishes and denounces the weaknesses in others that he hates in himself.

Most therapists agree that the masochist is also consumed by a sense of guilt, and that he or she accepts abuse as an act of expiation.

According to reports from prostitutes, many masochistic men who pay to be abused are, in real life, powerful businessmen and politicians. These men are among many who subscribe to the success-at-any-price philosophy. As a result, they have a history of doing things they don't feel good about. In masochism they rid themselves of some of the guilt that burdens them.

Although some experts feel that the number of women sadists has been underestimated, most agree that the majority are men. You stand a better chance of meeting a sadistic male who will want you to be his masochistic foil, than of a masochistic male who will want you to play rough with him.

The sadist may appeal to your ingrained conventional notions of femininity if he comes on—as many do—as a would-be protector. He may promise to make your life easier by taking all decisions out of your hands. If you are feeling harassed, this promise may seem tempting.

To my surprise, a woman doctor who had worked hard to get where she was, recently fell for the blandishments of a sadist who promised her relief from her demanding practice. Since she had to make life and death decisions every day, she found it tempting for a while to renounce all decision-making and just follow the sadist's orders. She played his game for a couple of months, but finally realized it was no answer to the pressure in her life. She asked for more rights in their relationship, but that was not where his kicks lay, so he left her.

For men who pressure you to engage in sadomasochistic practices the same role applies as to any other form of kink. Don't do anything that upsets you, or that you object to, just to get a man or keep him. He must allow for your tastes and needs, or you don't have a viable relationship.

Chapter 12

Other Impossible Lovers

Here are short rundowns on some other neurotic types who are plaguing women—and themselves—today:

Men Who Find Women Possessive and Demanding

"You are possessive and demanding!" Sound familiar?

Almost every woman has heard those two magic words—"possessive" and "demanding"—at some time in her life. They are staples in the male vocabulary. "Possessive" and "demanding" are schlepped out when a woman objects to her "steady" sleeping with the blonde down the block, when she wants to see him more than once a month, when she doesn't *always* want to do everything his way.

Although any man is liable at any time to use either word, there are P and D specialists. Their affairs always turn out the same: P and D. There are two variations on the P and D theme—the Portnoy Ploy and the No-Involvement Ploy.

THE PORTNOY PLOY: Portnoy is the man who still lives with his mother, even though he moved out years ago. Portnoy's Martyred Mom ran the roost. Guilt was the wand she waved over her son's head to wring compliance to her slightest wish, her every command. "How could you do this to me when I am sacrificing my whole life for you?" was her eternal message. Rather than be racked with guilt, little Portnoy learned to follow orders promptly and tried to anticipate her desires.

Portnoy, grown up, reacts to every woman as he did to his Martyred Mom. Everything is rosy until he is into a close relationship where he feels he must please. He tries to ferret out a woman's every wish, divine her every desire.

In the process of anticipating her wishes, Portnoy often reads things into a woman's mind. He thinks she wants what she really doesn't. He reacts to both imaginary desires and real ones like a soldier in the field. He snaps to automatically, obeys efficiently. Trying so hard to please, he begins to feel burdened by obeying orders. He feels his love has turned into a virago and that he is henpecked. "Why doesn't she do anything for me?" he kvetches to himself. "Why do I always have to do everything for her?"

Portnoy, in fact, has *made* the woman dominate him, or he lives as though she does. But, oblivious to his self-enslavement, he soon resents his wife or girlfriend. He sees her as terribly possessive, impossibly demanding. He feels he can never live up to her expectations (which are really *his* expectations) and he rebels. He criticizes, he quarrels and, finally, Portnoy and his mate become the Alienated Couple or they split.

The Portnoys of the world are doomed to find all relationships with women oppressive. They learned their lesson from Mom well. The price of love is obedience, and the price is too high.

The syndrome can set in quickly. If a Portnoy regards sexual contact as emotional intimacy, he may start to feel edgy soon after sleeping with a woman. For most P and D Lovers, however, the sense of being possessed and demanded of doesn't start until commitment, in marriage or an affair.

THE NO-INVOLVEMENT LOVER: An important variation on Portnoy is the man who starts off his relationships by telling a woman immediately, "I can't get involved." A charming woman writer I know cherishes two cocktail napkins on which two separate doodlers had written that phrase in answer to her question about their intentions.

At the same time that this P and D Lover is telling a woman he can't get involved, he is also acting as if she is the most important thing in the world to him. He calls her every day on the telephone, he sees her regularly. Sooner or later, because he is so attentive, the woman does get emotionally involved and begins to press for more commitment. He protests, again, that he can't get involved, but continues to act as if he is. He keeps calling and seeing her. Pressure mounts from her. She starts to feel bitter at his unwillingness to commit himself. In turn, he begins to feel resentful and hurt. After all, he is only doing what he warned her he would—not get involved. The relationship goes on as before, nevertheless. They see each other all the time. She keeps wanting more from him, and by now he is reading this as a sign that she is "possessive" and "demanding."

She is getting more and more confused because his actions do not match his words. He obviously wants to be with her, no matter what he says. She doesn't know where she stands. As her demands escalate, the P and D Lover feels sad. "This is how it always ends up," he tells her. "Every time I start to get too close I feel I don't have a life of my own," and they either hang together in no-involvement-man's land, with the woman becoming progressively bitter, or they part.

He, too, has set it up so that the woman turns into a shrew. He rarely calls her "possessive and demanding" to her face, but inwardly he labels his beloved a demanding bitch.

Men Who Try Too Hard to Please

Close in action, but not interaction or motivation, to the P and D Lover, is The Man Who Tries Too Hard to Please. He does not react to love as though it were a series of orders; nevertheless, he conforms to the woman he is with. He has only the faintest notion of his own needs, of what he likes and dislikes. His greatest desire in life is to be unobtrusive and liked.

In trying to please you he is also trying to assume your identity as a way to find one of his own. Your enthusiasms become his. If you dislike chocolate, he shares your distaste. If you love modern art, so does he. Men Who Try Too Hard to Please don't arouse strong emotions. They are essentially passive, pleasant, sometimes bland, always inoffensive. They are what is sometimes referred to as "nice schnooks."

Many women like such men, even if they can't love them, and many settle for one of them in marriage. He can have a sweet charm, and, anyway, he is so nice to you, how can you resist? Pleasers often attach themselves to strong, opinionated women, whose outward assurance covers a multitude of insecurities. Strong/vulnerable women respond to Men Who Try Too Hard to Please because they feel secure with them. Pleasers can be counted on and trusted. Their goal in life is to satisfy your every need. Sometimes a Pleaser and a strong/vulnerable female make a successful match. He assumes her strong identity, she gains security from him. No high romance, but a lot of peace. Sometimes, however, down the marriage road trouble looms. She may discover, finally, that his pleasing ways are really a cover-up for weakness. He never has an opinion of his own. She may begin to feel bored by him, or become irritated by his noncommittal ways. He, on the other hand, may start to blame his own ineptness on her. How can he take a stand on anything? She took over his life! Or he may accuse her of not giving him enough time or helping him enough with his problems. If divorce occurs she may feel guilty about it, remembering, in retrospect, all the nice things he did for her.

A second kind of Man Who Tries Too Hard to Please is not as benign as his passive counterpart. The Barter Pleaser comes on like a paternal, well-meaning mentor. He is someone you can go to with your troubles, and he will give you sympathy and advice. For him, helping and pleasing are a trade-off. An adding machine is constantly running up the tariff in his head. You end up owing him for his many kindnesses.

The Barter Pleaser wants to control you, and he does so by guilt. He *expects* you to feel obligated to him because he is so good to you. When it comes time for him to extract payment, watch out! If you don't go along with what he wants, you're dead. He explodes and will bear a grudge forever. He is not above saying, "After all I have done for you..."

Partners in love and marriage often end up subservient to the Barter Pleaser. You are eternally in his debt simply because he is so good to you, even if you don't want what he is "giving." Sneaky fellow, he manages to take charge by deciding what to give you and when.

Health Freaks and Exercise Nuts

He jogs, he works out at the gym religiously, he plays tennis every day, he does push-ups.

He may eat health foods, swallow dozens of vitamins every day, and be on the fashionable diet of the moment—low cholesterol, vegetarian, Zen macrobiotic.

He is the Exercise Nut or the Health Freak, and often both, simultaneously.

Freaks and Nuts have a glowing inner vision of themselves as strong and vigorous, an image they are constantly trying to live up to and maintain. Frequently Freaks and Nuts are overly concerned about retaining their youth. They may or may not be young in years, but they have trouble accepting adulthood and maturity. They prefer to remain semi-children.

What always eats at the healthy, vigorous insides of the Freak and Nut is a preoccupation with death. He sees it all around him—in the food he eats, the air he breathes, his sedentary life. Feeling more vulnerable than most, he tries to protect himself from the inevitable by scrupulously taking care of his body.

In personal relationships, a Health Freak or an Exercise Nut can be very controlling. He is picky about what he will or will not eat, so you have to cook only things he likes, or only go to health food restaurants. He has to be up every morning at six, so you have to go to bed early with him. Freaks and Nuts whose regimes are their primary preoccupation outside of work are often escaping from the confines of a relationship which makes them anxious and uncomfortable. They play tennis or jog in preference to being close and intimate. They are often so concerned with food or exercise—their talismans against death—that they put little warmth or thought into the relationship.

If you do not share his obsession, the Freak or Nut will often criticize the "condition" you are in. He complains that you are overweight or flabby, and if you get a cold it's because you haven't been taking vitamins or eating the right foods. His attitude is competitive, almost hostile. He is capable, for example, of walking at an extremely rapid pace to prove that you can't keep up with him and that he is in better shape.

This kind of tactic succeeds in eroding the intimacy that makes him fearful. It also serves as a rationale against rejection. If you leave him, who needed you, anyway? You were soft and flabby, not a fit mate for a strong and vigorous person like himself.

The Fastidious Compulsive Lover

He's the man who wants everything just so. The house must be tidy at all times. A speck of dust drives him crazy. A pile of papers sends him up the wall. His clothing is always neatly hung up, and you had better not leave a pair of pantyhose slung over a chair. He's the Fastidious Lover for whom life is a never-ending, rigorous ritual.

The Fastidious Lover's fussiness is a compulsion. Sometimes a compulsive man isn't only tidy. Often he has to have everything exactly the way he wants it in every other area of life as well.

He is a take-charge man. Unless he can dominate he becomes anxious. Fastidiousness is a way of controlling the environment—and that includes you. You have to comply with his wishes. If you break any of his rules (and he has one for almost every aspect of life) it upsets him and he complains, or attacks, or sulks.

To get their way, Compulsive Lovers use devious means unless they are very macho. The macho Compulsive will order you around up front and insist on having things done his way, because the man takes charge.

The majority of Compulsives are not as brutally domineering on the surface, but they manage to arrange to get their own way, anyhow. For example, one Compulsive who started to live with a woman kept telling his partner how much he admired her taste. He insisted they shop together to furnish their new apartment because she had such exquisite sensibilities. On shopping trips, however, he would let her wander around stores looking at things, and while she did, he ordered furniture. By the end of a month of shopping trips the Compulsive had ordered everything without consulting her, and the apartment was furnish exactly the way he wanted it without any sign of her taste at all.

Compulsives must keep things shipshape or control every small detail in their lives, because they basically feel inadequate. They experience life as overwhelming, and in order not to be crushed they keep a tight rein on their environment.

Compulsives are people who need distance between themselves and others. They are not usually very warm or affectionate. Their concentration on minutiae keeps them from thinking about their wives or girlfriends. They are incapable of being empathetic, sympathetic, or even trying to understand another's point of view.

Life with them is a constant round of criticisms and "suggestions" which are really demands. They are always making themselves unhappy, or you, or both; in that way they don't have to be loving.

It is difficult for Compulsives to be spontaneous; they are rarely able to loosen up enough to take pleasure in anything. The only thing that tickles them is order—*their* sense of order, not yours.

Compulsives are in great need of a close affiliation; at the same time, they can't stand relationships. Intimacy frightens them. Besides, a woman tends to louse up their meticulous universe.

Women in relationships with Compulsives tend to feel constricted and smothered. Sex lives are often erratic. In some periods the Compulsive is full of desire. At other times, if he feels overwhelmed by anxiety or depression, which always stalk him, he turns off.

Occasionally one meets a Compulsive whose compulsion is sex. He wants to have intercourse all the time, often without regard for his partner's desires. It is he who calls the shots about when and how often you make love.

The Fastidious Lover often came from Fastidious Parents, either a mother who sublimated her own unhappiness in a constant search for dust, or a father who demanded that his son be just so in everything: his room always neat, his bed always made, his manners impeccable. He had to leave for school exactly on time and could never dawdle on the way home. Sometimes his family background was so tumultuous that the growing child tried to create order in his own possessions as a way of avoiding anxiety.

Compulsives tend to marry because they need the security of a relationship. (But then they often divorce, because, although they require closeness, it frightens them.) They effectively sabotage the marriage with their controlling, critical ways. When breakups occur, the Compulsive may blame himself for causing the rift, but inwardly he knows it is the woman's fault.

Jealous Lovers

Some men drive you crazy with their suspicions, accusations, and fits of jealousy. One green-eyed monster always becomes the third party in a triangle. He is continually attracted to women who are involved with another man, married or not. A second type becomes obsessive and hysterically jealous in a one-to-one relationship. Both kinds suffer from low self-esteem, and their jealousy is a product of it.

THE TRIANGLE LOVER: This man tries to counteract his feeling of inadequacy by competing with someone else. In love his rival is the other man. The essence of the relationship is not nearly as important to the Triangle Lover as the answer to the question which makes him quiver with passion: "Am I going to win or not?"

Although the Triangle Lover entered the affair with his green eyes wide open, he reacts throughout as if the other lover had just walked into your life. He becomes enraged when you see him, has temper tantrums if he telephones, has scenes when he sees a gift the other man bought or if he even hears his name. His love affairs are in constant turmoil. His jealousy distorts his perception of the relationship. It may be nothing more than a pleasant dalliance, but jealousy keeps him in such constant heat that he imagines it to be true love.

He wants to possess you and he often tries to get you to dump his rival and be his one-and-only. If you do, the Triangle Lover has won, but you have lost. Without the sense of competition that created a fine edge to the relationship, it goes flat. The Triangle Lover feels disappointed. You aren't the girl he thought you were. He wants to call it quits and, not too long after his rival disappears, he does.

THE ONE-TO-ONE GREEN-EYED MONSTER: If irrational jealousy rears its ugly head in a one-to-one relationship, it is because the One-to-One Green-Eyed Monster is projecting his own feelings about himself onto his mate. He feels inadequate, but he imagines it is you who thinks that about him. Because he is sure you dwell on his imperfections, he pictures you constantly attracted to other men, forever flirting, always on the verge of leaving him.

Anything you do or say is interpreted as a sign of your disloyalty. If you merely glance at someone in the street, if you admire an actor on television, if you drop the name of a male coworker, he flies into a fit of jealousy. He torments himself—and you—with his fantasies.

The Jealous Lover's suspicions, accusations, innuendos, and anger are tactics. He wants to control and manipulate you. "If you really loved me you wouldn't even think about another man," he seems to be saying, which makes you question yourself: "Am I really giving him cause to be jealous?" Since everyone fantasizes about members of the opposite sex, even handsome movie stars, you feel guilty although you are blameless. Afraid of his scenes, you begin to curtail your life. You are loath to talk to another man casually, and you avoid even looking a man in the face. You watch yourself constantly. You don't want to do anything to make your lover's jealousy erupt.

Some women feel flattered by insane jealousy—for a while. They interpret it as a sign of a man's love. But eventually even these women find the turmoil and guilt the Jealous Lover creates in them too much to bear. They leave.

Men Who Won't Sleep Over

If the man you are having an affair with refuses to sleep over and/or doesn't want you to bed down at his place either, regard it as a message. He is telling you: "This relationship isn't to be taken seriously. I don't want to be trapped."

Men like this feel uneasy in the open-ended quality of sleep-over dates. At night there is a clear-cut ending—sometime in the late night or early morning either you or he will go home. If you wake up together he's not sure when the date will be over. Breakfast is next, then dirty dishes. When will he escape? The man who is allergic to spending the night regards sleeping over as a symbol of commitment.

Some men object to all sleep-overs, others set limits. They will sleep over sometimes, but not every time, or not all the time. One patient, in theray, would stay at his girlfriend's house on weekends, but although he saw her midweek he drew the line there. To him sleeping over in the middle of the week as well as weekends would lead to the next step—living together—and he didn't want that to arise even as a possibility. Men like this have problems with closeness. It makes them anxious.

Men Who Seek Women with Status

It may be great beauty, wealth, social standing, or fame he is after. The Status Seeker looks for a woman who represents something out of the ordinary to the world, and therefore adds to his own luster. He regards women not as human beings but as desirable objects to be competed for and shown off like a dazzling trophy.

The relationship *per se* is not what interests the Status Seeker. He is more intrigued by what he may accomplish through it. He yearns for the respect and envy of other men, but because he feels he lacks the qualities to attract it, he tries to obtain it through association with glamorous women.

Status Seekers, particularly if they are beauty lovers, often have rating systems for women. They score potential candidates: "On a scale of one to ten, she is 9.3."

It is important for the Status Seeker to enslave or dominate his trophy. Unless he is in control, he doesn't feel that the relationship is doing for him what it should. Being clearly the master of a glamorous woman is like having a prize dog do tricks for friends. One Status Seeker would always bring home guests unexpectedly so that his talented Status Woman would have to hustle up a fast dinner for them all.

The mirror image of the Status Seeker is the man

who is intimidated by women who are beautiful, of high social standing, or accomplished in other ways. He feels inferior and runs like hell, because glamorous women make him feel even more inferior. One man even refused to date a woman who was a secretary in a firm that handled famous clients. He was attracted to her, but was afraid she would compare him to famous people. A subtype of the mirror-image Status Seeker will engage in relationships with Status Women but be entirely subservient to them.

The Just-So-Far Lovers

Flora met Frank through a friend. They turned out to be a good match. They both liked to go camping and biking, enjoyed the same people, and read the same books. After a year of seeing each other, Flora moved into Frank's apartment. They have lived there for two years now. Flora is in love with Frank and wants to marry him. She has dreams of bearing his child. But Frank, although he loves Flora, cannot take that final step. He makes all kinds of excuses: "What do we need a contract for? This is just like marriage." "Maybe when I get a better job." But Frank in his inner self is aware that these aren't the reasons he won't marry. He just gets uptight at the thought. He *can't.*

Claudia and Michael have been going together for five years. They see each other all the time. Claudia wants to move in with Michael, but he won't let her. When she suggests he give up his apartment and stay with her, he refuses. He can't take a decisive step in the relationship. He wants it to go on as it is.

Flora and Claudia are struggling with Just-So-Far Lovers, a growing breed of men who can make only limited commitments. There are different commitment strokes for different folks. For some, living together is the dread step. For others, it is the marriage contract. For a third type, it is sustained close contact. These are men who ration the time they spend with you. The assume you are a couple, they are not afraid to express their devotion—but they will only see you on weekends, for example, or once a week at the most.

Almost all of the Just-So-Far Lovers are basically passive. They don't want to make decisions—in fact, they can't. Often they want you to resolve matters for them. They arrange it so that you will pressure them for commitment. But when you do, since they also fear being controlled, they react negatively. They cannot, will not, take the plunge.

If a woman threatens to leave the Just-So-Far Lover who rations his time, he will become more available, but just for a while. When he feels secure again in the relationship he slowly evaporates once more. He unconsciously fears that his inadequacies would be revealed in a closer relationship.

The live-together type who balks at marriage often fears responsibility. He need not have the same sense of obligation to a mere roommate. Very often he is a young bachelor who is afraid of grown-up responsibilities. Or he may be a divorced man who was left emotionally or financially wounded and now uses his past experience to rationalize his present fear of commitment.

Just-So-Far Lovers frequently don't know why they can't make final commitments. All they know is that the very thought makes them feel clutched up and sweaty. That's enough to stop them dead each and every time.

They have trouble ending relationships too. Rather than take that final step, they manage to be so difficult or obnoxious that the decision is taken out of their hands. The woman leaves them.

Men Who End Affairs Badly

The normal, healthy man ends relationships by being as forthright and honest as possible. If a woman is particularly fragile, and the reason for the breakup is a neurotic problem of hers, he may spare her feelings by inventing an excuse. But he tells her directly, no matter what, and in as humane a way as possible.

Most men, however, are not normal, and, as a group, they tend to end affairs atrociously, in the following typical ways:

THE VANISHING LOVER: Here one day, gone the next— he's the guy you've been having a nice relationship with who kisses you goodbye one night as if business will go on as usual, and then, as if a magic wand had been waved over him, disappears totally and mysteriously. Because his vanishing act is so sudden, most women see it as a brutal, insensitive, and irresponsible way to cut out. He sees it, however, as simply making things easier. It is the ultimate evasion. The Vanishing Lover feels guilty about having to reject you, and rather than face his guilt or any possible recriminations, he steals away as quietly as possible.

THE FAULT-FINDER: He hates rejecting women as much as the Vanishing Lover does, so he avoids it by torturing them instead. He picks on his girlfriend, finds fault with the way she dresses, cooks, or keeps house. He may even arrange to be seen at a party with another woman—anything to make himself so hateful and obnoxious that the woman will reject him, allowing him not to feel guilty about rejecting her.

THE "IT'S MY FAULT" FELLOW: He is a variation on the Fault-Finder. Instead of attacking a woman to make her reject him, he belittles and berates himself to accomplish the same end. He tells her he is not good enough for her, that he's selfish. He lists all his faults. He breaks dates to prove how irresponsible he is. This behavior is all part of a conscious game plan to make himself so undesirable that she will consider herself lucky to be rid of him. He, too, feels guilty about rejecting her and is trying to spare his own feelings under the guise of sparing hers. The woman, of course, isn't that dumb. He is so unsubtle about what he is doing that she catches on very quickly, and so, although she may give him the brush-off, as he desired, she feels rejected and hurt anyway.

THE BREAK-IT-OFF GRADUALLY BOY: He turns the lights off slowly. He gradually cuts down on the time he spends with you, and calls you less and less frequently on the phone. If you ask, "What's wrong?" he acts innocent. "Nothing's wrong, I'm just busy." Sooner or later, no matter what he says, you get the message. A man like this will hang in there for as long as it takes to make you decide to end the agony.

THE TRADERS: Some men placate their guilt about rejecting you by attempting to sell you off: "You know, you're a pretty good kid and I know somebody else you may be interested in. You're not for me, but you may be for him." Instead of making you feel better, you feel like a baseball card being traded between the boys.

Some Men Who End Affairs Badly are afraid of rejecting anyone—man, woman, or dog. Others are afraid only of women. They often have a fantasy that motivates their devious finales. The woman is so in love with them that she is liable to do anything when they leave—do away with herself, tell his boss and friends what a rat he is, come after him with a gun.

Occasionally, this fear has a realistic basis. The woman may have been so volatile in the relationship that she *is* capable of anything. One woman draped herself in sheets her ex-boyfriend had bought her and marched into his office wearing them.

More often, the man's fear is imaginary, often induced by a more generalized terror of women's anger that almost all men share. Women tend to get angrier than men and stay angry longer. They have been trained to suppress their anger and not show it, so when it does erupt it can come out like a volcano. Men, on the other hand, have been allowed to show anger their whole lives—it is one of the few emotions men are allowed to express in our culture. They have also learned to deal with it somewhat rationally while playing sports and in offices, where temper tantrums are not accepted. Men fear women will be hysterical and irrational if they make them mad, so they prefer to avoid confrontations when ending affairs, and in almost all other situations as well.

Chapter 13

Normal Men

David met Jennie six months ago. She was applying for a job in the firm for which he worked. Although someone else was hired, David thought Jennie attractive and interesting and called her. He took her out to dinner and to a movie on their first date, and then asked her out again for the following week.

He took Jennie out every Saturday night for three weeks then started to see her midweek as well. He also spoke to her more and more frequently on the telephone. By the end of six months they were seeing each other practically every night and talking on the telephone whether they saw one another or not.

So what is wrong with David? Surprise! Nothing. David is a Normal Man.

Normal Men really do exist, although if you tangle with enough Other Men, you may begin to doubt it. It is important to know what Normal Men are like so that, if by some miracle one crosses your path, you'll be able to recognize him. I use "Normal" here not to mean the norm, for they *aren't*, but to mean healthy—in tune, well-balanced.

Don't make the mistake of thinking that Normal Men are perfect, however. They are, after all, human beings. Normal Men are not immune to transitory feelings of depression, anxiety, and tension any more than Normal Women are, but they tend not to let their problems get in the way of intimate, long-term relationships.

They may, like Other Men, have some concerns about adequacy and acceptability—that is normal, too—but there is an essential difference between the way Normal Men and Others react to inner insecurities. The issues of adequacy and acceptability do not color the Normal Man's view of the world, nor distort his sense of reality. In contrast, Others tend to become self-protective and self-absorbed; they see the world only through their own eyes and are blind to the needs of women they are with.

Normal Men seldom are unaware or insensitive to the needs of their mates. They can empathize and identify with their partners in love. They expect, of course, that their mates will do the same for them.

Relationships with Normal Men do not erupt like firecrackers. Not that a strong sexual or emotional attraction may not be present from the beginning, but no matter how excited the Normal Man feels, he reserves, in the back of his head, the crucial knowledge that he really doesn't know this person to whom he is attracted.

This was the case with Ted. He met Dolores while they were both waiting for a bus. She asked him for information and they started to talk. He found himself drawn to her immediately. The way she moved was very sensual to him, and she had a sense of humor he loved. He asked her out to dinner the following evening.

On their first night together Ted found her incredibly sexy, and her wry way of looking at the world intriguing. He knew he wanted to go to bed with her and to see her more. But although Ted was immensely interested, he realized Dolores was still essentially a stranger to him. He didn't withhold his company or his emotions, but he continued to see her during the next few months as part of the process of getting to know her better. He accepted the fact that, until later in the relationship, he was unable to decide what role Dolores might play in his life. He knew his instant attraction did not constitute love. He judged it for what it was—simply an infatuation with a woman he still had to get to know.

On the other hand, if it had been George who met Dolores, the affair would have been different. George would have fallen for the same things—Dolores' sensual way and her wry humor. He, too, would have felt a strong urge to go to bed with her, but he would have mistaken his initial attraction for true love. From the moment he met her he would have assumed this was the real thing and that she was the most wonderful, wise, witty, and sexy woman in the world. He would not have taken into account the fact that he barely knew her and that, therefore, his thoughts and feelings were the product of fantasy, or at least that they might be.

Normal, healthy men approach relationships with optimism but a realistic caution. They don't set up dreams that are impossible to fulfill. Less normal men, on the other hand, are more prone to lose all perspective and surrender to illusions. They are doomed to disappointment because reality rarely, if ever, matches their hopes.

Normal Men don't rush into seeing a woman constantly, nor do they deliberately hold back out of fear. Instead, they go along with their feelings of response, permit the relationship to develop, and gradually increase physical and verbal communication with her.

The buildup, if neither party is seeing anyone else at the time, may take place quickly. Soon the couple may be seeing one another frequently. Or it may take longer, depending on the emotional status or life situation of the Normal Man and the woman he is seeing.

Relationships with Normal Men *never* reach a plateau. They either intensify or dissipate.

Other men tend either to start a relationship off with a bang and then back off, or let an affair flounder.

The earmark of a relationship with Normal Men is trust. They are honest with women and require the same in return. They are also reliable.

Relationships with Normal Men are not without ups and downs. Even Normal Men are normal; stresses and strains in a relationship can make them become insulated, uncommunicative, or angry for a while. But these are passing states that are direct responses to a specific situation. A Normal Man gets angry at something that has happened rather than at something that hasn't, something in the present rather than something in the past.

After an appropriate time, this anger or withdrawal

will pass and life will continue without constant reminders or recriminations. The Normal Man is not a grudge-bearer or an injustice-collector.

When no disharmony occurs in a relationship, many couples assume that the relationship is healthy. This isn't so. Total peace is generally the earmark of something else at work. Someone in the relationship is suppressing too much by keeping quiet or giving in. Differences are normal between two humans in constant close contact, and it is through clashes that a couple learns how to solve things as a unit, thereby building a stronger relationship.

The Normal Man tries to work out differences through discussion and compromise, while his counterpart reacts quite differently. Other Men have a low tolerance for frustration and they frighten easily and intensely. They attack problems that make them uptight inappropriately, generally in one of four ways: (1) by pushing problems out of their minds, ignoring them, and hoping they will go away; (2) by running away; (3) by overpowering the other person, shouting them down or threatening them; (4) by subordinating their feelings to those of the other person.

In general, Normal Men are able to take all problems, including their own, in stride. A good example of this would be the man who finds himself impotent one night. The man who isn't normal tends to become gravely concerned about the experience, feels full of self-pity or blames it on the woman. He may want to leave and never see her again. The Normal Man, on the other hand, realizes that impotence is not normal for him. Instead of blaming himself or the woman, he considers the possible cause. Was he upset because of conditions at work? Or were his emotions untuned that night?

He accepts the occasion for what it is—a passing episode—and tries again later.

Once intimacy is established with a Normal Man, the relationship can survive despite traumas or ordinary difficulties. He does not flee in the face of trouble. He attempts to work things out.

Although Others worry about being absorbed or controlled by a woman, the Normal Man feels no such threats to his existence. He is able to live with a woman without giving up his autonomy or becoming overly dependent.

Coexistence is the keynote of his marriage. The Normal Man is willing sometimes to subordinate his own needs for the good of his partner, and he counts on her to do the same. Decisions are made not on a competitive basis but on grounds of mutual understanding. His basic strength comes from within. This is why he does not feel threatened and why he does not seek a sense of security from another person, although within a good partnership each serves as a protector to the other.

Nevertheless, occasionally, even in healthy relationships, situations occur in which one partner may need to be more dependent than usual. This is a transitory state, and dependency as such is not the basis for the relationship. Situations that might create higher dependency needs are illness, getting fired, or the death of a loved one. Everyone needs to lean on someone else at such a time.

The Normal Man does not overly prize the external trappings. He doesn't insist that his wife or girlfriend be young, beautiful, famous, or wealthy any more than he pines away because he hasn't any of these attributes. Since he is sure of his own self-worth, he doesn't have to use his partner to impress the world.

He looks for other things in a relationship: Can he and the woman talk to one another? Does she understand and empathize with him? Is she responsive to him in an appropriate way—is she too demanding, or doesn't she demand enough for herself? He looks for the ability to communicate on a verbal and nonverbal level, and he seeks to find out how the other person operates in life. He gives a woman room to breathe without getting envious, jealous, or frightened that something is wrong, and he expects the same from her.

Based on such signs, the Normal Man knows whether it is possible for a long-term relationship to exist. If he finds, after a period of time, that the woman he is seeing is unable to compromise, or is too self-centered, too frightened or worried—and there can be a modicum of these things without bothering him unduly—then he may decide to end the relationship. Normal Men do this honestly. They talk things over and explain the real differences that exist between them, but without tearing the other down.

Although Normal Men are not necessarily monogamous until they have decided that a commitment exists, once that commitment is made, they are more faithful than the Others.

Not only are they able to delay or forsake outside gratification, if it is in the best interest of the couple to do so, they are also concerned with the effect an affair might have on their wife or girlfriend, or the effect her affair might have on them both. They expect monogamy— or non-monogamy—to work both ways.

A fair number of relatively Normal Husbands have an affair now and then, but most of them maintain marriages that are monogamous.

The decision to marry is always a mutual one for a Normal Man. He discusses it with the Normal Woman he loves and they jointly decide—not only to unite their lives, but to maintain a certain kind of lifestyle, to have children or not, to share money or not. Attention is paid to the contractual aspects of marriage as well as the emotional ones.

If the Normal Man decides not to marry the woman he has been seeing, the decision may not be mutual. It is rare that a Normal Man gets close to marriage without its actually taking place, but occasionally reservations he has harbored all along will surface. If he feels that essential differences exist between them and if the differences ultimately outweigh the positive aspects, he may break off the relationship. He realizes it can go nowhere. The woman may feel differently and want to marry anyway, but if he feels otherwise, the Normal Man does not allow himself to feel unduly pressured or guilty.

As a husband, the Normal Man helps around the house because he respects his spouse. He never feels that his obligation to the marriage is satisfied simply because he brings home a paycheck. He feels that sharing is part of the relationship, so he'll pitch in whether his wife is working or not. He never assumes that his wife is idle while he is away, but realizes that she, too, is busy with her own interests, and he respects her for them.

The Normal Man feels a sense of obligation to his mate. He feels he is there partly to serve her needs and be helpful to her. He never resents his obligations, as so many Other Men do. They are a price he is willing to pay. He understands that the relationship gives him more than total self-indulgence or freedom would.

The Normal Man may be somewhat threatened if his

wife decides to return to school or work, but he adjusts quickly and never lets his initial fears create irrational behavior. He involves himself in helping his wife, whether by taking care of the children more often or by encouraging her.

The Normal Man is only minimally chauvinistic. He may have ingrained attitudes he is unaware of—residues exist in all men—but he does not consider a woman who wants to be independent a threat or a "crazy, bra-burning ball-breaker." He thinks of her, instead, as a sane, rational human being.

He is quite comfortable with the growing number of women bosses and coworkers in the business world, and he treats women workers as peers.

Even in pre-Liberation days, the Normal Man did not look for excessively passive or dependent women. He understood instinctively what men who married such women found out after a number of years of marriage— that such a person becomes a burden, makes a man feel trapped, and creates unhappiness rather than contentment.

The Normal and Healthy Man, either consciously or unconsciously, is aware that life involves decision-making, from minute to minute and day to day, and he approaches this important responsibility rationally.

There is some debate as to whether "normal" also means the choice of a long-term commitment. Perhaps it doesn't, but Normal and Healthy Men are more apt to opt for a lasting relationship than Others, who are afraid of closeness.

Healthy Normal Men are nice. Try to find one. Here is the way a Normal Man would approach a woman. Use these five points to evaluate any prospects:

(1) He has basic respect for her as a person.

(2) He treats her with consideration.

(3) He believes that a woman is entitled to her rights.

(4) He is concerned with satisfying and fulfilling a woman.

(5) He regards a woman as his peer.

Chapter 14

Society and the Love Crisis

As we have seen, neuroses in men make them allergic to love and commitment. They use various tactics to avoid or sabotage closeness because it frightens them.

Women define the Love Crisis through their complaints about skittish men who play destructive games with them. These men are created by the psychodynamics I have described, but also, in part, by the world we live in.

There is much in our culture, past and present, that encourages men to feel inadequate, to be loners, to fear women, to search for the impossible. There are forces in our society that create a trend toward impermanence, in general. Let us see what they are.

Families

GROWING UP MALE: The Love Crisis has deep roots in the typical childhood of the American boy.

Patriarchy died at the turn of the century in this country, when men entered the world created by the Industrial Revolution. It was a world that took men from their homes and kept them working longer and longer hours at jobs that became increasingly competitive.

America is the home of the absentee father—the average man spends twelve minutes a day with his children, according to one study. Not only is father not around much, his spirit is not even felt in his absence, as it is in many European homes where father is still feared and revered. The sense of father as the authority in the home is lacking in American families.

The absence of Father has made Mother the heir to all parental functions. Unfortunately, American mothers find themselves without support from their husbands and also without confidence in their own abilities to mother adequately. The media in this country have bombarded mothers for generations with advice from experts who issued stern warnings about the potential harm they could inflict on their offspring.

Mothers in this country approach parental duties with anxiety and a sense of danger. Determined to do no wrong, they shower their children with attention. They watch over them anxiously, shepherd them to school, to music and art classes, to Little League games, to friends' houses.

They do all the right things—the things they have been told they should—and yet, while being such good mothers, they often feel resentful about their loss of freedom, and bored from being locked into a world of mothers and children in the suburbs.

They resent the anxiety that comes from mothering according to others' prescriptions. They resent their husbands' not being around to help or give them the affection and company they crave. Distracted and inwardly discontented, their child care is a curious combination of smothering and lack of real warmth. They attend to the children punctiliously, but they often wish they were elsewhere.

This combination of mother and father, unique to America, creates future troubles for the male child. He needs a father to model himself upon. If his father is absent and there are no significant other adult males around to substitute, he will grow up insecure about his masculinity.

From his distracted, unhappy mother who smothers him he inherits other problems. He picks up her vibes and blames himself for her unhappiness: There must be something wrong with him. From her he also comes to associate certain qualities with all women. He learns to see women as both devouring and rejecting, and himself, in their presence, as inadequate and vulnerable.

The way he is disciplined is another source of trouble. In other countries and at other times in this country, kids were smacked or spanked if they did something wrong. The current middle-class way to control and train a child is to give him love when he is good, and deny him love or make him feel guilty when he is bad. This ever-present threat makes him chronically insecure about love. He becomes intensely preoccupied with the possibility of losing it.

Love-related disciplinary techniques create certain typical characteristics in human beings. They become passive, dependent, insecure. They are not able to shoulder responsibilities easily, and they fear trying.

Let us now examine the picture of a man who emerges from a childhood with an absentee father and a smothering but distracted mother who gives and takes love from him at will. He is insecure, passive, dependent, and apprehensive about responsibility—hardly what a man is supposed to be in our culture.

The American boy learns from other sources—television, movies, books, comics—what masculine attributes are. He knows he is supposed to be aggressive, assertive, independent, domineering, reliable.

There is a gross dichotomy between the basic character structure of the American man—the product of his upbringing—and how he feels he should be, based on cultural mandates.

As a result of the contrast between his true feelings and what he aspires to be, the American male cultivates a pose. He tries to appear aggressive, domineering, strong, but he's always afraid someone will see through his mask and perceive the real man below the surface.

The intrinsic insecurity of American men who have fears about their masculinity, who are afraid of being rejected in love as adults, as they continually were as children, are powerful factors in the Love Crisis.

The man who feels inauthentic, who has a poor sense of self-esteem, who craves love but also fears it, is a man who has trouble relating to women. We have seen its manifestation in some of the various lovers I have described.

Intimacy makes them anxious. The woman who gets too close may find out how anxious they really are.

Also contributing to the Love Crisis is the view of women that such men have. They are afraid of them. In close relationships women may become like Mother. They may devour him, or reject him, or both.

With the rise of the working mother this picture may change. There is the danger that in the future there will be many homes with two absentee parents instead of one, a situation that may either breed insecurity or help children to look out for themselves. But the children of today's working mothers are not yet adults. The men that women have trouble with today are often crippled from growing up male in a typical home.

THE NUCLEAR HOUSEHOLD: Whatever effects the individual family has upon the psyche of the child are intensified by the death of the extended family. Grandparents, aunts, and uncles who lived nearby in earlier days often gave children alternative adults to model themselves upon, or love that could compensate for a mother or father's faulty parenting. Now "Daddy and Mommy and Baby make three." We have only the nuclear family, living apart from relatives. The effects of absentee fathers and unhappy, smothering mothers, and any damaging psychological games played within the nuclear family, have the potential of being more profound. There is no one around to dilute the interaction.

DIVORCE: Today it often isn't even Daddy, Mommy, and Baby. Frequently Daddy is cut out of the picture by divorce. Father becomes a weekend visitor. He is likely, through enforced absence and the diversions of his new life, to become increasingly estranged from his children. With Father gone from the house, a boy's problems in establishing his male identity are increased.

Mother may parade a series of lovers through the house, creating havoc for a child. Not only didn't Mommy and Daddy's relationship last, but the child begins to observe that all relationships between men and women are short-lived.

If a mother gratifies her sexual needs under a son's nose, it can arouse in him erotic fantasies about her, destructive to the boy's own budding sexual orientation.

Other sections of this book point out that the incest taboo, in which all women become unconsciously associated with Mother, often intrudes into the sex life of neurotic men. It can take hold forcefully in the psyche of the child who has eroticized his mother in his fantasies.

Children of divorced parents are bad risks in their adult relationships. They tend either to avoid marriage altogether or to compulsively relive their parents' experience and divorce themselves. Never having had a chance to observe Mother and Father disagree, then compromise and reconcile, they have not learned to resolve differences. When trouble arises in a relationship, children of divorced parents often overreact. A problem seems to them to be the end of the road. They can also underreact. They may be so intent on not repeating their parents' mistakes that they pretend problems don't exist, until those problems get out of hand.

Statistics confirm what sociologists and mental-health practitioners tell us: Divorce begets divorce. With more than one out of three marriages currently ending, we can look forward to a deepening of the Love Crisis in future generations.

MOBILITY: The fact that families move so often in our society is also taking its toll on the ability of American children to form long-term relationships. It is not uncommon for a family to pack up every two years because the father changes jobs. High mobility increases the isolation of nuclear families because they are unable to put down roots in communities. There is, in turn, more strain on relationships within the family. High mobility also fosters a sense of impermanence in children. If they move often, children learn that nothing ever lasts, that friends are made and lost, that people come and go. They decide early in life not to invest themselves in others emotionally because they'll be moving on. Men and women who have grown up with the moving-on experience are cautious and often incapable of making deep commitments.

WORK: Work is what makes men absentee fathers. Men in our country from early childhood are taught that the most important thing in life is achievement. For women, until very recently, it has been loving and being loved.

Men pin their identities on work and measure themselves
by how successful they are in their jobs. Women pin their
identities on their relationships with men, and generally
feel that if they aren't having some kind of love relationship, they are failures. As a result, we are a nation of
male work addicts who don't pay enough attention to personal relationships, and of female love addicts who have
not paid enough attention to their capabilities.

American husbands have traditionally disappointed
wives by disappearing into work after the babies are born.
Sometimes work is used as a flight from intimacy, as
other sections of this book indicate. But one cannot discount the strong societal pressures that compel men to
neglect their emotional lives for their jobs. There are no
points given to men for being loving husbands and fathers. No one rewards them for that. But a man who is
successful in his job gains status and a sense of fulfillment. Ironically, American women have helped men
along the road to success by considering success an aph-
rodisiac.

It is interesting how our culture set the stage for the
Love Crisis by training men and women from birth to look
for their satisfactions in seemingly opposite areas. Men
need love too little, and women need it too much.

Women's attitudes seem to be changing now because
of their new goals. Current surveys of college-age women
indicate that they want both marriage and careers.
Women of the future will achieve their identity from work
as well as love, which will be healthier for them. But another danger is growing. Mental health practitioners are
beginning to see a new breed of career woman. She has
embraced the male ethic and is as hell-bent on success as
any man. Sacrificing human emotions and relationships
to work has done great harm to men both psychologically
and physically. Their high death rates due to stress-re-
lated diseases are well known. The success ethic will harm
women too. Attaching too much importance to love isn't
good either for women or the men they relate to, but giving it too little importance is no answer either. Work-
addicted women joining men already swallowed up in the
marketplace can lead only to a deepening of the Love Crisis.

Media

ADVERTISING: The advertising industry has contributed immeasurably to the present Love Crisis. It has created the idea that everything should and can be replaced by a newer, better model. By emphasizing youth and freshness, ads produce a fertile climate for divorce, separation, and relationships that are clearly temporary. The middle-aged man shucks off his middle-aged wife and starts life anew with someone younger and better.

Advertising, by catering to the growing singles market, glorifies the single state. The unattached young girls in bikinis, the glowing-skinned goddesses with hair blowing in the wind, look like great fun. They encourage men to remain single and try harder to achieve that mythical "good life" they see pictured in commercials. The ads also entice the married man. They make him fantasize about what it would be like to be single again, and tempt him to try it out.

Men who are single, however, know better. Many of them are jaded, tired of running. They want to settle down, but they find themselves looking for the wrong things in a woman. Advertising has projected fantasies of perfection that are doomed to disappointment. Men look for the women associated with products—those gorgeous, smart women who live, it is often implied, in order to satisfy a man's needs.

Advertising teaches people to look for surface attributes. If he has the right car, uses the right toothpaste, smokes the right cigarette, he will be virile and irresistible. If she has blue eyes, looks good in a bikini, wears provocative clothing, she's sexy and desirable. Advertising ignores what goes into the making of a truly desirable member of the opposite sex—the ability to empathize, cooperate, and respect another person. And so do many people who are searching for love and not finding it.

CONSUMERISM: Making oneself feel good by buying things—a byproduct of advertising which creates the demand for products—is a significant trend in our time. Consumerism plays a role in the Love Crisis. Men shy away from marriage because they see it as an overwhelming economic burden. The needs of middle-class life have escalated to include luxuries formerly reserved for the rich—a second home, private schools for children, costly college educations, household help, two cars, and all the other expensive trappings that any of us who have been married and have children know all too well.

Consumerism has also contributed to zero population growth. Men and women would rather spend money on nice things for themselves than on children. Without the desire to have children, the pull toward marriage lessens. It has anyway. Society exerts much less pressure on men and women to marry than it used to.

TELEVISION: The television set, that extra presence in our homes, serves as a physical barrier between men and women, reducing intimacy. Husbands and wives and lovers sit in front of it for hours—watching instead of interacting.

The programs they watch set up unrealistic expectations that make men and women disappointed in their real lives. Why can't I be as witty and as handsome as that actor? Why doesn't my wife look as good or sound as good as that actress? Why isn't my family as much fun as they are in those sitcoms?

Television, in this respect, caters to the sense of dissatisfaction that permeates much of contemporary life.

Television also perpetuates some of the myths about masculinity that undermine relationships with women. The heroes of action series are free-wheeling cowboys, cops, and secret agents who live in an emotional void. The Kojaks and Barettas have few friendships and no love lives except for the quick sexual encounter. Despite Women's Liberation, women are still treated, by and large, as sex objects. Charlie's Angels may be women of action, but they operate under orders from a man, and they are all gorgeous enough to be *Playboy* centerfolds. They personify male sexual fantasies. TV heroines are slender, young, and beautiful.

In contrast to single heroes who are emotionally unconnected to women, we see the awful consequences of marriage. In sitcoms, husbands are nincompoops manipulated by smart-ass wives. Men are never shown in search of women, but women are shown as husband hunters. Marriage is never portrayed as tender or warm, or as a co-operative venture in life between a man and a woman.

Boys in America who have absentee fathers often

turn to television for models of masculinity. And what they see can be damaging. They learn that real men are prone to violence, that they are vibrant and alive and strong only when they are unattached, and that they become weak and victimized with commitment. By the time a child is sixteen, he has watched an average of twelve to fifteen thousand hours of television. Its impact cannot be taken lightly.

MAGAZINES: *Playboy* and other men's magazines extol the concept of the swinging bachelor, exploitative of women, eternally elusive, surrounded by the right equipment that will attract and seduce women—the softly lit pad, stereo music, a well-stocked bar. Women in *Playboy*, *Penthouse*, and *Hustler* are accessories, playthings for a man's pleasure. These female playthings invade men's minds. "Why is it that no woman in real life ever looks like them?" one swinging bachelor, who has seduced thousands of women, lamented to me.

Pornography emphasizes the extraordinary even more—penises ten inches long, multiple sex partners, continuously orgasmic females, constantly erect males. Men's magazines and pornography add to male insecurity by creating sexual expectations that can never be realized. Unfortunately, when men don't measure up they often feel inferior.

Men's magazines and porno films show men and women getting together in only one way and for only one purpose—brief encounters solely for sexual pleasure.

In sharp contrast are the women's magazines these days. They used to deal in destructive myths and set up impossible expectations. A *McCall's* invention, "Togetherness," which made women slaves to men and children, was a goal for many years in this country. Today, however, women's magazines have turned practical. They are full of advice about sexual problems, ways to achieve intimacy, and improve communication between spouses. Women's magazines reflect the fact that women are still deeply interested in relationships and making them work. Men's magazines reflect the fact that men, at least in fantasy, try to elude relationships. The dichotomy between them reflects the Love Crisis.

Psychological Trends

THE GROWTH OF NARCISSISM: The media call it the "Me First Generation." Referred to are the growing number of men and women in our culture who have narcissistic personalities. As defined by Dr. Otto Kernberg and Christopher Lasch, who have written on the subject, narcissistic personalities are infantile in their outlook. They are concerned with their own gratification only and feel justified in exploiting others to get whatever they want. Filled with grandiose conceptions of themselves, they are only dimly aware of others. They find it impossible to empathize with another person's viewpoint or needs. They need others, however, for constant approval and admiration. Nevertheless, they are afraid of attachments because they fear dependency. The narcissist wants love but is incapable of giving it. The narcissist often cultivates a charm which seduces people into giving him what he wants. Narcissists who have a voracious appetite for experiences have a tendency toward promiscuity. Their relationships are shallow and often brief. The fact that a growing number of men and women want love but are unable to return it, are totally selfish and self-absorbed and unable or unwilling to delay gratification, is another contributing factor to the Love Crisis.

THE HUMAN POTENTIAL MOVEMENT: Arising out of California, the human potential movement, spearheaded by Essalen group encounters and Fritz Perls and Gestalt Therapy, is a growing conglomeration of post-Freudian therapies that focus on fulfillment of the self. The most recent heir of the human potential movement is EST. In most of these therapies the achievement of what is good for one's self takes precedence over any sense of obligation to the community or to another person. The personal (the gratification of one's own impulses) is emphasized at the expense of the interpersonal (the need for commitment and loving interaction with another). As a result, the human potential movement has contributed to narcissism and the growing alienation of men and women in this country. Two people looking out only for themselves cannot exist in a long-term relationship where co-operation and occasional deferral to another's needs are necessary for survival.

Myths and Male Sexuality

Men and women, alike, believe many of the popular myths in our culture about male sexuality. They believe: (1) men are always ready for sex; (2) male sexuality is less complicated than female sexuality; (3) men know all there is to know about sex; (4) men aren't afraid of sex.

Men are *not* always ready for sex. Their sex drive is variable. Some men have a stronger need than others. Men's sex drive and performance are subject to psychological moods and fears, as are women's. Previous chapters should already have made that clear. Inability to perform and lack of desire may be caused by fear of intimacy, anger within a relationship, fear about one's ability as a lover, and a variety of other problems. Men—like women—can be turned off by money worries, stress, the presence of a stranger or relative in the house, the sound of a child in the next room. Masters and Johnson learned, from their clinical observations of humans during sex, that men are even more subject to distractions in the first stage of intercourse—85 percent of the sexual difficulties that occurred during tests happened to men. Male sexuality is no less complicated than female sexuality.

Men also carry with them a fear of many things when they approach a woman sexually. To begin with, they are always afraid of rejection and wait for a signal that a woman is receptive. "It may be the way she touches your arm," explained a real estate broker, "or a look in her eye, or the way she moves when you dance with her, but I wait for that 'something.'"

Men have great concern about their penis size as well. Rare is the man who is satisfied with his equipment. Most worry that their penis is not big enough to satisfy a woman. There is also a subliminal, almost universal, fear of injury to genitals. Sometimes this fear is projected onto the female. The *vagina dentata* myth handed down through the ages pictures women's genitals with teeth that can bite and hurt—and contributes to the feeling many men have that the vagina is a dangerous place. In *Rabbit Redux*, John Updike imagines a vagina with razor blades in it, a lethal refinement on the vagina with teeth.

Karen Horney claimed that every male analysand she treated was afflicted in some way with dread of the vagina.

The idea of women as harmful, in general, has been handed down to men through another myth, that of the evil seductress out to destroy a man. Two examples of this myth are the stories of Adam and Eve and Samson and Delilah.

Some men are more afraid of hurting than being hurt, however. They picture the woman as frail and easily damaged. Most men don't know much about the female sexual apparatus, since it is hidden inside. This fact tends to make them think of it as mysterious, sometimes unclean, and often more fragile than it really is. Despite the prevailing notion in our society that men know everything about sex, as a group they tend to be quite ignorant. Their sex education at home is often perfunctory. As a result, boys often turn to their peers for knowledge. The tendency among adolescent boys is to brag, exaggerate, and lie. The picture the boy gets is confusing and undermining. If he believes his companions, he often begins to believe that everyone else knows more about sex than he does, that his friends are more attractive, experienced, and better lovers, which is rarely the case. According to many experts I spoke to, men spend their entire lives hoping they are doing the right thing with women but are never quite sure. The sense of insecurity engendered by sexual ignorance is compounded by women who, at least in the past, have been loath to show a man or tell him what it is they like and need. They assume that men *should* know. Women also have been afraid of appearing unfeminine if they were assertive. More women are now taking responsibility for their own pleasure and are willing to guide men, but this attitude is far from universal. Many women, perhaps the majority, have learned their lessons about female behavior all too well—they are still inhibited about showing and telling. Of course, if a man is slave to a rigid view of women as passive and unassertive, he may react badly if a woman does try to communicate her desires. He may feel resentful that she is trying to order him around, which in turn may interefere with his sexuality. Most men, however, would be grateful for a little guidance.

The notion that men have a stronger sex drive is under attack these days. Many women I interviewed said they knew their sexual appetite was stronger than their husband's or boyfriend's, but they had adjusted to his desires. Psychiatrist Mary Jane Sherfey, in *The Nature and Evolution of Female Sexuality*, has made a case for female superiority. She writes, "...the more orgasms a woman has, the stronger they become; the more orgasms she has, the more she can have. To all intents and purposes *the human female is sexually insatiable.*" She goes on to theorize, "...a woman could go on having orgasms indefinitely if physical exhaustion did not intervene." Masters and Johnson proved the greater orgasmic capacity of women as well.

Many men feel threatened by this knowledge. Spectacular musings like those of Dr. Sherfey, whether they are true or not, play into another myth, one that has also haunted men through the ages: the myth of the insatiable female who enervates. The myth surfaces and is perpetuated in many jokes, such as this one:

Joe hates his wife and wants to kill her. He asks a friend how to do it. The friend tells him, "You have to screw her twelve times every day for six months. At the end of that time she will die."

When six months are over, the friend comes to see Joe. As he approaches his house he hears a female voice singing loudly and happily.

A little old wizened man stumbles out the door. "Heh, heh, heh," he croaks, "little does she know she is about to die."

Dr. Ray Birdwhistle, a specialist in nonverbal communication and the father of "body language," points out the growing contrast between myths about male sexuality and reality: "We liken the male to an Eveready flashlight—press the button and he's ready. The female is supposedly an engine without power, until engaged by the male piston. The female is regarded as an old-fashioned telephone: 'Grind and grind and you work up enough power to send a signal to Central.' When they marry, you run into the dreadful reality that he has weak batteries and she's attached to Norris Dam."

These days men don't have to be married to feel like weak pistons. There are Norris Dams all over town. Anxieties and fears about sexuality always existed among men, but the fall of some of their myths may have increased doubts about their real capacities. Despite the realities of male sexuality, despite their inner fears, men still aspire to be superstuds, and women are generally as disappointed as they are if they don't succeed.

Chapter 15

What to do about Men who make You Miserable

Now that you understand more about why the men you meet are the way they are, what do you do about them?

The first rule to apply to men and relationships with them is: Be realistic. Most women feel as if their whole life hangs on the man they are involved with, or on men in general. We have all been brought up to believe that men are our Destiny, that we cannot be fulfilled as women unless we have one of our very own who will automatically supply us with Security, Love, a Place in Society, an Identity, a Reason for Living.

We surely have heard the message from the Women's Liberation movement that we are people in our own right. But how many of us, even if we are career women, believe it on a gut level?

Believe it! Women—you—are "people" without a man. This doesn't mean that it wouldn't be nice, even wonderful to have that special man as a companion and/or husband. But if you can't find someone suitable, life is still worth living. Also, don't believe the myth that there is just one person for you. There are many possibilities.

Being realistic means that you don't hang around the house waiting for a man to call, or to ask you out, or that in your spare time you run only to places where you will meet men—a common trap women fall into. It means making sure you fill up your life with things you enjoy, even if they are simple, like movies, shows, and concerts. Many women don't allow themselves to enjoy small things because they are in a state of suspended animation waiting for the big thing—Romance. They also subscribe to the myth that life is somehow *supposed* to be satisfying. They don't realize you have to go out and do something to *make* it satisfying. By becoming active on your own you will find yourself less dependent on men—or A Rat, if you have one—for your happiness.

Women who believe love affairs are life and death matters approach men with illusions that tend to blind them to who Mr. New really is. After one date, some women begin to refurnish a man's whole apartment in their heads. They are already moving in.

Being realistic means understanding that most—not just a few, but *most*—of the men you are going to meet will be neurotic or unsuitable in one way or another. It means accepting this as a fact of life in a complex society. It means you don't get completely involved too quickly, as most women do. You start out by dating Mr. New, calmly, instead of wonderfully expectant or cynically detached, with the knowledge firmly fixed in your mind that you don't really know Mr. New well enough to know what you are getting into. You can make a few *tentative* judgments. If he has told you his history with women, you may decide: "He has never been involved with anyone for more than three months. I don't stand a chance of entering a long-term relationship," or, "He looks like he has possibilities—this stands a fair chance of working out." Bear in mind that the first guesses you make are subject to change. Mr. New may turn out to be Mr. Impossible or Mr. Possible, he may even be Mr. Right. But he can also turn out to be A Rat. You won't know until you are further down the line.

Being realistic means that you may not get a chance to get further down the line in some relationships. The man may turn out to be a Hit-and-Run Lover, someone who flip-flops from woman to woman, a Divorced Man wreaking vengeance on all women, or he may simply not dig you. If you are deceived or dumped, or even dumped on, it doesn't mean that you are ugly or undesirable. If you realize that these possibilities exist with Mr. New because you don't really know him yet, you may be deceived or discarded, but you won't fall into despair or be embittered if it happens. Being realistic means understanding that Hit-and-Run Lovers and guys who flip-flop or dump on women as a way of life have problems—but they are their problems, not yours.

Being realistic means not deceiving yourself about The Man, if you find A Man to have a relationship with. Many women are so desperate for the security of the relationship—*any* relationship—that they deliberately don't face facts. A Man, for example, may not see you as often as you would like, after the trial period is over. You know he's interested but unavailable, and this makes you anxious and unhappy. Don't pretend it isn't happening, and don't just bitch to your friends, and, by all means, don't let him sweet-talk you into a false sense of security just because you really don't want to go back to man hunting again.

He may tell you that business is occupying his time, but sit down and consider: What are the other possibilities? Are there other women in his life? Does he not want to get too close? Is he avoiding you in order to avoid sex? If he is really making you unhappy, don't pounce on one of the possibilities as the cause. Try to get him to clarify. Have a discussion with him. In an unhostile, unaccusing way tell him how he is making you feel and ask him to tell you what is really going on. Talking it over will make you feel better about yourself. At least you won't be passively letting it happen to you.

Being realistic means understanding that a man may not necessarily tell you the truth under these circumstances, or, even if he does, that an honest discussion will not necessarily lead to change. Ultimately, being realistic means recognizing that if the same conditions that make you miserable persist for any length of time, *you*, not *he*, The Rat, are responsible for what is happening. *You have options.*

Being realistic means understanding that clearly. You can go on seeing The Rat and give up false expectations, stop believing that something wonderful is going to happen between you. By so doing you can at least enjoy what you have. Or you can decide that he isn't giving you what you want or need, and never will, so you split.

Most women who are unhappy in relationships are determined sufferers. They continue to deny reality: He will change. He will come around. They see the relationship as stronger than it is. How many women do you know whose miserable affair with The Rat has gone on for years? They are partners in the crime.

By seeing the relationship as stronger and bigger than it is, women sometimes drive their man away. They press him to commit himself to a relationship that obviously is more casual to him. "What do I need this kind of hassle for?" he thinks, when she starts complaining, and takes off. Of course, driving him away is one solution. Sticking around for years with an impossible, isn't.

Frequently a woman continues an unhappy relationship because of her own insecurities rather than his charm. She may be afraid to re-enter the singles scene, afraid of rejection, loneliness, afraid of feeling worthless and unfulfilled because she's without a man again.

Sometimes women with these fears grab any man who's available, whether he is obviously Mr. Wrong or not. They may sense he's a man with problems from the beginning, but they need a man—any man—and he is interested. They forget how it all started and begin to get involved. Then they feel sorry for themselves because he turned out to be A Rat. He isn't giving them what they want, even though they knew he never had it to give. If you make desperate decisions, be prepared to accept the consequences.

If being completely without a man is too terrible an alternative to you, there is another option—look around for someone else while continuing to see The Rat. Women often find this hard to do. They are afraid of losing The Rat altogether, or they imagine they must be monogamous. Losing A Rat is a remote possibility. Because of the pressure you're putting on him, he's probably giving you lots of room to breathe and play, anyway. The monogamy argument generally plays only a small part in a woman's reluctance to start hunting again. It is a barrier erected by women who have little confidence in themselves. They are afraid of the anxieties, tensions, and rejections of the singles world. For some women the known, even in the form of A Rat, is better than the unknown.

At least The Rat is there and always comes back to you. No matter what he does otherwise, he makes you feel somewhat desirable.

Helping a Man Change

Should you try to change a man? Only if the relationship is worth it. Relationships that are worth it are those in which the symptom that is making you miserable is relatively confined. For example, sex life with a Stingy Lover may be off, but the rest of the relationship may be on. He's worth it. The Bastard who makes your life miserable in a thousand ways is not worth it unless you are married to him and you want to give it one last try. Chances are small that you can help a man whose entire lifestyle has to be radically altered, or a man whose symptoms are not making him feel conscious pain.

Most men can change to some degree. The ones in this book who are least amenable to change are Bastards (who are psychopathic) and Complete Asexuals (who have made a good adjustment to life and see little reason to alter their lives). Hit-and-Run Lovers, of course, don't give you a chance to know them, let alone help them. Men Who Never Make Passes at women they think are "good" rarely give you a chance to start a relationship. The easiest person to change instantly is the Passive Man Who Never Makes a Pass. Just create a receptive atmosphere, put a record on, give him a glass of wine, then make a move and you'll get what you want.

A prime requisite for helping a man is the existence of a true relationship. He has to be as involved as you are. Mutual trust is important also. This rule means that you can leave, without a second thought, Jugglers who deceive you. You may be reluctant to help a Romantic change for fear of destroying what you already have—his blind devotion. But if you manage to bring a little reality into his life and he starts to look at you as a person rather than a fantasy, and he doesn't like what he sees, what have you lost anyway?

The best time to try to help a man is when, for some reason, his lifestyle has become unacceptable to him. It may be because of you. You are threatening to leave him and he cares. It may be because stresses in the business world have made him feel he isn't functioning well. It may be that he sees all his friends settling down and he is unable to. It may simply be age. He wants different things as he matures, maybe a long-term relationship, but he can't seem to make it happen, or he is tired of the same old rat race but is running anyway, with less and less pleasure.

When you set about trying to help a man, the same rules apply to all types:

1. *Have an open, honest discussion with him.* The purpose of talking things over is twofold. It will help him to confront his own problem. (As I pointed out in previous dissections, Lovers often deny that anything is wrong with them.) It may also help him to understand the nature of the problem and the origins of some of his behavior. For example, if your husband is a sexually Stingy Lover, you may ask questions that would lead him to make the connection between intimacy and sex. If you find you are too embarrassed or anxious to discuss the matter, try writing out the things you want to talk about. Tell him it's a love note. It is, or you wouldn't be bothering.

2. *Make sure he understands that the relationship is imperiled.* If he really cares, this fact may serve as motivation for change.

3. *Don't try to change him overnight.* Do things gradually. Let's use the example of the Stingy Lover again. He may be afraid to express affection because it will lead to sex. Ask him at first to just hug, hold hands, and touch for a while. Once holding and touching are established, you can ask him to try sex a little more often. Ask him to even force himself, for the sake of the relationship.

4. *Get him to read self-help books.* Find those that cover his particular problem. If you can't find anything specific, any good book on improving one's self-esteem may be helpful. As a first, or last, resort, give him this book, with a bookmark inserted at the appropriate chapter.

5. *Set a time limit on your efforts.* Six months, a year. But don't be prepared to spend a lifetime playing nurse.

6. *Get the man into therapy,* where his problems can be dealt with by a trained professional. This tactic is your best bet. If he's a Bastard, choose a male therapist. The

Bastard will react to a woman therapist negatively, as if she were in league with his wife. She will not be respected. For other Lovers, the sex of the therapist doesn't matter.

Breaking Up

If you have tried to help and failed, and you feel that you can't go on living with your man, or if you decide that the relationship isn't worth the effort, you should get rid of The Rat. There are two ways to split: the right way and the wrong way. The wrong way is to get angry over the situation, quietly seethe for a while, then either attack him furiously, leaving on a note of hysteria, or disappear from his life without any explanation, thus becoming the female equivalent of the Vanishing Lover.

The right way to end a relationship is to do what you would like to have done to you. Have an honest, calm discussion of the facts. A barrage of accusations will only lead to counteroffensives, and will leave both of you upset.

Before you start any terminal proceedings, you should know why you want to get out of the relationship. You should know exactly what about the man's conduct is unacceptable to you.

With these things in mind, you should arrange a meeting for the express purpose of talking about your decision. Again, be careful not to accuse. In a way that is not hostile, simply tell him how he is making you feel by his actions. Ask him for clarification of vital issues. Is he dead set against closer involvement? Does he have other women in his life? Do you turn him off sexually? If he appears to answer you honestly, you are in a better position to decide what to do.

If you have been wrong in any of your assumptions, you may want to stay to see what happens. If you find that nothing he says makes the situation more tenable, then tell him you don't want to continue the affair and why.

Even if you are acting in a completely reasonable and honest way, some men may become defensive and angry during your discussion. Don't respond to his hostility with your own. Prepare yourself for this contingency ahead of time. If you are sure your behavior has been rational and not deliberately provocative, then the best way to handle his anger is to say something like: "I understand you may be feeling bad about my wanting to end the relationship, and maybe you don't agree with certain things I've said, but I'm trying to do this in a reasonable way."

During breakup discussions, funny things can happen. Both of you may feel regret and interpret it as love. He, in particular, will be prone to this feeling. If he is being rejected he may experience it as a narcissistic wound. His sense of self-esteem is under attack. He feels bad about himself and he feels he has to make you like him again so that he can feel better. This feeling is experienced consciously as a sudden surge of love for you. He may plead with you: "Don't leave. I really love you. I can't live without you."

The Rat's protestation of love after your long siege of feeling unloved may be tempting, but keep your cool and proceed cautiously. Cover your bets. Tell him that you think you and he should take a break and not see each other for a month. If his love is real, it will be there in four weeks. If his ego just needs some salve, his love for you will dissipate.

After breakups, even those initiated by the woman, it is not uncommon—particularly if you are sitting home without a new man, and have not busied yourself with other things—to think: "Why did I do it?" The any-man-is-better-than-no-man syndrome sets in. You must remember that you just found out, perhaps for the nth time that any man is really not the solution to your cravings for security, love, and companionship. The way to be secure is to feel better about yourself. And one way to feel better about yourself, and solve loneliness at the same time, is to get up and go about the business of life, as well as love.

Love is only a crisis if you permit it to be.

Appendix

Twelve Ways to Spot a Loser Lover

1. *He comes on too strong too soon.* Beware of the man who loves you instantly and insists on seeing you all the time from the minute he knows you. He is responding to his fantasy of what you are rather than to the real you. He is sure to be disappointed when you don't—because you can't—live up to his dream. Relationships that start out with a bang generally end just as quickly, and not necessarily with a whimper.

2. *His behavior is erratic, uneven, or mysterious.* He becomes unpredictable soon after the relationship starts. He disappears mysteriously for days or weeks. Or, after initial ardor and interest, he suddenly seems to withdraw. Or he forgets to call you to confirm a date. Or he's never home at night, and you know he isn't working because you called his private number in the office. Or he calls you only at the last minute, or can't ever meet you until 9:30 or 10:00 at night. Erratic, unpredictable, or mysterious behavior is generally symptomatic of men with inner conflicts that interfere with their ability to enter into good relationships. Such behavior can also indicate that the man has another life, whether with women or with work, that leaves little room for decent personal relationships.

3. *The relationship reaches a plateau and stagnates there.* When a man freezes the relationship in one spot—he sees you only once a week or only on weekends or only during the week—watch out. Good relationships always grow. They move in a positive direction with increased contact and more intimacy. The man who establishes a pattern and keeps it there has no intention of going any

further. You are being kept on hold—forever.

4. *There is inconsistency between what he says and what he does.* He promises that you'll take a trip together in the spring, but when spring comes he never mentions it and the trip never materializes. Or he tells you about his fascinating or famous friends. "You'll meet them soon. You'll love them," he says. But time passes and you never meet any of his friends—fascinating, famous, or otherwise. Often those friends do not exist, and he never had any intention of taking the trip. Men like this tend to say what they think you want to hear even if it has no basis in reality. They are trying to compensate for underlying feelings of inadequacy. They are out to impress you because they don't feel acceptable when they are just being themselves.

5. *He confuses you.* Again inconsistency plays a part in your bewilderment. He may tell you he adores you, but he never sees you more than once every two weeks. Or he tells you he doesn't want to get involved, then sees and calls you all the time. In general, anytime there is a sense of confusion it is a warning signal that something in the relationship is not straight.

6. *He has a bad history with women.* Ask him to tell you about his past relationships. If you find out that he has never had an affair that lasted more than a year or two, or that he has been divorced for fifteen years and hasn't had a long-lasting relationship since, it's a very good indication that things are not going to be different with you.

7. *The rest of his life has not jelled.* Beware of the man past the first flush of youth who has flitted from job to job, or has changed careers three times and is still not settled into what he is doing. A man incapable of being consistent in his work will have as much trouble settling down into a personal relationship. Do not confuse the man who jumps around in the marketplace with the man who has had a consistent career but was fired, or with someone whose business had failed. It's the man who can't seem to make anything work for long that you have to watch out for.

8. *He is completely self-centered.* The man who thinks only about fulfilling his own needs is a bad risk. If he never cares about what you think, if he always decides for the two of you where you will go and what you will

do, if he cuts you off in the middle of sentences because he obviously hasn't been paying attention to what you were saying, take it as a warning. You can expect more of the same if you continue the relationship.

9. *He behaves badly with others.* Even if he seems to be nice to you, you can often spot a Loser Lover by his behavior with others. Many men put their best foot forward while they are trying to capture a woman, but if your guy is dishonest, unthinking, or cruel with others, think twice about him. The way he functions with the rest of the world is the way he will ultimately function with you.

10. *He always blames other people.* When anything happens to him it is always someone else's fault. If he steps in a puddle it is because some schmuck blocked his vision so he couldn't see it. If he gets a ticket it's because the cop was hiding behind the bushes looking for someone to nab. If he is not successful at work it is because his boss is impossible. A man like this is unable to see himself as anything but right, and inevitably he will start blaming you too for things that go wrong.

11. *He tells you what to expect.* If he tells you he can't get involved, or that he's selfish or not good enough for you, don't give him the benefit of the doubt. Believe him. He knows himself a lot better than you do.

12. *Trust your gut feelings.* If something tells you that your man is hiding something, or that he isn't being completely honest with you, if you feel he is anxious, insecure, neurotic, or that he really cares only about himself, chances are that you are right. Many women are so intent on nailing a man that they tend to ignore their instincts. If you tune into your gut feelings you may find he is no one you want, anyway. Make sure, however, that what you feel about him is the way he always is, rather than just a temporary state. A man who has lost his job, for example, may be more distracted, self-absorbed, or anxious than he normally is. If you are not sure whether what you are feeling is temporary or permanent, stay with the relationship until you find out.

About The Authors

CAROL BOTWIN has written about human behavior, sex and other topics for such publications as *The New York Times Magazine, Family Circle,* and *Redbook.* In the late '60s, her by-line column, "Young World," appeared in *This Week* magazine, a Sunday supplement for 43 major newspapers. She lives in Manhattan and is the author of one previous book, *Sex and the Teenage Girl.*

JEROME L. FINE, Ph.D., is a clinical psychologist connected with the William A. White Institute of Psychoanalysis and Mount Sinai Hospital in New York City.

Bantam Book Catalog

Here's your up-to-the-minute listing of over 1,400 titles by your favorite authors.

This illustrated, large format catalog gives a description of each title. For your convenience, it is divided into categories in fiction and non-fiction—gothics, science fiction, westerns, mysteries, cookbooks, mysticism and occult, biographies, history, family living, health, psychology, art.

So don't delay—take advantage of this special opportunity to increase your reading pleasure.

Just send us your name and address and 50¢ (to help defray postage and handling costs).